Career Choices and Changes

A Workbook to Discover Who You Are, What You Want, and How to Get It

Your Path to Personal Success and Self-sufficiency

Written by Mindy Bingham and Sandy Stryker

Edited by Tanja Easson

Academic Innovations

This book belongs to _____

Started on _____

Completed on _____

I dedicate this work to _____

Copies of this book, along with the optional corresponding web site
www.my10yearplan.com, are available from the publisher. Visit
www.academicinnovationshighered.com or call (800) 967-8016
for information.

Library of Congress Catalog Card Number: 90-81785

ISBN 978-1-878787-66-8   Hardcover
ISBN 978-1-878787-67-5   Softcover

Photo Credits:
Front Cover: © iStockphoto.com/Mlenny, 2011
Photos throughout text: © Melinda Bingham, 2012
Photo for pages 362–363 © G.K. and Vikki Hart, 2011

 Published by Academic Innovations
(800) 967-8016   FAX (800) 967-4027
www.academicinnovationshighered.com
supportccc@academicinnovations.com

My10yearPlan.com® is a registered trademark of Academic Innovations

NOTE ON THIS EDITION: This volume is a derivative of our earlier book,
*CAREER CHOICES: A Guide for Teens and Young Adults: Who Am I? What Do I Want?
and How Do I Get It?* It has been rewritten in part and edited throughout to
meet the needs of a more mature audience.

*We have taken the privilege of substituting certain words in the quotations cited here
("person" instead of "man," "people" instead of "men") to make them more inclusive,
with the certainty that, had they been said today, this is how they would have been stated.*

20   19   18   17   16   15   14   13   12

Manufactured in the United States of America

In memory of Dr. Ken Hoyt

Know thyself

SOCRATES

Contents Overview

Contents Detail

Section Two: What Do I Want?

Section Three: How Do I Get It?

One of the most common questions asked of children is: What do you want to be when you grow up? Today this question is being asked of young adults and mature workers alike. The U.S. Department of Labor reports that the average worker will change jobs or careers at least seven times in their lifetime. This workbook is designed not only to help you answer that question now, but also to teach you a systematic process for choosing your future career and life direction.

Work plays a large part in all our lives, and this fact underscores the importance of choosing a career that enhances life satisfaction. While work is a way to occupy your time and earn money, it is also a way to define yourself, express yourself, and leave your mark in the world. It may be your major life activity. It will certainly claim much of your time. If you give the matter some serious thought, you can be among the small percentage of workers who say they are "completely satisfied" with their jobs, rather than the majority who, all things considered, would rather be doing something else.

Before you can make a good choice, however, you need to have more information than just the top ten job categories for the coming decade or the average annual salaries for 2,000 different careers. While your earning potential and the projected growth of your industry of choice are certainly things to consider, you need to start with information a bit more fundamental — like who you are and what you want. Once you have this information, you may find dozens of ways

to flourish. Without it, any career decision you make is likely to be less than fully satisfying. That's why this book devotes so much space to helping you find personal answers to these most important questions.

It also focuses on an inescapable fact of life: "All things change except the love of change." Written by an anonymous author nearly four hundred years ago, that statement has never been so true. In twenty-first century America, change is a way of life—like it or not. As a result, success in the contemporary workforce will require flexibility and mastery of a process for dealing with change.

If you don't believe this, ask the former steel or factory workers who, not so long ago, thought they would always have a dependable income. Talk to the white-collar workers who never expected to be standing in line to collect unemployment checks. Speak with the young professionals who grew up thinking they would be at least as prosperous as their parents.

This is a challenging time, but also a time of great opportunity. If there are fewer secure jobs than in previous years, there is more room in the global marketplace and emerging industries for innovation, imaginative endeavors, and entrepreneurial drive. For those with the necessary self-knowledge, skill, and courage, the potential for real job satisfaction has probably never been greater

You are about to embark on one of the most important journeys of your life — that of discovering who you are, what you want, and how to go about making the future you envision a reality. Along the way you'll come to understand that determining your life path is one of the most complex decision-making processes anyone makes. That may be why far too many people have never reached the point of being truly satisfied with their life choices.

The choices you'll be making as you work through the exercises and activities in this book will impact not only your happiness and life satisfaction but also your feelings of self-worth. With patience, an open mind, and hard work, you can master the process and learn to navigate these important choices. When you've finished, you'll have developed a 10-year Plan that will help you realize your dreams and goals.

Your life is defined by the choices *you* make. No matter what path you choose to follow, this process will help to ensure it is your own.

Your Path to Personal Success and Self-sufficiency

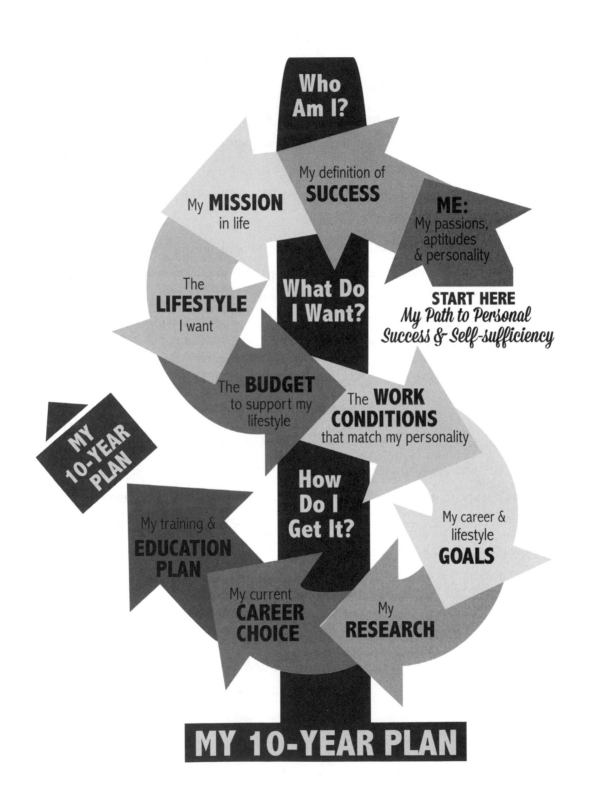

Who Am I?

My definition of **SUCCESS**

My **MISSION** in life

ME: My passions, aptitudes & personality

The **LIFESTYLE** I want

What Do I Want?

START HERE
My Path to Personal Success & Self-sufficiency

The **BUDGET** to support my lifestyle

The **WORK CONDITIONS** that match my personality

MY 10-YEAR PLAN

How Do I Get It?

My training & **EDUCATION PLAN**

My career & lifestyle **GOALS**

My current **CAREER CHOICE**

My **RESEARCH**

MY 10-YEAR PLAN

Learning the Process Pays Lifelong Dividends

You won't choose a "lifetime" career as you work through this book. There is no longer any such thing. You will learn a process that you can use over and over again as you change jobs in a rapidly evolving workplace. Once you've learned its simple secrets, you'll find you can use this process for all major lifestyle decisions. You'll also find yourself better able to adapt and proceed in the face of change, no matter what your chosen career.

In the past, the battle was to get a job. Today, the goal is also to build a satisfying life. We strongly believe that, with meaningful contemplation, appropriate preparation, and the proper attitudes, achieving that goal is within the reach of all.

A couple tips as you proceed through this book:

1. Don't be fooled by the simplistic format. The lighthearted text and non-threatening design are meant to facilitate the contemplation and self-discovery required to make the process meaningful.

2. Start at the beginning and work through each chapter, in sequence, to the end. The insights and the data you gather in the earliest chapters will be explored more fully, enhanced, and used later in the process as you make choices and develop your plan.

3. You may be tempted to sit down and complete all of the activities in a few sittings. As simple as this seems, you must remember that these are important questions requiring reflection and thought. Take whatever time you need.

4. This is not a one-time activity. It is the beginning of a lifelong habit. Whenever you learn something new about yourself or encounter a change that impacts your career or lifestyle, revisit this process and update your choices and your **10-year Plan**.

This exploratory process will surprise you. It will either send you ricocheting in new directions you've never considered or confirm your current plans. Whether you are starting or completing your education, re-entering the workforce, displaced due to workplace changes, or looking for new professional challenges, taking the time to work through this journal and learn this essential process will pay lifelong dividends.

Becoming a Lifelong Learner . . .

Lifelong learning not only guarantees your success at work but also impacts how satisfied you'll be with life in general. Why? Have you noticed the speed with which everything changes? Just about the time you learn how to program your DVR to capture all your favorite shows, technology advances and you have a new application waiting to be mastered. In the past, you may have relied on a call to the airline to book your next flight; now you have the "honor" of paying an additional fee if you can't navigate their online ticketing process.

That's a lot to keep up with, it's true. The good news is some of the best learning resources are now as close as the nearest computer and as portable as your smartphone.

Using Keyword Searches

During the Scientific Revolution, Sir Francis Bacon believed, "Knowledge is power." As a learner living during an era of technological revolution, power comes from being able do more than just memorize or reproduce knowledge. Real power comes from an ability to find meaning in the information you encounter and use it **to produce new knowledge or new understanding.**

The last time you wanted to know about something what did you do? Did you go to your bookshelf and pull down an encyclopedia? Visit your local library? Or did you search for the information online using Google or Bing or watch an informational video that explored the subject using YouTube?

You'll find suggested keywords located at the bottom of pages throughout the book. You can use these keywords to direct an online search for appropriate in-depth resources. The keywords will give you a head start for additional knowledge and skills on the topics presented on that particular page.

The speed at which our world changes presents its own learning challenges, but it also presents wonderful learning possibilities. This book—or any book—can only provide a finite amount of information. **Your potential to learn is infinite!**

Means Being a Self-directed Learner

If you are like most people, you want control — control of your learning and, by extension, control of your future. In today's environment, if you want to successfully manage the changes and challenges that come your way, you'll want to be a **self-regulated or self-directed learner**. As a self-directed learner, you'll be aware of your own strengths and weaknesses in learning, and you'll employ appropriate strategies or techniques to tackle each learning challenge.

We've added features and tools throughout the book to help you master the important task of becoming a self-directed learner.

Checkpoints

Because the material you are about to encounter requires higher-order thinking skills, (analysis, synthesis, evaluation, and creativity), it is difficult to assess what you've learned by traditional testing methods. The answers are uniquely your own — your life, your choices, your plans — and only you know if they're right or wrong.

The Checkpoints at the end of each chapter were designed as a self-assessment. They will prompt you to take a moment to monitor and evaluate your own progress. If you feel confident in your understanding of the concepts and projects, you're ready to move on. If you feel less than certain, you'll want to go back and work through the corresponding activity or exercise, either on your own or with the help of an instructor, mentor, or learning partner.

Your Skills Inventory Chart and Education Plan

While in school, someone else — a teacher or professor — directs your learning through assignments and lectures. You've probably sat in at least one class and wondered "When am I ever going to use this?"

Well, what if you could create your own **Education Plan**, secure in the knowledge that the courses you take and the skills you learn will pay off in the future?

Beginning in chapter two, you'll start identifying the skills you have and the ones you need to learn in order to be prepared for the career and lifestyle you desire. This list will grow as you complete activities designed to help you discover more about yourself and the career(s) you'd find fulfilling. By the end of this process, through the development of your **Skills Inventory**, you'll have the information you need for a job-winning resume *(the skills you have)*. You'll also have a good start on an **Education Plan** that is focused on what you need *(the skills you want to learn)*.

Armed with your comprehensive **Education Plan**, you'll be in good shape for your lifelong learning journey, gathering the necessary resources along the way to help you get the skills and experience to land the job of your dreams.

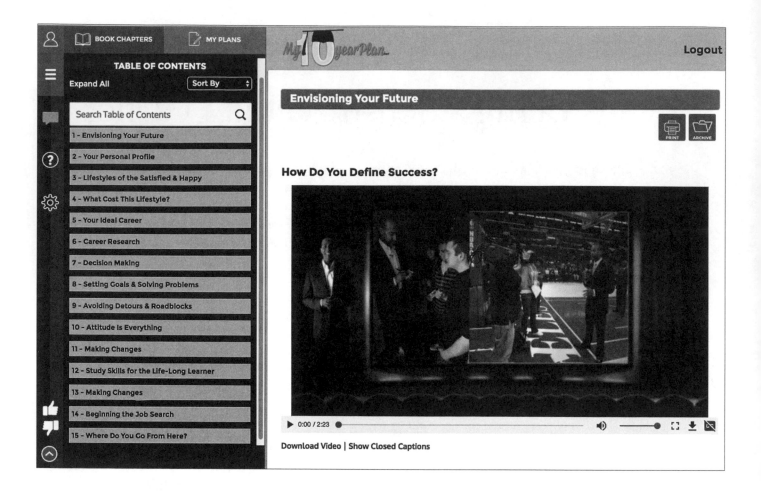

My10yearPlan.com®

My 10yearPlan.com®* provides an online planning area where you can enter and expand upon the work from your *Career Choices and Changes* workbook. While the program's content mirrors the nearly 100 *Career Choices and Changes* exercises, the My10yearPlan.com® system's dynamic and interactive structure prompts you to revisit, revise, update, and share the data related to the development of your **10-year Plan**. That information is then available for the seamless creation of your own personalized planning documents:

- 10-year Plan Summary Page
- 10-year Plan and Portfolio report
- My Skills Inventory
- My Education Plan

Together these documents provide an overview of the goals you've set for the next decade regarding your education and training, career, finances, and lifestyle choices.

*To order visit www.careerchoices.com/store/category/highered

4

How Do I Benefit from this Extra Step?

Because your **10-year Plan** is online, you can update it as you experience new things, learn more about yourself, and refine your vision of the future. The online format also makes it easy to share your plan with advisors, counselors, teachers, family, friends, and mentors in four different formats.

The **10-year Plan Summary** Page provides a snapshot of you—your dreams, goals, and plans. Anyone taking five minutes to read this document will know a lot about you: who you are, what you want, and how you plan to go about getting it. Sessions with counselors will be more productive. Family and friends can more effectively support your dreams and goals. Anyone reading your carefully-thought-out plan will be more likely to take you and your goals seriously.

Your 10-year Plan and Portfolio report is a multi-page document that provides a more detailed picture. An autobiography of sorts, it's a collection of all the work you enter about yourself in an easy-to-read format. As you gain new understanding and update your plan, this dynamic report will be revised automatically.

My Skills Inventory expands on the **Skills Inventory** chart you'll create beginning in chapter 11. My10yearPlan.com® easily tracks the skills identified as those you have and those you want to acquire. Because the inventory is a fully integrated part of the system, skills can be linked to specific career options and can be sorted and selected based on the career path you decide to follow.

My Education Plan will evolve from your **Skills Inventory** chart. As you identify your chosen career paths, the necessity for certain skills, particularly those that are transferable, will become apparent. Using this knowledge, you'll build your lifelong Education Plan.

The career you choose for your initial **10-year Plan** is meant for the duration of the course, not necessarily for the rest of your life. As you discover careers that hold even more interest, the online nature of My10yearPlan.com® allows you convenient and secure access so you can easily re-work some key activities and keep your plan current as you change and grow.

How to Use My10yearPlan.com®
and the *Career Choices and Changes* Workbook Together

It's important to remember that your workbook and My10yearPlan.com® are designed to work together in a two-step process.

1. After the classroom or online discussion and the personal reflection that follows your reading of *Career Choices and Changes,* complete the activities and exercises in your workbook using your initial thoughts, ideas, and plans.

2. Then, when you have access to the Internet, enter your data into your online **10-year Plan** for each of the corresponding activities. These are listed by chapter and appear in the same order as in the textbook.

Here are some important points to remember:

• Complete the activity in your workbook first.

• Like most of your writing assignments, the work from your *Career Choices and Changes* workbook will go through a number of different editorial stages. Think of your workbook as the place where you'll create your draft for each activity and think of My10yearPlan.com® as the place for you to review, revise, edit, and polish your draft.

• After you've completed the activity in your workbook, log in to your My10yearPlan.com® account and enter your information online. This can happen whenever you have access to the Internet — whether it's during class time, between classes in the library or career center, or at home during the evening.

• Before you just start typing away, take a moment and read through the responses you've written in your workbook. Maybe you've given the activity more thought since you first completed it. Do your answers still seem like the best possible response? If so, go ahead and enter the information into My10yearPlan.com® as written. If not, you might want to update your answer as you type.

• Keep in mind that the information you input into the activity pages of My10yearPlan.com® will flow into your **10-year Plan Summary Page** and your **10-year Plan and Portfolio** report. This is your chance to pay attention to your spelling, check for typos, and make sure you've answered in complete sentences when appropriate. Because you'll want to print and use parts of your portfolio for job interviews, scholarship interviews, performance reviews, and more, you'll want to make sure that your spelling, grammar, and punctuation are correct.

• Many instructors will use your **10-year Plan Summary Page** and your **10-year Plan and Portfolio** report as part of your final grade, so make sure you're always putting your best work into My10yearPlan.com®. That way your grade will reflect all of the thought and hard work devoted to this process and your final product will be something you'll be proud to share with the special people in your life.

• If you've completed online interest inventories and/or personality tests such as those found in your career center or on the Department of Labor websites, you already know that these tools provide interesting but very general information. Wrapping your mind around how to make use of these broad conclusions can be frustrating. However, once you learn and complete the comprehensive process of developing your **10-year Plan** advocated in *Career Choices and Changes* and My10yearPlan.com®, you'll understand how to apply this information. When you've reached that point in the process, it may be valuable to review these surveys again from a more informed and self-aware perspective.

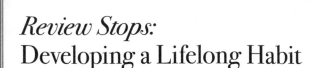

Logout

Review Stops: Developing a Lifelong Habit

As you work through the *Career Choices and Changes* activities and enter them into My10yearPlan.com®, you are embarking on one of the most important and complex decision-making processes of your life. You're determining not only how you want to spend the majority of your waking hours for the forty-plus years of your career, but also how to structure a lifestyle that is uniquely yours. This requires contemplation, reflection, flexibility, and research.

Throughout your process of developing your online **10-year Plan**, you will encounter a series of *Review Stops*. **These have been strategically placed to remind you to pause and consider earlier information or decisions you've made.** Each time you encounter one of these *Review Stops*, the system will help you look back at previous activities and build on your self-knowledge in order to make new, more complex choices and decisions. Think of these prompts as a friend reminding you to step back for a moment and take a look at that wonderful, multifaceted being...YOU.

Technology is a wonderful thing, especially when it allows us to streamline or eliminate tedious processes or tasks that, when done the "old-fashioned way," would take much longer. However, you don't want to overlook the role your own brainpower should play in the process of planning your unique life. Don't be in a hurry or get impatient. The *Review Stops* enhance the decision-making process by coaching and guiding you to reach the depth of self-reflection and critical thinking necessary to make meaningful choices. From their examples, you will develop a lifelong habit that can propel you to a self-actualizing life of your own design. Their assistance, in the end, will lead to a **10-year Plan** that will help you determine, articulate, and then realize your most cherished goals and dreams.

*Personal success is simply the fulfillment
of what makes you happiest.*
—Anonymous

Vision is the art of seeing the invisible.
—Jonathan Swift

If you can dream it, you can do it.

—Walt Disney

CHAPTER ONE
Envisioning Your Future

How do you define success?

Section One:
WHO AM I?

MIA EARNS THE MAGIC CLEATS

Walking down a cobbled street in Florence, Italy, Mia Hamm noticed a rugged beggar looking for enough change to buy a meal. Several people pushed past the old man before Mia reached him. "Here you go," she said, offering the stranger her last five euros. "My child, your compassion is touching. Please take this token of my appreciation." the man said, pulling a shiny pair of soccer cleats from inside his shabby coat. "If you lace and unlace these cleats three times before each match, they will set records for you and carry you to championships, medals, and halls of fame." Mia replied, "So three times before each match. Okay, I'll try it!"

ELON GETS A SHOCK

Elon Musk really needed to sell his car. He had been working for days to repair the engine on a limited budget, but with no luck. Taking a long overdue break, Elon plugged his old TV into the adapter, adjusted the antenna, and leaned the seat back, ready to enjoy another episode of Top Gear. Out of a clear, blue sky, a bolt of lightning struck the car roof, traveled through the TV antenna, and electrified the engine, which roared to life. Weirder still, the car continued to run long after the gas tank ran dry. Turning to Tesla (the cat he had named after his hero, Nikola Tesla), Elon exclaimed, "Now I can post my car on Craigslist for at least $100,000, and I can use the money—and my TV antenna—to make more electric cars!"

10

OPRAH GETS DISCOVERED

Oprah Winfrey got on a downtown bus to go shopping one Saturday. The bus was crowded, and she accidentally stepped on the foot of a man sitting near the front. "Excuse me," she said. The man looked at her. "Would you say that again?" he asked. "Excuse me?" said Oprah. "That's it! People, this is the one!" the man exclaimed. "This is our star!" As he made his announcement, a dozen people jumped up from seats further back in the bus. A camera crew descended on Oprah with microphones and glaring lights. Someone from make-up began highlighting her cheekbones. A costumer told Oprah she'd be stunning in chartreuse. "Wait a minute," Oprah demanded. "What's this all about?" "You're going to be the star of our new talk show," the first man told her. "You'll have your own production company, and you'll make some movies, too. The job pays about 75 million dollars a year. How does that sound?" "Sounds good to me," said Oprah.

WARREN FINDS A JOB

While vacationing in Manhattan, Warren Buffett saw a "Help Wanted" sign in a window of the New York Stock Exchange. He was between jobs at the time, so Warren decided to check it out. "We're looking for someone to be the most successful investor in history," the woman in the office told him. "You have to know a little about business, and you had better like math." "I do like math," said Warren. "Plus I used to sell newspapers, and now I own half of a pinball machine. Do I get the job?" "I don't see why not," the woman said. "When can you move to New York?" "Well, I don't know. I like living in Omaha. Could I think about it for a day or two and get back to you?" "Sure. Take your time. No pressure."

Vision + Energy = Success

You can safely assume that there is not one kernel of truth in any of the preceding stories. Successful people do not depend on luck or magic to get what they want. Nor do they let others make their career choices for them. Most people who are successful in their work don't just *find* a job. They *make* one. They have a *vision* of what they would like to do, how they would like to use their minds, talents, and interests. And they have the *energy* to make their dreams come true. They believe in their vision.

Vision and energy (or action) are the two most important elements in getting what you want from life. Your vision of what you'd like to do or be, or how you'd like to live, will help you know when you've succeeded. A goal is like a compass that will help keep you on track. And your energy or actions will take you, step by step, to the realization of your vision.

It is essential to have both elements. Vision without action is just daydreaming. Alone, it won't get you anywhere. Undirected action is equally useless. It leads only to exhaustion and frustration. Together, though, they are a dynamic duo. And they can work for you, no matter what your goal. (Not everyone can — or wants to — be a superstar. You need to have your own definition of success. More on that later in this chapter.)

What do you think are the real stories behind the successful people we talked about on the preceding pages? For the following exercises, write a statement that you feel might reflect their visions. Then list some actions they may have taken to realize their goal.

Mia Hamm's chart, for example, might look something like this:

Mia Hamm

Vision: To join the women's national soccer team, win championships, and build the popularity of women's soccer.

Actions in school and work: Throughout junior high, high school, and college, train, train, train; learn to work on a team; keep up grades to remain eligible to play; stay healthy.

Actions at work: As a player, continue to train, train, train and maintain health; as team captain, encourage other players, support the coaches, and focus on team success over personal success.

Complete charts for the following individuals.

Elon Musk

Vision: _____

Actions in school: _____

Actions at work: _____

Oprah Winfrey

Vision: _____

Actions in school: _____

Actions at work: _____

Warren Buffett

Vision: _____

Actions in school: _____

Actions at work: _____

Envisioning *Your* Future

What about you? Do you have a vision for your own future? You need to begin imagining one, if you don't. It's an important first step. Once you have a vision, you start expecting to realize it. What you *expect* for yourself tends to become what you *get*. So imagine a *positive* future for yourself.

Sit quietly, close your eyes, and imagine your ideal career. What kind of setting are you in?
What tasks are you performing? Are you working alone or with others?
How do you feel about yourself? Describe your vision in as much detail as possible.

_____

_____

_____

_____

_____

_____

_____

_____

_____

_____

Was that a difficult exercise for you? Don't worry about it if it was. The rest of this book is designed to help you begin to clarify who you are, what you want, and what you need to do to get it. So keep reading!

Why People Work

People work for many reasons, but, basically, they work to bring personal meaning and satisfaction to themselves, as well as benefits to society. All human beings have a need to work, to do, and to become someone through that process. According to Kenneth B. Hoyt, known as the "father of career education," we work to "discover both *who* we are and *why* we are."

☐ *Of course, people also work for survival.* In early history, that meant — literally — bringing home the bacon (or the wooly mammoth), gathering fruits and grains, and finding shelter from the elements. Today the transaction is less direct. People work for *money*, which they use to fulfill the same basic needs. But, you probably already knew that. You may be less aware, however, of some of the *other* reasons people go to work each day. The following come from Dr. Jay B. Rohrlich's book, *Work and Love: The Crucial Balance*.

☐ *People work to define themselves.* Ask most people who they are and they will respond with their occupation: "I'm a mail carrier," "I'm a software designer," "I'm a teacher," and so on. It may be just as accurate to say "I'm an emotional person" or "I'm very creative." But, somehow, statements like these seem more ambiguous. They provide less concrete information. Being able to provide a job title or a list of accomplishments makes us feel more *real* to ourselves and others.

☐ *People work to have a sense of security.* Many people find it difficult to get all the love or approval they need from their relationships with friends and family. For them, work can be a constant source of security and pleasure. They may not know what kind of mood they will find their spouse, partner, or roommate in on any given night, but they can be fairly certain that their work will be the same.

☐ *People work for self-respect*, or to feel competent and powerful. It isn't always easy to feel powerful in the world. Some people will always be more powerful than you are. Discrimination based on sex or race is real, and robs its victims of the feeling that they can direct the course of their lives. Doing a particular job well gives a worker a sense of control and responsibility that adds greatly to his or her self-respect.

Keywords: reasons why people work

☐ **People work to conquer time.** We are aware from an early age that our time on earth is limited. The days that pass simply vanish. One way we can "conquer" time is to fill each day with achievements or accomplishments. Over time, these experiences become a real and lasting part of what we see ourselves to be.

☐ **People work to measure their self-worth.** Working is one way of "keeping score," of seeing how we stack up in comparison to others. Who is the most accomplished? Who got the award or promotion? Who earned the respect of the group? Who makes the most money? These are all ways we use to measure our self-worth. We feel better about ourselves when we succeed at a *difficult* task than we do when we accomplish something easy. We also tend to place importance on public recognition: the more lives you touch, the longer you may be remembered.

What are your motivations? Why do you work, whether it's at school, at home, or at a job? Prioritize the previous statements by placing a "1" in the box next to the statement that resonates most with your feelings about work. Continue to score each item, with "6" being what you find least matches your personal drives. This basic understanding of why you work and what it brings to you may help you later as you examine your possible career choices.

In the long run, though, true job satisfaction comes only from inside. You are the final judge of your own achievement. Whether you make a fortune or just a living is less important than knowing that you made a contribution and that you did your job well.

Everybody Works

Whether you currently earn money from a job or not, you are a worker. You may be a student. Chances are you work to maintain your home. Perhaps you are an athlete or a musician, a computer whiz or a movie fanatic, a cook or a gardener. For the purpose of this exercise, consider all your studies, tasks, hobbies and any job you perform for money.

Think about a typical "working day," one in which you spent time on most of your "jobs." List the tasks and activities you performed below. Make your list as complete as you can.

_____

_____

_____

_____

_____

Based on that list, how would you define your jobs? Write your titles on the following lines.

I am a _____

_____

_____

What would be your accomplishments at the end of the day (a new blog post, a clean kitchen, a solved problem, and so on)? List them below.

_____

_____

_____

_____

Which accomplishments are most satisfying? _____

_____

How do they make you feel about yourself? _____

_____

Do your feelings relate to any of the reasons people work listed on the previous page? Which ones?

_____

_____

Defining Success

According to the dictionary, success is "the achievement of something desired, planned, or attempted." Since your desires and plans are very personal and are not exactly like anyone else's, you will need to define success for yourself.

This is not an easy thing to do in our society. Success is often equated with wealth and fame, luxurious homes and fancy cars. These outward displays may *look like* success to others, but they do not make those who possess them *feel* successful. The feeling of success comes only when *you achieve* what is *most important to you*. True success is a personal feeling, not a public display.

What does success mean to you? What would make you feel that you are a successful human being? In addition to thinking about what you do, contemplate the type of person you want to be.

Other people have made their opinions known as well. We've listed some of them below. Do any of them match your definition? Indicate whether you strongly agree, agree, are not sure, disagree, or strongly disagree with each statement.

	Strongly Agree	Agree	Not Sure	Disagree	Strongly Disagree
Money, achievement, fame, and success are important, but they are bought too dearly when acquired at the cost of health. — Anonymous					
It's great to be great, but it's better to be human. — Will Rogers					
Nothing succeeds like excess. — Oscar Wilde					
Success is a journey, not a destination. — Ben Sweetland					
The fastest way to succeed is to look as if you're playing by other people's rules, while quietly playing by your own. — Michael Korda					
She could not separate success from peace of mind. The two must go together... — Daphne Du Maurier, *Mary Anne*					
All of us are born for a reason, but all of us don't discover why. Success in life has nothing to do with what you gain in life or accomplish for yourself. It's what you do for others. — Danny Thomas					
I've never sought success in order to get fame and money; it's the talent and the passion that count in success. — Ingrid Bergman					

	Strongly Agree	Agree	Not Sure	Disagree	Strongly Disagree
The two leading recipes for success are building a better mousetrap and finding a bigger loophole. — Edgar A. Shoaff					
Success is something to enjoy — to flaunt! Otherwise, why work so hard to get it? — Isobel Lennart, *Funny Girl*					
Success is knowing what your values are and living in a way consistent with your values. — Danny Cox					
Success can only be measured in terms of distance traveled... — Mavis Gallant					
If at first you don't succeed, you are running about average. — M. H. Anderson					
I think success has no rules, but you can learn a great deal from failure. — Jean Kerr, *Mary, Mary*					
Success can make you go one of two ways. It can make you a *prima donna,* or it can smooth the edges, take away the insecurities, let the nice things come out. — Barbara Walters					
Six essential qualities that are the key to success: Sincerity, personal integrity, humility, courtesy, wisdom, charity. — Dr. William Menninger					
The people who try to do something and fail are infinitely better than those who try to do nothing and succeed. — Lloyd Jones					
The wealthy man is the man who is much, not the one who has much. — Karl Marx					
Winning isn't everything — it's the only thing. — Vince Lombardi					
Only those who dare to fail greatly can ever achieve greatly. — Robert F. Kennedy					
If at first you don't succeed, try, try again. Then give up. There's no use being a fool about it. — W. C. Fields					
I'm opposed to millionaires, but it would be dangerous to offer me the position. — Mark Twain					

Making Career Choices

Later in the book, you will learn a technique that will help you make good decisions in most situations. For now, though, as you begin making choices about your future career, try to be aware of the decision-making patterns you use most often. Some of them work better than others. Some of them don't work at all. Do you recognize yourself in any of the following stories?

ERIC has a tendency toward wishful thinking. He concentrates on the outcome that seems most attractive to him, but he pays little attention to the risks involved or the probability of his wish coming true. Eric has decided to be a professional tennis player, even though he's not an exceptional player.

LOUISA is an escape artist. She takes pride in determining the worst thing that could happen in any situation. And, even when there is little chance of that outcome, she chooses a safe alternative. Although Louisa was a straight A student in math, she was afraid she wouldn't do as well in that subject in college. She'd like to be an engineer, but she's decided to enter a medical coding/billing program instead.

MAGGIE likes to play it safe. She knows she could be successful as an insurance agent, so she plans to follow that course. Really, though, she'd rather be a politician.

WADE is impulsive. He makes decisions without giving them too much thought. He's thinking of being a flight attendant because he likes the way they dress.

ANDY usually leaves things to fate. He plans to move to California this summer, just to see what happens.

ELENA is compliant. She usually lets someone else make her decisions. Her husband thinks she should become a computer programmer, so she probably will.

HAROLD procrastinates. He puts off decisions until the last minute. He plans to think about his future someday, when he has more time.

YOKO agonizes over every decision. She examines each alternative so closely — and so repeatedly — that she never seems able to make up her mind. She says she wants to interview several dozen more people before selecting a career path.

ARTURO makes decisions intuitively. Some things just feel right, he says. He's always liked the idea of being a wildlife biologist, but he isn't exactly sure what they do.

KENISHA has a rational approach to making decisions. She considers the alternatives, the pros and cons of each, and the likelihood of succeeding before making her choice. She is interested in technology and sees a bright future in high-tech careers, so she plans to train for a job in that field.

Which of these patterns do you use most often?_____

Explain: _____

_____

Keywords: improve decision making

Your Definition of Success

Write your own definition of success here:

_____

_____

_____

_____

_____

                                   _____
                                          your name

Throughout this book we will be talking about success. As you read about and ponder
this concept, make sure to keep **your own definition** in mind.

*Accept no one's definition of
your life; define yourself.*

—Harvey Fierstein

There Are Jobs . . . and
There Are Careers

Although we often use the terms interchangeably, there is a difference between a *job* and a *career*. A job is
a particular task or undertaking. It may be paid or unpaid. You will, undoubtedly, have many jobs during
your lifetime.

However, you will only have one career. Your career encompasses *all* of your life's work. You have already
begun your career. The work you have done so far will help determine where you go from here. Future
occupations grow out of past experiences. That is why people speak of career *development*. The path may
not always be obvious, but the connections are there, so the choices you make now are important.

MAKING CHOICES THAT ARE RIGHT FOR YOU IS WHAT THIS BOOK IS ALL ABOUT. BEFORE
YOU CHOOSE WHAT YOU WANT, HOWEVER, YOU NEED TO KNOW WHO YOU ARE. THAT IS
A SUBJECT WE WILL TACKLE IN THE NEXT CHAPTER.

CHAPTER 1 CHECKPOINTS
Envisioning Your Future
How do you define success?

You have started thinking about your ideal future, which is the first step toward achieving it. Before you move on, check to make sure that you've reached the goals listed below.

☐ I realized that success does not come from daydreaming, but from combining a vision with appropriate actions.

☐ I am beginning to imagine the kind of future that I would find most satisfying.

☐ I understand that work is more than just a way to earn a living; it is an important part of most people's identity.

☐ I can now recognize the diversity in individuals' daily accomplishments.

☐ I am aware of the methods that I typically use to make decisions and can evaluate their effectiveness.

☐ I learned there are myriad definitions of success, and I realize the one I want to strive to meet is my own.

☐ I am now on a life-long path toward determining my own personal definition of success.

What lies behind us and what lies before us are small matters compared to what lies within us.

—Ralph Waldo Emerson

Self-trust is the first secret of success.

—Ralph Waldo Emerson

CHAPTER TWO

Your Personal Profile

Getting what you want starts with knowing who you are

Section One:
WHO AM I?

The Chamber of Commerce was sponsoring a career fair at the city auditorium. When Letitia arrived, she found her friend, James, standing outside, looking bewildered. "I didn't expect to find a scene like this," said James. The meeting hall was packed with representatives from dozens of technical and professional schools, as well as graduate programs. All branches of the armed forces were represented. There were all kinds of corporate representatives, prospective employers, and people working in a wide variety of careers.

"Isn't it great?" said Letitia. "Every one of those people stands for a possible future, a different way of life! But I guess it could be confusing. It's a good thing we have some ideas about what we want to do."

James cleared his throat and stared at his shoes.

"You do have some ideas, don't you, James?"

"Oh, sure," he replied. "My family think it would be good for me to take over my parents' business. And Tom, my best friend, thinks I should go to graduate school. He wants me to talk to the admissions officer from his university. Of course, everyone says computers are the way to go, and that might be fun."

"Yes, but what do you think? What kind of future do you want? You're the one who's going to be living there, you know. Have you considered who you are and what you want?"

"What's there to think about? I'm my parents' son and my friends' friend. I go to work. I hang out. I'm just me. And who are you, if I may ask?"

"Well, I have thought about it," said Letitia. "In a lot of ways, I'm like you and my other friends. But people are like snowflakes or fingerprints—no two are the same. And it seems to me that it's the differences that make life interesting. We have to consider those things when we plan our lives.

"For example, I enjoy being on the college's debating team. I love to argue and discuss and try to persuade people, even though most of my friends think that kind of thing is boring. I'm also really interested in civil rights. So, I'm thinking about going to law school, maybe even running for Congress someday. And those things, James, are all part of who I am."

Letitia has a head start on her friend, but it's not too late for James to consider who he is and what he wants to do. This is a process that can start at any time — and should continue throughout life.

Learning about yourself is a little like painting a picture. When you are very young, you have little more than a sketch — who takes care of you, what you like to eat, what you like to play with. As you grow and change, you learn more and more about yourself and begin to develop a vivid self-portrait. But, the portrait is never complete. Some things will change. Many details will be added.

It's important, though, to keep a sort of running tab: "Who am I now? What's important to me at this point in my life? What do I do well? What do I most enjoy?" Your answers to these questions will help you make the decisions that will lead to a satisfying short-term future. By asking them again and again, you will be better able to make the necessary changes and adjustments that lead to a fulfilling life.

You may be tempted to rely on internet-based or computerized interest surveys. After all, you can complete these in an hour or two and you "magically" get the answer to one of your most important questions — what career(s) match with your interests and needs. However, there are compelling reasons for you to not take this shortcut. You'll see as you work through this book that choosing a career is complex and multi-dimensional. In the next fourteen chapters you'll be evaluating data and feelings that only you can assess.

These feelings and realities will change over the course of your life. Knowing the decision-making process so you can re-evaluate as needed, you'll have a stronger sense of direction and a better handle on your own career options. Then when opportunities or challenges present themselves, you'll be ready to confidently take action to keep yourself and your career on track with your own personal desires and requirements.

So, where do you start? The following exercise should help.

Choosing a career is complex and multi-dimensional.

25

Write your name in the center of the chart, then add as many words as you can that describe your own passions, values, strengths, and so forth.

As you fill out your chart, keep in mind that everyone has many different sides. Don't worry if some of your answers seem incompatible with others. Remember, too, that it's natural to want to "belong." Because you want to be like your peers, you may try to deny interests or abilities that are not shared with your friends. For this exercise — for your own sake — try to be complete and honest.

Don't get frustrated if you have a hard time completing your chart at this time. It will get easier as you work through this chapter. For now, do your best. Use a pencil so you can make any necessary changes as you go along.

Here are some short definitions to help you:

Passions: A passion is something you feel very strongly about, something for which you have boundless enthusiasm. You might be passionate about music, sports, art, computers, horses, cars, gardening, politics, the beach, marching bands, penguins — you name it. The happiest people are often those who find a way to incorporate their passions into their career. These are the people you'll hear say things like, "I can't believe they pay me to do this."

Values: Your values are those qualities or things that are most important in your life. Some people may value family or security, while others place more importance on adventure or power. You might value beauty, knowledge, social justice, or independence. Your career and life choices should be compatible with your values if they are to bring true satisfaction.

Personality traits and strengths: Are you tactful? Bold? Sociable? Quiet? Thoughtful? Energetic? Funny? Sympathetic? Inquisitive? Reserved? Dramatic? Intelligent? List as many traits as you can.

Skills and aptitudes: What have you learned? What comes easily for you? Do you have a special talent for anything in particular? Are you good at working with your hands? Solving problems? Working with people?

Roles: Your roles are the different parts you play in your life. Most of these are temporary, though some can go on for many years. You may be a spouse, a son or daughter, a student, a friend. You might also be an employee, an employer, a volunteer, a sister or brother, a girlfriend or boyfriend, and so on.

Occupations and vocations: Here we mean both work you do for pay (occupations) and recreational activities (vocations). For example, you might be a grocery clerk, research assistant, bus driver, flute player, cook, Little League coach, or basketball player.

Your Personal Profile

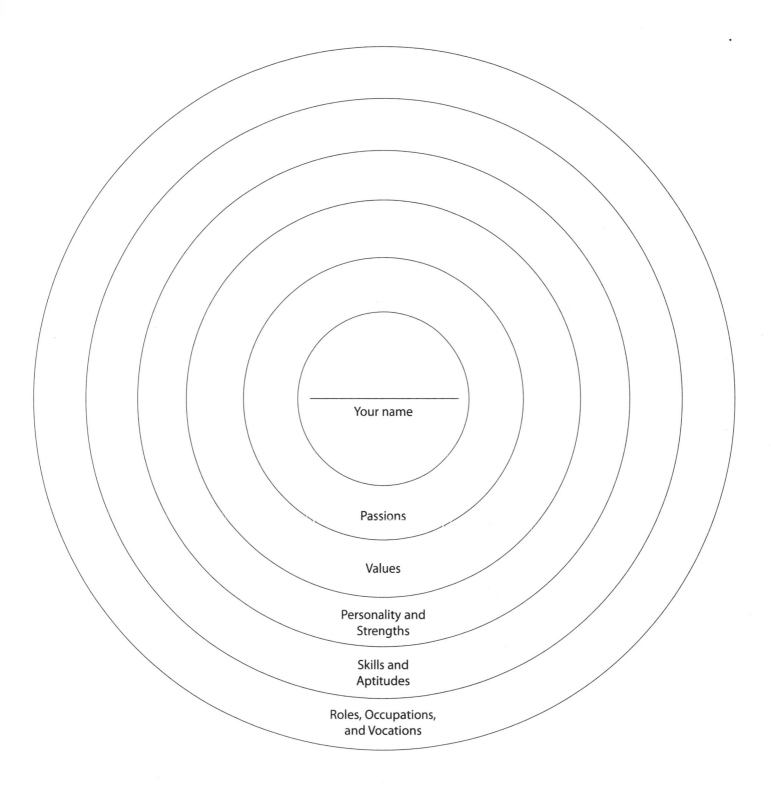

_____
Your name

Passions

Values

Personality and
Strengths

Skills and
Aptitudes

Roles, Occupations,
and Vocations

Back at the auditorium, Letitia had just finished discussing law school admission requirements with a representative from the state university when James tapped her on the shoulder.

"Okay," he said, "you seem to know a lot more about this than I do. I don't know who to talk to or what questions to ask. Where do I start?"

"You can start by identifying your passions," she replied.

James grinned in what he imagined was a worldly and sophisticated way.

"That's not what I mean," said Letitia. "This is serious stuff. Aren't there things you really love to do? What could you do all day without getting bored or tired?"

"Well, last summer I taught my nephew and his friends how to play baseball and I really enjoyed that. I had a part in a play and I guess I got kind of choked up when the audience gave us a standing ovation. I saw the movie *Top Gun* 14 times."

Passion: energy and enthusiasm wedded to a sense of purpose.

"That's a start," said Letitia. "What kinds of occupations does that list suggest? Do you want to be a teacher or a coach? Do you want to take acting lessons? Maybe you'd like being an Air Force or Navy pilot. Talk to some of the people here tonight about those possibilities. But, you need to give your list more thought. Keep adding to it. See where it takes you. You want to be sure that, whatever you end up doing, you'll be able to fit in activities that give you that kind of natural high."

The dictionary defines passion as a "powerful emotion; boundless enthusiasm; deep, overwhelming feeling; or avid interest." Clinical psychologist Carl Goldberg says, "Passion is the energy and enthusiasm wedded to a sense of purpose that gives life meaning and pleasure." Preparing for a career, or changing one, is hard work. It takes time and patience. If you choose a field that you truly love, one that excites and energizes you, you will be motivated to *do* the work, to *find* the patience. You are more likely to stick with your plan and realize your goal.

The interests, activities, or accomplishments that cause this special feeling are different for everyone. It's up to you to discover your passions. Answering the following questions should get you started, but don't stop here. Be aware of your reactions to all the ordinary and extraordinary events in your life. Keep building your list.

Identifying Your Passions

These are some of the items on Letitia's list:

Winning a debate	Chocolate	Red shoes
Dancing	The Lakers	Long walks
Texting	Social justice	*The Star-Spangled Banner*
Politics	Movies that make me cry	Writing

Complete the following statements. Don't be frustrated if you can't do it immediately, but start being aware of these feelings. As more ideas occur to you in the next weeks, turn back to this page and add them to your lists. You will continue to discover new passions throughout your life.

My heart pounds with excitement when . . .

_____

_____

I feel especially good about myself when . . .

_____

_____

I get a lump in my throat when . . .

_____

_____

I lose track of time whenever I am . . .

_____

_____

If I could be any person in history, I would be . . .

_____

_____

When I dream about my future, I see myself . . .

_____

_____

If I could change one thing about the world, it would be . . .

_____

_____

When Letitia came home, her phone was ringing. "Sorry to bother you, but I have another question."

"Yes, James, what is it?"

"I did what you suggested," he said. "I talked to a recruiter about a career in the Navy, and I also had an interesting conversation with an actor I met. Now I feel kind of uneasy."

"What do you mean?"

"Well, I'd like to wear a uniform and get a bunch of medals and ride in parades and stuff, but being a fighter pilot is, like . . . dangerous, you know? And it would be fun to get fan letters and have my picture in magazines and all that. But the guy I talked to said it can take years before you even get a small part—some people never make it. And all that time, you have to take classes and go to auditions—and you still have to find some way to make money, you know? So, I'm confused. Part of me would really like to do these things, but another part thinks it wouldn't be that great."

"James, I think you have a values conflict here," said Letitia.

"What do you mean by 'values?'"

"Values are the standards or guiding principles that are most important to you. It sounds to me like you are seeking recognition, but you also need security. The careers you're considering are risky. You may not feel comfortable in those roles. What you need to do now is figure out what your strongest values are, and then think about careers that are compatible. Be sure that the values are yours, though. Don't just try to please others. If you aren't really committed to your goal, you won't be able to take the necessary risks or feel good about what you are doing while you're in school or just starting out. This is something you really need to think through on your own, James."

WORK VALUES SURVEY

What are *your* values? Is having plenty of time to spend with friends and family important to you? Or would you rather be off on some kind of adventure? Do you want to help other people? Do you want to exercise power? The following exercise should give some indication of what you value most. For each statement below, check the column that comes closest to matching your feelings.

	Very True	Some-Times True	Not Sure	Not True
1. I'd rather donate to a good cause than join a prestigious club.				
2. I'd rather have good friends than a lot of money.				
3. I'd rather have my savings in a bank account than in the stock market.				
4. I'm too adventurous to be tied down by a family.				
5. I'd like a job where I set my own hours.				
6. I enjoy books and movies where the moral to the story is not obvious.				
7. I'd rather be a scholar than a politician.				
8. I would not want to work while my children are young.				
9. I would rather write a fictional story than a research paper.				
10. When I lend money to a friend, I don't worry about being paid back.				
11. I'd rather be famous than wealthy.				
12. I would rather associate with influential people than intellectual people.				
13. Teachers should be paid as much as business executives.				
14. I'd rather go to an art museum than a sporting event.				
15. I will contribute to my retirement account before I buy extras.				
16. I prefer jobs where the duties are varied and challenging.				
17. I prefer jobs where the duties are consistent and goals are clear.				
18. I feel a person's salary indicates how much he or she is valued on the job.				
19. I would not want a high-powered job because it could strain my marriage.				
20. It is important to me that my surroundings are attractive.				
21. My reputation is worth more to me than all the money in the world.				
22. I'd rather visit a place than read about it.				
23. I'd rather know something than be *known for* something.				
24. I'd rather have a secure job than a powerful one.				
25. I'd like to be my own boss.				
26. I believe a percentage of my income should be used to help others.				
27. I would turn down a promotion if it meant I had to travel away from my family too much.				

	Very True	Some-Times True	Not Sure	Not True
28. "Money talks."				
29. I would take a cut in salary if I were offered a position in the President's Cabinet.				
30. I'd rather own a special work of art than a fancy car.				
31. I'd rather have time than money.				
32. I will always stop to watch a beautiful sunset.				
33. If my brother committed a crime, I would turn him in.				
34. I don't like to do things the same way all the time.				
35. My friendships are more precious to me than possessions.				
36. The fact that most careers that "help others" make lower wages would not stop me from entering these lines of work.				
37. It is important that I get recognition for what I do.				
38. I'd rather *work* for an exciting company than *run* a dull one.				
39. I would like to run for office in my community.				
40. I'd rather work for someone else than have my own business.				
41. The first thing I would consider when deciding on a career is how much it pays.				
42. I always take time to be a good friend.				
43. The mundane work of feeding the hungry or caring for the sick would not bother me.				
44. I don't like my decisions questioned.				
45. I'd rather have a job with a high income than one with a lot of security.				
46. It is important for me to understand how things work.				
47. I like to organize the activities of my friends and family.				
48. If I were famous, I would enjoy signing autographs.				
49. I'd rather have a secure job than an exciting one.				
50. Owning nice things is important to me.				
51. I like to do things my own way.				
52. I feel good when I volunteer my time to make my community a better place.				
53. I would never testify in court against someone in my family.				
54. It is important to me that my home is beautiful.				
55. I like to be in charge.				
56. I would rather work together with other people than alone.				
57. Books and reading are important to me.				
58. I would stand up for my beliefs even if I were punished for it.				
59. I like to solve problems.				
60. I expect to be consulted when a group I am in is making a decision.				
61. If I believed strongly in a "cause," I would make it my first priority.				
62. I have expensive tastes.				
63. If a member of my family committed a crime, I would turn him or her in to the appropriate authorities.				
64. I don't like my friends to be too dependent on me.				
65. I'd rather be married than single.				

32

	Very True	Some-Times True	Not Sure	Not True
66. I like to make things.				
67. My appearance is important to me.				
68. I'd love to travel around the world alone.				
69. I am sensitive to colors that clash.				
70. Someday I'd like to own my own business.				
71. I'd rather be a leader than a follower.				
72. I'd rather follow someone else.				
73. I like to learn something new everyday.				
74. I would never marry someone who had less money than I do.				
75. It is important that my mate is good looking.				
76. I would borrow money to go on a vacation.				
77. Charity begins at home.				
78. With enough money, I could be happy.				
79. I think it would be exciting to be famous.				
80. I value my privacy…I wouldn't want to be famous.				
81. I believe I should be home every night with my family and not out with friends.				
82. "Don't rock the boat."				
83. I would not take a job that I felt was unethical, no matter how much money it paid.				
84. I enjoy people who do things differently.				
85. I will go out of my way to help a stranger.				
86. I would like to have a building or street named after me.				
87. I would not lie even if telling the truth might hurt a friend's reputation.				
88. I'd rather live in a cabin in the wilderness than a beautiful home.				
89. I like to look at problems from many different angles.				
90. It is important to me to be an influential person.				
91. I'd like to be known as being one of the best in my field.				
92. I like to try new things.				
93. I will not change my views just because they're unpopular.				
94. I think you should question "rules" if they don't make sense to you.				
95. I wouldn't want to travel alone.				
96. If asked, I would serve Thanksgiving dinner to the homeless and miss my family's celebration.				
97. I always stand up for what I believe in.				
98. I wouldn't like doing the same task all day long.				
99. I like to be called in an emergency.				
100. My family will be more important to me than my career.				
101. Trophies and awards are important to me.				
102. I like to help friends with their problems.				
103. My title at work is very important to me.				
104. It is important to share my life with someone.				

Now, assign a numerical value to each of your answers. Statements in the "very true" column are worth 9 points. Those you marked "sometimes true" get 6 points. Allow 3 points for each "not sure," and zero points for every "not true" answer.

In the columns on this page and the next, write the numerical value of your response next to the statement number. For example, if you answered "very true" to the first statement, you would write a 9 on the line next to the number 1. When you have entered a number on each line, go back and total the columns under each heading.

ANSWERS

ADVENTURE	FAMILY	POWER	RECOGNITION
4. _____	8. _____	12. _____	11. _____
16. _____	19. _____	29. _____	37. _____
22. _____	27. _____	39. _____	48. _____
38. _____	53. _____	47. _____	79. _____
68. _____	65. _____	55. _____	86. _____
76. _____	77. _____	60. _____	91. _____
88. _____	81. _____	71. _____	101. _____
92. _____	100. _____	90. _____	103. _____
Total _____	Total _____	Total _____	Total _____

PERSONAL INTEGRITY & MORAL COURAGE	MONEY	SECURITY	CREATIVITY
21. _____	18. _____	3. _____	6. _____
33. _____	28. _____	15. _____	9. _____
44. _____	41. _____	17. _____	34. _____
58. _____	45. _____	24. _____	59. _____
63. _____	50. _____	40. _____	66. _____
83. _____	62. _____	49. _____	84. _____
93. _____	74. _____	72. _____	89. _____
97. _____	78. _____	82. _____	98. _____
Total _____	Total _____	Total _____	Total _____

HELPING OTHERS	KNOWLEDGE & TRUTH	FRIENDSHIP & COMPANIONSHIP
1. _____	7. _____	2. _____
26. _____	13. _____	10. _____
36. _____	23. _____	35. _____
43. _____	46. _____	42. _____
52. _____	57. _____	56. _____
85. _____	61. _____	95. _____
96. _____	73. _____	102. _____
99. _____	87. _____	104. _____
Total _____	Total _____	Total _____

BEAUTY & AESTHETICS	INDEPENDENCE & FREEDOM
14. _____	5. _____
20. _____	25. _____
30. _____	31. _____
32. _____	51. _____
54. _____	64. _____
67. _____	70. _____
69. _____	80. _____
75. _____	94. _____
Total _____	Total _____

In which category did you have the highest total? Right now, that value is most important to you. Remember, though, that values often change over time. You might want to come back to this survey every year or whenever you are considering a change in your plans.

Did you have high scores in more than one category? If so, you might want to try to find a career that satisfies both or all your top values. If you value both beauty and adventure, for example, you might be happier tracking down international jewel thieves than you would be working in an art gallery or museum.

Each values category is described below:

Adventure

If you value adventure, you would be happiest in a career that offers some degree of variety or unpredictability. You don't necessarily have to be a spy or a soldier of fortune, but you won't want a job with too much structure or routine. Since you are probably willing to take risks, you might make a good entrepreneur.

Family

Those who value family are usually happiest with careers that don't call for evening or weekend work or a great deal of travel. Flexibility is helpful, as is the opportunity to work at home. A career with a salary high enough to allow you to work part-time might be attractive.

Knowledge and truth

If you value knowledge and truth, you might find a career that lets you pass on your knowledge — teaching, for example, or being a librarian — rewarding. Or you might prefer a job that keeps teaching *you:* doing research, investigative reporting, and the like.

Values: standards or guiding principles that are most important to you.

Power

Those who value power need to prepare for leadership. Usually, that means some type of advanced education or years of experience in your trade. Most political leaders, for example, have law degrees. Business leaders quite often have a master's degree in business administration. If you value power, make sure that any job you take offers room for advancement, or consider starting a business of your own.

Personal integrity and moral courage

You will be most satisfied in a career that mirrors your sense of purpose if you value personal integrity and moral purpose. Perhaps your *field* of work is less important than what you do *within* that field. For example, if you are a lawyer, you would probably be more satisfied working in legal aid than in corporate law. It is important for you to feel that your work is worthwhile to society.

Money or wealth

Many career fields have the potential to pay very well. Make sure that the one you choose meshes with your other top values. If you also value security, for example, you might find it more satisfying to be an engineer than an entrepreneur. Remember, too, that you will probably need to spend the majority of your time working. Is there a job you would enjoy so much you wouldn't mind if it also had to be your hobby?

Friendship and companionship

If this is your highest value, you will want to make sure that your chosen career involves working closely with others. Things to consider: Would you prefer spending your time with co-workers or clients? Do you like to see the same faces every day, or would you like to meet new people on a regular basis? Do you have a circle of friends for whom you want to reserve time?

Recognition

You may be recognized by more people if you are a TV star than if you are the best caterer in town. But, generally, you can earn recognition in just about any field if you do your job well. Choose something for which you have the necessary skills or talents, and work hard.

Independence and freedom

If this is your highest value, you may find unstructured sales — real estate or insurance, for example — rewarding. In this type of job, you can set your own hours and work without constant supervision. You might prefer to work part-time, or you might want to be self-employed. Stay away from strict schedules or jobs in which you are constantly accountable to someone else.

Security

If you value security, you will be most comfortable in a job you know will be around for a while. No new companies or risky ventures for you. You may prefer to have clearly defined duties, rather than a loosely structured job.

Beauty or aesthetics

If this is your top value, *where* you work may be almost as important a consideration as *what you do.* Your setting must be one that you find visually attractive, whether it's a garden or a cathedral. You might want your work to center on beauty, as well — perhaps you'd be happy as a designer, an architect, or a florist.

Creativity

Creative people need room to exercise their imaginations, whether they are creating a work of art, inventing a better way to display merchandise, or solving a problem in computer programming. If this is your top value, you should seek a flexible career that lets you put your ideas to work.

Helping others

If you value helping others, there are many ways for you to accomplish your goal. The service industry, in fact, is one of the fastest-growing parts of the economy. How do you want to help others? Some possibilities: you could be a paramedic, a physical therapist, a social worker, a nutritionist, a psychologist, a police officer, or a child-care worker.

Strengths and Personality

James was waiting by Letitia's car when she finished her classes the next day. "Hi, James!" she said. "What a surprise. What's going on?"

"Well," said James, "I thought about my values, and I think I know what they are. I really would like to be recognized, to have people know who I am. I want to keep learning, to know about things. And, I'd like some adventure in my life, too—as long as it's not too risky. I mean, I'd like to go to interesting places, but I'd rather not have people shooting at me on a regular basis, if you know what I mean. But what now? Values aren't jobs. I don't think anyone is going to hire me to be a well-known person."

"Probably not," Letitia agreed. "I guess the next step is to think about your passions and values and how they relate to your personality. How do you like to work? What are your strong points? How do you feel about this? How do you feel about that? Stuff like that."

"Okay," said James. "What do you think my strengths are?"

"Well, you're curious. You're not a bit shy, and you certainly are persistent! I'm late for class. Why don't you get some opinions from your other friends?"

Everyone has his or her own way of thinking, feeling, and acting. We are all unique. Our individual characteristics develop early in childhood and usually continue in a somewhat consistent manner throughout life.

In the four columns below, you will find a list of personality traits. Circle the 10 traits you feel best describe you.

Now total the number circled in each column.

a.	b.	c.	d.
forthright	enthusiastic	steady	analytical
adventurous	expressive	amiable	controlling
forceful	influencing	predictable	perfectionist
sharp	emotional	supportive	systematic
decisive	inventive	loyal	conventional
risk taker	spontaneous	methodical	respectful
demanding	trusting	team player	meticulous
authoritative	outgoing	calm	well-disciplined
direct	unselfish	thorough	diplomatic
curious	self-assured	dependable	precise
competitive	charming	self-composed	sensitive
self-sufficient	inspiring	possessive	accurate

_____	_____	_____	_____
Total from column a	Total from column b	Total from column c	Total from column d

People have a better chance of feeling successful when they know their own work style — including their strengths and their weaknesses. Understanding the way you are likely to behave on the job will greatly enhance your ability to choose a satisfying career and lifestyle.

The ancient Greek physician Hippocrates believed people exhibited four different behavioral styles. Today many career and profile tests also use four categories to distinguish types of behavior.

Complete the following self-evaluation quiz. Circle the letter under each situation that best reflects how you would be likely to act, feel, or think.

1. Your favorite projects are ones that are
   a. likely to have favorable results.
   b. enjoyable to take part in.
   c. clearly explained.
   d. detail oriented.

2. You are on the community hospital's fund-raising committee. You would be happiest
   a. chairing the committee.
   b. publicizing the event and selling tickets.
   c. decorating the hall.
   d. keeping track of the monies collected.

3. When doing a task, you
   a. complete it in the shortest time possible.
   b. allow interruptions to take phone calls from friends.
   c. are willing to take time to help another person with their assignment.
   d. take time to check all your work for accuracy and thoroughness.

4. When faced with a stressful situation, you
   a. take charge and sometimes override the decisions of others.
   b. confront and may act in an impulsive fashion.
   c. become submissive and allow others to make your decisions.
   d. resist change and withdraw from the situation.

5. When getting dressed in the morning, you
   a. know exactly what you want to wear without giving it much thought.
   b. try on three things before deciding which is best.
   c. put on the clothes you laid out the night before.
   d. have no problem coordinating outfits because everything in your closet is in color sequence.

6. Your family is moving across the country to a lovely new home. You feel
   a. excited.
   b. curious.
   c. cautious.
   d. worried.

7. When you ask someone a question about a problem, you like an answer that
   a. is direct and to the point.
   b. includes stimulating ideas on various ways the problem could be solved.
   c. outlines the process for solving the problem.
   d. includes data and background on how the solution was reached.

8. When solving a problem, you are
   a. decisive.
   b. spontaneous.
   c. considered.
   d. deliberate.

9. When going shopping for clothes, you
   a. will not need a list. If you forget something, you'll just get it later.
   b. buy whatever catches your eye. You don't worry how different outfits go together.
   c. have a list and visit every store in town before finalizing your purchases.
   d. know exactly what you want and have searched the mall website for sales.

41

On page 41, how many times did you choose each
of the letters below?

a. _____   b. _____   c. _____   d. _____

Did you choose the same letter four times or more?   Yes   No

If so, which letter? _____ (1)

Now turn back to page 39 and write the total for each column below.

a. _____   b. _____   c. _____   d. _____

Which column has the highest total? _____ (2)

Does the letter with the highest total on page 39 (line 2) match the
predominant letter from the self-evaluation quiz on page 41 (line 1)?
If so, you can start identifying your work behavior style.

The four styles are as follows:

a. Dominance

People with this behavioral style like to be in control of the work environment. They are decisive and focus on accomplishing goals. They work quickly and efficiently and like tasks that are challenging. They are usually happiest in leadership positions, such as manager, store owner, entrepreneur, school principal, contractor, office manager, and so on.

b. Influencing

These people's strength lies in their ability to influence others. They are good communicators and enjoy the relationships that they develop at work. Very personable, they want recognition and a stimulating work environment. They work best in a flexible setting. They are usually happiest in people-oriented jobs such as sales, marketing, teaching, counseling, coaching, customer service, and the like.

c. Steadiness

People in this category like tasks that have well-defined procedures. Known for their steadiness and follow-through, they excel at jobs calling for specialized skills. Maintaining relationships is a high priority for them, and their home life is important. Their decisions are considered, so they are often slower to accept change. They are usually happiest in specialized positions such as word processor, mechanic, assembly line worker, repairperson, lab technician, or scientist.

d. Compliance

This category of people is responsible for quality control. They are detail people who work from a prescribed set of rules and regulations. They enjoy systematic approaches to problems and strive for accuracy. They are very precise and are well prepared. They are happiest in "watch dog" jobs: working as accountants, law enforcement officials, editors, quality control managers, building inspectors, or zoning officials.

What you have worked through is a simplified approach to analyzing your work behavior style. Very few people exhibit only one of the four profile types. There are many different combinations. The intention of this exercise is to expose you to the concept and make you aware of the possibilities available to analyze your behavior patterns. As you become more serious about choosing your career path, you will probably want to take one of the more extensive, sophisticated tests available. Many corporations use these tests in helping employees evaluate how, they best work and relate to others. If you have this knowledge now, it should be helpful in your career planning search. We recommend the *Personal Profile System*® from Inscape Publishing.

Information on personality styles is adapted from the widely-used DiSC™ Dimensions of Behavior model and the *Personal Profile System*® assessment instrument, ™ copyright 1972, Carlson Learning Company. Used with permission of Carlson Learning Company, Minneapolis, Minnesota.

It is wisdom to know others; it is enlightenment to know one's self.

—Lao-Tzu

Your Strengths

Other things to consider in choosing an appropriate career are the strong points in your personality. Are you known to be friendly? Independent? Creative? Once again, there are no "good" or "bad" traits. It's just a matter of choosing a career that's compatible and takes advantage of your strengths. For example, a friendly, outgoing person is likely to do better at and feel more satisfied with a job that provides an opportunity to make use of these social skills.

What are your strengths? It may be hard for you to list them, so get some help. One of the best ways to identify your strengths is to ask people who know you well. We all tend to be humble about such things, so your friends' and family's opinions may be more complete than your own. Ask at least six people what they feel your strengths are. It may be easiest to do this in a small group. At lunch today, why not spend time discussing personality strengths with your friends or associates?

Turn to page 39 for a list of terms that might apply. Some other strengths might be:

adaptable, ambitious, assertive, caring, charismatic, charitable, clever, cooperative, courageous, creative, dependable, empathetic, energetic, enterprising, friendly, gracious, gentle, handy, hardworking, humorous, independent, innovative, inventive, knowledgeable, nonconformist, nurturing, open-minded, persevering, protective, realistic, reliable, resourceful, sensitive, tactful, trustworthy, unusual, versatile, well-read, willing, etc.

Now complete the chart below. Choose ten of the personal strengths you have identified and list them in the first column. Then, in the second column, describe a situation or personal experience where you used these strengths or where they might be helpful.

I AM:	I HAVE USED THIS STRENGTH TO:
1.	
2.	
3.	
4.	
5.	
6.	
7.	
8.	
9.	
10.	

Skills and Aptitudes

Letitia was ready for James when she found him back at her front porch later that afternoon. She took a sign she'd made at work from her purse and taped it to the door. "The Career Counselor Is In," it said. "Reasonable Advice at Reasonable Rates."

"Very funny," James said. "But you're the one who got me thinking about all this stuff. Who else am I going to ask?"

"Well, there is the workforce development center. You'll also find resources online. But I know those places can be kind of intimidating sometimes, so what can I do to help you?"

"I was just thinking. So far, we've talked about the kind of person I am and the things I like to do. But aren't we overlooking something? Like what I'm able to do?"

"Oh, you mean your skills and aptitudes. Sure, they're important. Of course, we'll keep developing new skills throughout our lives. But it's still a good idea to consider the things we can do now—especially the things we most enjoy."

"So where do I start?"

"Well, James, one way I've heard about is to list some of the accomplishments you're most proud of. You said you felt good about being in the play and teaching those kids how to play baseball. Take those experiences apart and think of the various skills you needed to succeed."

Though everyone has skills and aptitudes, many people are not good at recognizing them. Part of the reason for that is modesty—it seems boastful to announce that you are a terrific cook or a great musician. However, there is also an element of truly not thinking about all the skills involved in planning a party or writing a paper. James's appearance in the community play, for example, required many different skills: he had to *read* the play, *interpret* his part, *memorize* his lines, *cooperate* with others in the play, *project* his voice, and *perform* in front of hundreds of people. Many of these skills are transferable, which means that James can apply them in other situations. James has to *read* and *interpret* the reading assignments in his literature class. He also has to *memorize* lyrics and *project* his voice when he *performs* with the men's choir.

Since you develop skills by performing them over and over again, they are likely to be things you enjoy doing. That makes recognizing them doubly important when you plan your career: skills are things you not only *can* do, but *enjoy* doing.

An aptitude, on the other hand, is something for which you have a natural talent or something that comes easily to you. If you can sketch an accurate portrait or landscape without much effort, you can be said to have an aptitude for art. If people say you are a "natural athlete," you probably have an aptitude for sports. You may not enjoy all the subjects or activities for which you have an aptitude, but you probably will. People tend to enjoy those things that they do well.

As Letitia reminded James, you will continue to acquire skills throughout your life. In addition, some people develop skills and recognize their aptitudes later than others, so don't be discouraged if your list seems short right now. The fact that you have never built a house doesn't mean that you should give up your dream of being a carpenter.

Name That Skill

Use the following exercise to begin a list of specific skills you've mastered. Write three accomplishments that gave you the most satisfaction, or that you're most proud of, on the lines below. Then, in the middle column, list the skills you used in that enterprise. If you have a hard time identifying these skills, describe the experience to friends or family members and ask them to help you. (You'll complete the last column next.)

Accomplishment	Skills Required	Skills Category*
1. _____		
2. _____		
3. _____		

Do you see any pattern in the kinds of skills you used? Did they involve physical strength or coordination? Numbers or equations? Reasoning? Dealing with people?

* Basic Skills – Social Skills – Complex Problem Solving Skills – Technical Skills – Systems Skills – Resource Management Skills

Skills Identification

Each occupation requires a unique set of skills. Looking for common skill sets is one way of classifying jobs. Below are six broad **skill categories** used to group occupations on O*NET Online. Designed to group occupations that use the 35 general skills listed within these skill categories, you'll want to visit O*NET Online when you begin your research process in chapter six.

For now, review the list below and place a check mark next to each general skill that you feel competent in and an "X" next to those you want acquire in the future. Note: You're not required to select from more than one category of skills.

Basic Skills
- ☐ Reading Comprehension
- ☐ Active Listening
- ☐ Writing
- ☐ Speaking
- ☐ Mathematics
- ☐ Science
- ☐ Critical Thinking
- ☐ Active Learning
- ☐ Learning Strategies
- ☐ Monitoring

Social Skills
- ☐ Social Perceptiveness
- ☐ Coordination
- ☐ Persuasion
- ☐ Negotiation
- ☐ Instructing
- ☐ Service Orientation

Complex Problem Solving Skills
- ☐ Complex Problem Solving

Technical Skills
- ☐ Operations Analysis
- ☐ Technology Design
- ☐ Equipment Selection
- ☐ Installation
- ☐ Programming
- ☐ Operation Monitoring
- ☐ Operation and Control
- ☐ Equipment Maintenance
- ☐ Troubleshooting
- ☐ Repairing
- ☐ Quality Control Analysis

Systems Skills
- ☐ Judgment and Decision Making
- ☐ Systems Analysis
- ☐ Systems Evaluation

Resource Management Skills
- ☐ Time Management
- ☐ Management of Financial Resources
- ☐ Management of Material Resources
- ☐ Management of Personnel Resources

Within each of the skills listed above are more specific skills. For instance, your "repairing" skills may relate to computers or lawn mowers or jet engines. Review your skills on page 47 and, in the far right column on that page, indicate which of the six skills categories relates to each one. Do you have a preference for any one skills category? If so, which one?

_____

Below, list specific skills, expertise, or talents you currently have that are not listed on page 47.

_____   _____   _____

_____   _____   _____

_____   _____   _____

Can you think of skills you would like to learn but have not yet mastered? Expand the list above and be more specific. For instance, would you like to learn web design or contract negotiation, dog grooming or sales techniques?

_____   _____   _____

_____   _____   _____

_____   _____   _____

Roles, Occupations, and Vocations

The final ring on your chart asks you to list the roles, occupations, and vocations you now hold. These are very much a part of who you are, but they will change repeatedly as you get older. Today you may be someone's grandchild, for example. Some years down the road, you may be someone's *grandparent.* You will have many other roles in between.

The difference between roles and occupations or vocations is simple. A role is what you are (son, daughter, sister, brother, friend, and so on). It requires no specific actions on your part. (It might be nice if you spent an hour playing video games with your niece every night, but you will still be her uncle or aunt if you don't.) An occupation or vocation relates to what you do. It is something you spend time on. Occupations are paid employment. You may also be paid for your vocations, but not necessarily. A vocation is more like a special skill, something you are particularly suited to do. Right now, you may be a student. You may have other vocations or an occupation as well (waiter or waitress, clerk, cashier, computer wizard, basketball player, musician, artist, and so on). These are more easily changed or taken away. If you don't show up for practice, you may not be a basketball player for long.

Record your present roles and occupations or vocations below, and then transfer your responses to the chart on page 27.

Roles, occupations, and vocations, very much a part of who you are, will change repeatedly.

The Message Center

The next time Letitia saw James, he didn't seem his enthusiastic self. "Hey, James," she said, "are you okay? How's the career plan working out?"

"Oh, I don't know," he replied. "I thought about it a lot, and I finally hit on something I think I'd really like — broadcast journalism. But who do I think I'm kidding? I could never do that."

"I don't see why not," Letitia said. "You can talk. You can read. The rest of it you'll learn in the journalism program."

"Come on, Letitia. Can you imagine me on TV? No one in my family has ever even gone to college. My mom's always told me to remember where I belong, and my dad says I'm nothing but a dreamer. I guess they're probably right. I'd never make it."

"You're right. With that attitude, you never will find a way to create a future! Are you telling me your parents' fears and negative feelings are going to determine the way you feel about yourself?"

"You don't understand."

"Don't I? My father has never supported my dream of going to college. After I graduate, I'm expected to keep working at the mall until I get married. Sometimes I think he's right, that I'll never get into law school. But my mom believes in me. She says I can do anything I set my mind to, as long as I'm willing to work at it. And I tell myself she's right. I think it's reasonable for you to believe you can go to college and make your dream come true.

"I know it's hard to give up those negative messages, but you've got to believe in yourself, James."

"Do you really think I could make it in TV news?" he asked.

"James, I think if you really commit yourself and give it all you've got, your chances are very high. You have the talent. If you're willing to work diligently, with no guarantee of success, I think you can make it."

We all get messages about who we are and what we should be doing from the important people in our lives. Family, teachers, friends — all let us know in various ways what they think. Some messages are hard to miss. If your father added your name to the sign on the family business the day you were born, there's not much doubt where he thinks your future lies. More subtly, a parent who would step in to help you finish your homework, or would rewash the floor as soon as you put your mop away, gives the message that you are not competent to do something yourself.

Messages like these are limiting and destructive. They can make you feel that you have few choices in life, or that you just don't measure up. Other messages — like Letitia's to James, or her mother's to Letitia — are positive and empowering. They can build your confidence and help you achieve your dreams.

It's important to recognize the messages you get from your significant others because they are powerful and pervasive. They are like a recording playing over and over in the back of your mind, and they are difficult to erase.

Negative or limiting messages may come back to haunt you throughout your life, especially in certain situations. For example, if you've been given the message that you are too shy to have fun at parties, a little voice will crop up every time you get an invitation: "I'm no good at parties. I don't want to go." If you are aware of this fact, however, you can learn to dismiss the message and act more freely: "Thank you for sharing that, but I think I will go to the party and have a good time."

What messages have you received? For the following exercise, write what you think the significant people in your life would tell you about your future. Imagine them leaving their message on your voicemail.

Hello, you have reached _____ *'s message center.*

What would you like to tell me about my future? BEEP!

Mother's message: _____

_____

Father's message: _____

_____

Instructor's message: _____

_____

Other significant adult's message (coach, mentor, boss, relative): _____

_____

_____

Best friend's message: _____

_____

Girlfriend or boyfriend's message: _____

_____

Some of the strongest messages we receive come from society. Sex, age, race, nationality, religion, physical appearance, physical or intellectual abilities, financial status, social class — any of these can be the basis for taunts and jeers or praise and affection, great expectations or limited hope. What messages has society given you?

Society's message:

_____

_____

_____

Now go back and circle the messages that are limiting or negative. How much importance should you place on other people's opinions of you and their plans for your life? Should you have to live up to other people's goals and ideals? Whose life is it, anyway?

Positive Messages to Yourself

What positive messages can you give yourself about your future? Write them below. Recite them to yourself often, or read them into a digital voice recorder and play them again and again while you're relaxing.

1. _____

_____

2. _____

_____

3. _____

_____

4. _____

_____

5. _____

_____

When you have completed all the exercises in this chapter, go back to page 27 and add what you've learned about yourself to the diagram there.

Who you are, of course, cannot be summed up by a bunch of words on a chart. You are a complex and constantly changing person, an individual unlike any other who's ever existed. The exercises in this chapter should, however, provide some insights that can help you make sound decisions for your future. The next step is deciding what you want.

CHAPTER 2 CHECKPOINTS
Your Personal Profile
Getting what you want starts with knowing who you are

You have now made good progress toward answering the question "Who am I?" which you will continue to investigate throughout your life. You also recognize that knowing yourself well is essential to living the most fulfilling life possible. Make sure you are ready to proceed by confirming that you've accomplished the goals below.

☐ I am starting to outline the many qualities and characteristics that make up my unique identity and understand this self-knowledge is a necessary and ongoing part of any rewarding life.

☐ I am learning to identify and articulate things that are extremely important to me on an emotional level.

☐ I clarified which work values are most meaningful in my own life.

☐ I determined my work behavioral style and understand it as an important trait to consider when evaluating my career interests.

☐ I identified the strengths that make me unique and valuable, and I am starting to synthesize how my interests, values, and traits relate to education and career choices.

☐ I understand the standard skills categories, and I'm cataloging the skills I've developed over the years.

☐ I recognized and evaluated my roles, occupations, and vocations.

☐ I am more aware of the messages—verbal and otherwise—I get from society and from significant people in my life, and I understand how these messages can affect the way I feel about my future or my potential.

☐ I completed the first draft of my bulls-eye formatted **Personal Profile**, with the recognition that I will build on this as I discover more about myself.

There is only one success—
to be able to spend your life
in your own way.

—Christopher Morley

Happiness is not a state to arrive at,
but a manner of traveling.

—Margaret Lee Runbeck

CHAPTER THREE
Lifestyles of the Satisfied and Happy

Keeping your balance and perspective

Section Two:
WHAT DO I WANT?

Deciding what you want from life is not an easy task. What you want today is probably quite different from what you wanted 10 years ago. And, in another 10 years, your wants may well have changed again. That's to be expected. What you want usually depends on who you think you are at the time. As you change, so do your needs and desires.

In general, though, most people want happiness, peace, and life satisfaction. However, the things that will *give* them these feelings vary greatly. Contrary to popular opinion, money and outward signs of success don't have much to do with life satisfaction. That comes from *inside,* from your own unique achievements and sense of self.

Again, though, these will change. Perhaps this section of the book should be titled "What Do I Want *Now*?" This is something you need to re-evaluate on a regular basis. The processes you'll learn in the following chapters should help.

To paraphrase Mick Jagger, "You can't get what you want 'til you get what you need." Fortunately for us, someone has already determined the things we all need in order to be fully satisfied — and the order in which we must have them. The psychologist Abraham Maslow developed what has come to be called the Maslow Triangle. It graphically illustrates this hierarchy of human needs.

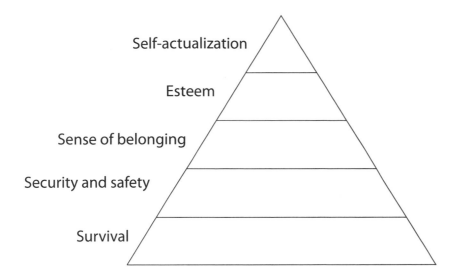

It's important to become familiar with this diagram. Deciding what you want from life is difficult. If you can place yourself on a particular level of the triangle, you will have a better understanding of what you need to do next.

Think of the triangle as a ladder, with the bottom rung at the triangle's base. You cannot jump over a rung or two. You must take each step in order if you want to reach the top. (It's quite possible to slip down the rungs, but let's not get ahead of ourselves.) Let's look at the triangle.

According to Dr. Maslow, our first need is simply to **survive**. We must have food, water, clothing, and shelter. Until we have these basic necessities, we cannot move on to consider our next need, which is for **safety and security**. The first two rungs deal only with physical and emotional survival—not a very satisfying way to live for most people.

When you hit the third level of the triangle, your need for other people becomes apparent. Some people are more dependent on relationships than others, but we all need to feel connected to other human beings. We all need to have a **sense of belonging**.

As we near the top of the triangle, we find that we have a need for **esteem**. We want other people to feel that we are worthy of respect. We also want to respect ourselves. At this point, we become capable of thinking about what we want, rather than simply about what we need.

Finally, at the peak of the triangle is the need for what Maslow calls **"self-actualization."** Self-actualized people are those who have done what they set out to accomplish, who have reached their goals. Not many people reach this point (only about 10 percent), and not everyone who gets there stays there. Some people continue to set new goals every time they reach their old ones.

Other people can quickly slide back to a lower rung. For example, people who lose their jobs or their health may find themselves back seeking survival and safety. Until they re-achieve these needs, they cannot approach — or probably even give much thought to — their higher needs.

As you think about your current place in the hierarchy of needs, it is important to remember that achieving life satisfaction is a *process*. It can only be accomplished one step at a time.

So be patient with yourself. It may be years before you can say exactly what you want from life. Even then, you may change your mind. The world is full of middle-aged people who are still trying to decide what they want to be when they grow up.

The process of thinking about your identity and your future can be rewarding in itself. It can get you headed in the right direction. It can help you realize that you have some control over your life.

58

Where Are You Now?

Answer the following questions to determine your present location on the Maslow Triangle. If you answer yes to the questions in each section, color in the corresponding section on the triangle below.

SURVIVAL

Do you have enough food and water to survive?	Yes	No
Do you have a place to live?	Yes	No
Do you have enough clothes to keep you warm?	Yes	No

SECURITY AND SAFETY

Do you feel safe?	Yes	No
Do you feel secure?	Yes	No

SENSE OF BELONGING

Do you feel you belong somewhere?	Yes	No
Do you feel loved?	Yes	No

SELF-ESTEEM

Do you feel good about yourself?	Yes	No
Do you feel worthwhile or valuable as a human being?	Yes	No

SELF-ACTUALIZATION

Do you feel accomplished?	Yes	No
Do you feel mature?	Yes	No
Do you trust your judgment?	Yes	No
Do you feel in control of your life?	Yes	No

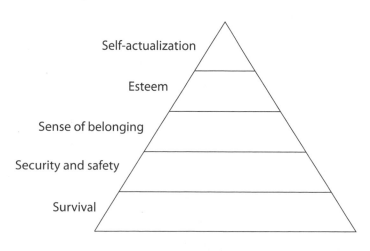

Self-actualization
Esteem
Sense of belonging
Security and safety
Survival

59

How Do You Want to be Remembered?

The goal is not to live forever, but to create something that will.

— Chuck Palahniuk

Walter Johnson always seemed to be three steps ahead of everyone else. When other children his age were learning to crawl, Walter was learning to in-line skate. "A much more efficient means of transportation," he explained to his mother.

At five, Walter was memorizing Homer's *Odyssey* — in Greek. "Such a musical language," he said. Few people were surprised when Walter graduated at the top of his college class at age 14.

However, even his mother was shocked to find 16-year-old Walter carving his own tombstone in the family basement. "What are you doing?" she exclaimed. "Are you sick? What's going on? You have to tell me!"

"I'm fine, Mom," he said. "No sense putting this off until the last minute. Besides, I have a use for it now. I need it to show me how to live."

"What do you mean?" she asked.

"I've carved it right here — what I want to be remembered for. For now, it will be my guide. It will help me make decisions and make the best use of my time."

He held up the stone. WALTER JOHNSON, it said. HE GAVE IT HIS BEST SHOT.

It may seem odd, but Walter's idea is a good one. One of the best ways to determine what you really want out of life is to think about how you want to be remembered after death. Caught up in the demands of day-to-day living, we often lose track of our fondest dreams, our mission in life, our legacy.

We all want to be recognized or acknowledged for some action, way of being, or accomplishment. This is a basic human need. Taking the time now to think about the contribution you would like to make in your lifetime will help give your life direction.

How would you like to be remembered? Do any of these epitaphs strike a chord?

JACK LITTLE: BEST COOK IN CHICAGO

SARITA PATEL: EVERYBODY LOVED HER

FARID MANSOUR: A NEW CAR EVERY YEAR

BERTA SANTINI: CRUSADER FOR JUSTICE

MAURICIO PEREZ: HE MADE PEOPLE LAUGH

AN NGUYEN: FIRST WOMAN PRESIDENT OF THE UNITED STATES

SAMUEL STEVENS: TEACHER OF THE YEAR

LUCY BARTON: PROUD OWNER OF 139 PAIRS OF SHOES

CONNIE FITZPATRICK: WORLD TRAVELER

LEWIS JONES: PEACEMAKER

ROBERTA ZIMMER: SUPERSTAR

HAROLD CLAUSSEN: FAMILY MAN

MARGARET GONZALES: PHILANTHROPIST

LEE CHUNG: POET

In the space below, write your own epitaph. How do you want to be remembered? At the end of your life, what would you have to have done in order to be thought of that way? You don't have to limit your answer to a single line, but keep it brief.

Try not to get hung up on external forms of success, such as making a million dollars. You are more likely to be remembered — and to feel good about yourself — because of what you do with the money. If you must have that million, consider how you would use it. Would you set up a scholarship fund? Build a wing of a hospital? Assure the future security of your family? Save the whales? Retire and become a community volunteer?

Consider your personal heroes. These might be world figures like Anne Frank or Mohandas Gandhi, or they might be known only to a few, such as the coach who made you believe in yourself or the stutterer who landed the lead in the class play. What do these people tell you about your values?

Think about your passions and your dreams as well. And remember that, unlike Walter's, *your* mission is not carved in stone. It may change as you develop new beliefs, dreams, and goals.

_____ : _____

Your Name

_____

_____

_____

Your Lifestyle

As you may be beginning to see, your career choice will affect more than the 40 hours a week you'll spend on the job. A job title often suggests a whole way of life. Rock star, scientist, farmer, carpenter — when we think of people in these occupations, we immediately visualize what they wear, where they live, who their friends are, perhaps even the person they voted for in the last election. (We may be *wrong,* mind you. However, in general, you won't find too many farmers in Manhattan, and most scientists are not close personal friends of Beyoncé.) In short, your career will help define your lifestyle.

What do we mean when we talk about lifestyle? Until recently, the word didn't even appear in the dictionary. Sociologists and psychologists have, however, come to realize that the way people live, the way they think and feel, what's important to them, and how they spend their time, money, and energy help explain not only individual lives, but how and why our society works the way it does. The term *lifestyle* is a composite of your income and education, your attitudes, your political and spiritual beliefs, where you choose to live, how you earn and spend your money, what is most important to you — even how secure and happy you are likely to be.

Before you begin researching possible careers, it is important to try to determine what type of lifestyle you want. Your career choice will have a great impact on the type of lifestyle you will lead.

COMPONENTS OF LIFESTYLE

Lifestyle has many components. Think about your ideal future life and then complete this questionnaire.

RELATIONSHIPS

Are you or do you want to be married, in a committed relationship, or remain single? _____
Have children? _____ If so, how many? _____

What kinds of people would you like to be your friends? _____
_____

How much time (hours per week) will you want to spend with your family? Your friends?
_____

WORK

How much time do you want to spend at your chosen profession? Less than 20 hours per week? 20 – 40 hours per week? 40 – 50 hours? As long as it takes?
_____

What is your mission in life?   What sort of commitment do you want or need to make to some larger goal?
_____

What are your other priorities that require time and attention?
_____

PERSONAL

How much time each week would you like to spend on:

Recreation _____ Individual pursuits _____ Contemplation and relaxation _____

How much flexibility do you want in your life? _____

What will be the "pace" of your life? Are you a high-energy person who always needs to have many projects at once, or are you a person who likes to tackle one thing at a time?
_____

How will you meet your spiritual needs? _____

MATERIAL ITEMS

Where do you want to live? Describe the location and housing. _____
_____

What income level would you like to reach? _____

Describe the possessions you want most. _____
_____

Happiness Is a Balanced Lifestyle

Emma is a stockbroker who is totally dedicated to her work. She seldom gets home before 10 at night, and is back at her desk by 7:00 A.M. She devotes her weekends to reading annual reports and books and articles dealing with her job. She hasn't taken a vacation in five years and has no close friends or outside interests.

I've learned that you can't have everything and do everything at the same time.

—Oprah Winfrey

Isaac is a police officer in a small town. He and his wife have two children. He volunteers at a homeless shelter two nights a week and coaches his daughters' softball team. In order to save money, Isaac and his wife are renovating their house by themselves. He attends night school, working toward a degree in criminology. Issac is also a guitarist with a small band that plays for local social events. He tries to do his share of the housework and thinks it's important to spend time with his children each day. Isaac and his wife go out alone at least once a week. His parents are getting older, and he likes to see them often. He enjoys going out with his friends.

Emma and Isaac have little in common — except that both have problems balancing their lives. Emma's life is incomplete. There are times when it is necessary to center your attention on one part of your life (finishing a project at work or recuperating from an illness, for example). However, Emma may never be truly happy if she keeps up her current pattern indefinitely. She needs to look at Maslow's Triangle.

Isaac is probably already aware that his life is *too* full. Some people have enormous amounts of energy and are able to juggle a wide variety of interests, activities, and responsibilities, but there are only 24 hours in a day and everyone has to sleep *sometime.* Isaac needs to decide which activities are most important to him and which ones he can most easily give up.

The exact makeup of a balanced lifestyle will be different for everyone. Some people want to give most of their attention to their work. For others, family is most important. Some people want or need to give priority to health concerns. But, in general, an emotionally and physically healthy life will include time for the following:

Physical health: Time to sleep and eat wisely must be built into every balanced lifestyle. Healthy people need time for both exercise and relaxation. Other health needs vary.

Work: Work is a central activity and source of identity for most adults. How important is it for you? Will you work part-time? Full-time? More than 40 hours a week? Would you like to be able to take time out when you have small children?

Family/relationships: Are you married or will you marry and have children? Marry and *not* have children? Surround yourself with a group of close friends? Today, there is a wide range of acceptable ways to meet your needs for close relationships with others. Your best choice might depend on the weight you assign other parts of your life. For example, Emma would almost certainly be happier if she had good friends and a circle of acquaintances she could socialize with regularly. Whether she would be happy being married with three children is questionable.

Do you want to have children? They take time and attention, especially when they are young. How would you adjust your lifestyle to accommodate them? For example, could you earn enough money working part-time? Could you work at home?

Leisure and recreation: Your balanced lifestyle should include time for hobbies, avocations, and the leisure activities that add so much to life. Will you travel? Have a garden? Follow your favorite sport or athletic team? Read or go to the movies?

Spiritual life: The dictionary defines spirit as "that which constitutes one's unseen, intangible being" or "the essential and activating principle of a person." Many people realize their spiritual needs through their religion. Others choose to "give something back" to the world by working as a volunteer or getting involved with organizations that promote conservation, peace, or human rights. Some people meet their spiritual needs privately, through meditation, reading, walking, and the like.

With all these considerations, it's easy to see how a life can get off balance!

The key to keeping your balance is knowing when you've lost it.

—Anonymous

The Modified Maslow Triangle

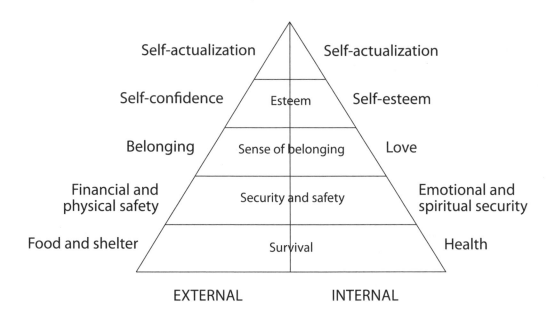

To make it easier to visualize a balanced lifestyle, we have divided Maslow's Triangle down the middle. Although the hierarchy of needs remains the same, *our* triangle differentiates professional, or external, needs (shown on the left side) from personal, or internal, needs (diagrammed on the right).

> **Our external lives** include such things as careers, the tasks we do, the possessions we accumulate, the roles we play, and the way others see us. Our social and educational systems teach us to deal almost exclusively with this side of life.

> **By internal lives**, we mean our physical and spiritual well-being, our values, and our personal relationships. This is the side of life society tends to ignore. This may account for the increased use of drugs, depression, divorce, and general discontent we are experiencing today.

If either side is given too much emphasis, our lives become unbalanced. Life satisfaction decreases. It is possible on our double triangle to achieve one level of fulfillment in career life and quite another in personal matters. The happiest people are those who engage in both aspects of life. They are less willing to sacrifice one part for the sake of the other.

However, it's often a difficult balancing act. Today, especially, people attempting to mix career and family are having problems finding the time for all the important activities in their lives. It takes careful and creative planning to balance all of the areas of your life.

Let's go through our divided triangle, level by level. It's necessary to repeat ourselves somewhat, so please be patient.

Just as the most basic external need is for **food and shelter** (left), **good health** is the most basic personal need (right). Until we have these, we are unable to satisfy the next level of needs—**financial and physical safety** on the left side, **spiritual and emotional security** on the right side. It is impossible for most people to experience life satisfaction unless they reach these first two levels of fulfillment. Yet many people begin to make trade-offs here. They sacrifice their health in order to make more money even though, without good health, they cannot hope to enjoy their lives.

Those who feel confident of the ability to support themselves—without giving up physical or emotional health—can move on to the next level of need: **love** (on the right or personal side) and **belonging** (on the left or professional side). Although it is important to "belong," to have a circle of acquaintances and casual friends, it is also necessary to have at least one deeper relationship. This might be with a spouse, a best friend, or someone else to whom you feel particularly close and committed.

People who do not have satisfying relationships with others cannot move on to achieve **self-confidence and achievement** (on the external side) and self-esteem (an internal need). At this level, you like yourself and feel good about what you are doing. Again, we see the necessity to consider the needs on both sides of the triangle. You might feel confident of your ability to succeed by cheating, lying, or manipulating, but if success comes at the expense of your **self-esteem**, it is not likely to make you happy. Shortcuts, even when successful, carry costs that will lessen good feelings.

Once you have attained both confidence and self-esteem, you are on your way to becoming one of those rare **self-actualizers**, someone who is satisfied and happy with her or his life.

Life is not in having and getting, but in being and becoming.

—Matthew Arnold

How can you tell if you are neglecting one side of your life? Besides the obvious ways — losing your health, your job, your close relationship — listen to your inner voice. Be aware of your feelings. Do you ever begin sentences with phrases such as "if only," "I wish," "I should but I can't," or "If I had the time I would?" These are clues that your life is not as satisfying as it might be. It's time to take a closer look and make some changes.

Let's see what Emma's and Isaac's diagrams might look like:

Emma has a good job and the respect of her colleagues and superiors. She thinks her work is of value, and loves what she does. Because she puts in so many hours, however, she has no time for personal relationships or private interests, and the stress of her job has placed her health in jeopardy. Emma's triangle looks like this:

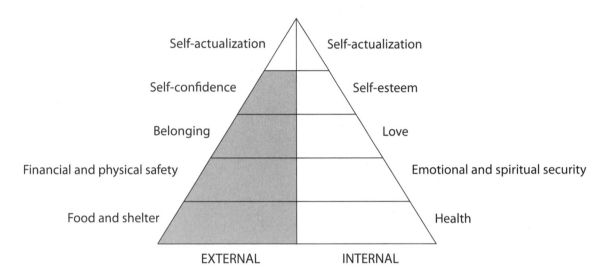

Isaac, too, has a good job and the respect of his community. He feels good about working toward his degree in criminology. He loves his wife and children and has many friends. Unfortunately, he seems to be exhausted all the time because of all he does, and he gets down on himself because he can't always do what he's promised. Many of his projects are done haphazardly or not completed. Isaac's triangle looks like this:

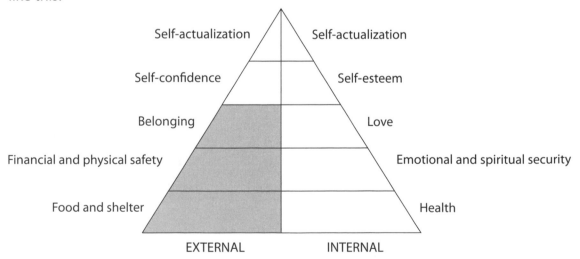

Especially when you don't make conscious changes in your life, things can get off kilter over time. That's why it is important to re-evaluate your situation regularly and try to become more aware of your feelings.

When Joanie was 25, she had a financially secure job that she loved, the respect of her fellow workers, and a circle of devoted and loving friends. Shade the triangle below to represent the levels Joanie had attained in both her professional and personal life.

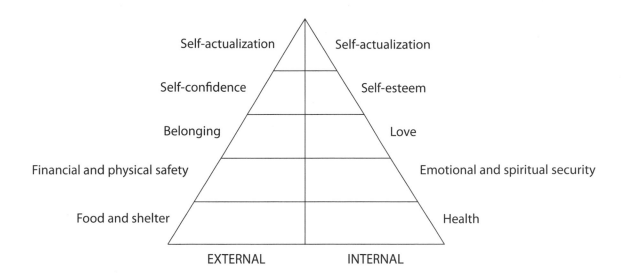

By the time she was 30, things had changed. Her job seemed less satisfying, though she put in many hours. The resulting stress caused health problems. Many of her friends had married and started families or moved away to take new jobs, and Joanie's social life dramatically changed. She thought she might like to have a family of her own, but she wasn't dating anyone at the moment. Shade this triangle to show how Joanie's life had changed.

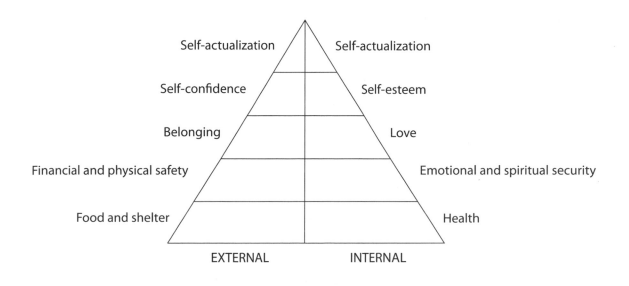

What About Your Life?

Describe your life right now:

How is your health? Do you get enough to eat? Do you have adequate housing? Do you feel financially secure and physically safe? Do you feel emotionally secure? Are your spiritual needs being met? Do you feel you belong to a group? Do you feel loved? Do you like yourself? Do you feel confident about your abilities and who you are? Are you satisfied and happy?

Shade the triangle below to show the balance in your life right now. Do you need to make any adjustments? What could you do to make your life more satisfying?

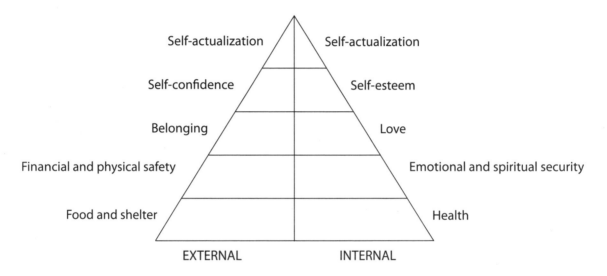

Now ask these same questions of one of your parents or older friends and interpret his or her responses.

Shade the triangle below to show his or her balance.

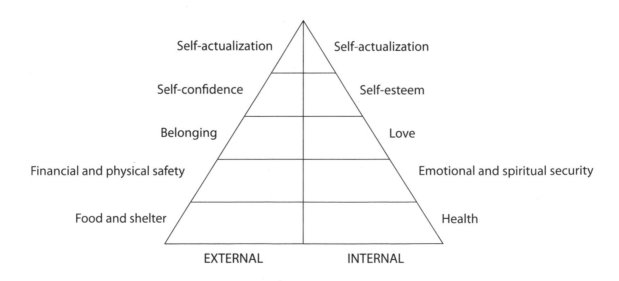

What do you think the triangle of a homeless person living alone would look like?

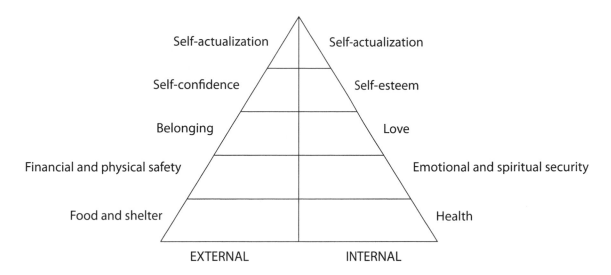

Self-actualization   Self-actualization

Self-confidence   Self-esteem

Belonging   Love

Financial and physical safety   Emotional and spiritual security

Food and shelter   Health

EXTERNAL   INTERNAL

Your desired lifestyle is something to be considered when making career decisions. As you will see in the next chapter, however, any way of life you choose involves costs as well as rewards. These might relate to finances, psychological rewards or sacrifices, or the degree of commitment required.

CHAPTER 3 CHECKPOINTS
Lifestyles of the Satisfied and Happy
Keeping your balance and perspective

You have begun to answer the question "What do I want?" as it relates to your ideal lifestyle. Check that you've reached the goals listed below, essential for living a balanced and satisfying life.

☐ I understand Maslow's hierarchy of needs and its impact on my identity and self-esteem.

☐ I started to identify an overall goal or mission for my life.

☐ I projected myself into the future and recognized the diversity of lifestyle options available to me.

☐ I identified the components of a balanced lifestyle and appreciate the desirability of balancing internal and external, personal and professional, private and public life.

☐ I experienced the balanced lifestyle evaluation process and realized the effect that outside forces can have on my life and my role in mitigating these.

It's good to have money and the things money can buy,
but it's good too, to check once in a while and make sure
that you haven't lost the things that money can't buy.
—George Horace Lorimer

I'd rather have roses on my table
than diamonds on my neck.
—Emma Goldman

CHAPTER FOUR
What Cost This Lifestyle?

Every career choice involves sacrifices and rewards

Ralph Tuttle, young business reporter for the *Daily Bugle*, was upset. His interview with Ivy Elms, the highest paid executive in the world, was not proceeding as expected. This was supposed to be Ralph's big chance. He could almost see the headlines: IVY ELMS REVEALS SECRETS FOR SUCCESS TO JUNIOR REPORTER. Instead, the famous executive was running on about things that made no sense to Ralph. Was she senile? Ralph cheered up a bit. Maybe that was another angle he could use for his story.

"Making a lot of money can be one of the most expensive things in the world," Ivy said when Ralph tuned back in to the interview. "I'm lucky I can afford this job."

"Wow," Ralph thought. "She really is going off the deep end." He decided to play along with her. "Just what do you mean by that, Miss Elms?"

Ivy poured herself a glass of mineral water from the crystal decanter on her enormous rosewood desk. She removed two tablets from a sterling silver pill box, explaining, "This one's for my blood pressure, and this for my ulcer. Been taking them for years. Fortunately, I've never had any real health problems. Health is one of the first things a high-pressure job like this can cost."

Ralph's face brightened. "OH! I get it. You mean making a lot of money is expensive because of the other things you have to give up, right?"

"I knew you'd catch on sooner or later," Ivy said.

"So what else has your success cost you?"

"One of the sad things is that you never know exactly what your life might have been. No one ever knows that, so you just have to go after what seems most important. I always wanted to be a big success in business. This company has been my family, my best friend, my only hobby. I invested my life in it, you might say. I never married or had children — didn't think I could spare the time. Now I often wonder if people are nice to me only because they want something they think I can give them.

"This power to affect so many lives is a big responsibility. I worry about it. What happens if I make a mistake and profits fall and I have to lay some people off? There's no one else to blame. I also worry about leaving the company in good shape. There are all those young, ambitious people out there wanting to take my job away from me. That makes me more determined, and then I work a little harder, which takes its toll on my health and my sense of humor.

Nothing is ever enough when what you are looking for isn't what you really want.

— Arianna Huffington

"But I got what I wanted and, more or less, I'm happy with that. I live very well — beautiful homes, expensive cars, even a corporate jet. I'm known and respected all over the world. I have the pleasure of knowing that I do an important job, and that I do it better than anyone.

"Always remember, Mr. Tuttle, every job has its costs as well as its rewards. I have wealth, position, and power, but I will always wonder what it's like to have a family."

After the interview, Ralph asked himself what Ivy's story might mean for him. He thought about the way he lived and the way he'd like to live. How important was money to him, he wondered. What did he need to make his life meaningful? Ivy had set her goal early, and she stuck to her plan. She invested heavily in her career. Ralph thought about the commitment that called for and wondered if he was willing to follow through in the same way.

How much will your
dream lifestyle cost —
in money, in physical
and emotional health,
in commitment?

Every job involves three different kinds of rewards — and sacrifices. The most obvious consideration is financial — how much money can you expect to earn at this job? Your salary will visibly affect your lifestyle. That is why it is essential to consider the cost — in dollars — of the material things you want to include in your life when making career decisions. Is it reasonable to expect that an elementary school teacher will be delivered to his classroom in a chauffeur-driven limousine?

The second consideration involves the physical, emotional, or psychological rewards and sacrifices of a given career. This concern is tied directly to your own values. What is most important to you? The idea is not to find a job that offers only rewards — as far as we can determine, no such job exists. However, one person's reward may be a sacrifice to someone else. Being a politician, for example, may offer large rewards to someone who values recognition. For someone who values privacy, though, this career would require a big sacrifice. When you look at potential careers, consider both the rewards and the sacrifices and try to find one that matches your own values closely.

The third consideration is commitment. Do you want this job or lifestyle badly enough to invest the required time, money, and energy to prepare for it? Some people decide to scale down their dreams when they find they don't have the "stick-to-itiveness" to make them come true, or if they think the sacrifices are too great. For example, one man we know who grew up believing he would be head of a major corporation abandoned that plan to work for a smaller firm. The change allows him to pursue other interests and to have more time for family and community affairs. He thinks the trade-off was worthwhile.

This chapter is designed to help you determine just how much your dream lifestyle will cost: in money, in physical and emotional health, and in commitment.

To begin, you need to consider the income you would need to support your ideal lifestyle.

Your Budget

For the Lifestyle You Envision

Let's talk about the kind of lifestyle you want to have — and how much money it is likely to cost. The following exercise asks you to make choices about everything from where you'd like to live to the vacations you'd like to take. Charts are provided to show approximate costs for many choices. Better yet, the Internet is a wonderful financial resource tool. The calculators and information available online will help you customize your budget to the penny. Once you make your choices in each category, enter your monthly expense in the space provided.

Since the point of the exercise is to help you make career decisions for your future, don't base your choices on what you think is realistic for you right now. Instead, think of the way you would like to be living at some specific point in the future, at least 10 years from now.

Choose an age and then complete this statement: Today, I am _____ years old.

In _____ years, when I am _____ years old, this is how I would like my life to look.

Family Profile

The first choice you need to make concerns your future family. In the real world, this choice is not totally under your control; for now, dream away. Check the marital status you see for yourself at the age you've chosen, and indicate the number of children you'll have, if any. Fill in the ages of your children.

MARITAL STATUS	CHILDREN	AGES OF CHILDREN
☐ Single	0 _____	_____
☐ Married	1 _____	_____
☐ Divorced	2 _____	_____
☐ Separated	3 _____	_____
☐ Widowed	4 _____	_____
☐ Other	5 _____	_____

What other dependants will you have? Is it possible you will be responsible for your aging parents?

OTHER DEPENDANTS

_____

_____

_____

_____

WHERE I WOULD LIKE TO LIVE

_____

_____

WHY?

_____

Housing

Housing is the most expensive item on most people's budget. It is possible that your spouse will inherit the family estate (tax-free, of course), but don't count on it. For the purpose of this exercise, assume that you will have to allot a portion of your income for a place to live.

Keep your own values in mind as you complete this exercise. It's *your* dreams we're interested in, not your best friend's.

Do you want to live in:

☐ Government housing   ☐ A farm or ranch

☐ A rental apartment   ☐ A cabin

☐ A cooperative apartment   ☐ A luxury home/estate

☐ A rental house   ☐ No permanent home

☐ Your own home   ☐ Other _____

☐ A condominium

How many bedrooms? _____ Bathrooms? _____

Other distinguishing features _____

_____

Check the classified advertisement section of a newspaper or a local realtor's web site to get an idea of the sales prices of homes and rental rates. The charts on the next page may help you figure your monthly costs.

Monthly payment/rent	$ _____
Monthly property taxes	$ _____
Monthly insurance	$ _____
Total utilities/phone	$ _____
Housing	$ _____ [1]

Enter at [1] on page 92, Your Budget Profile.

Keywords: factors rent versus buy, rent apartments [city], rent homes [city], property tax [city], home insurance calculator, average utility costs

Here are some interesting charts for comparison.

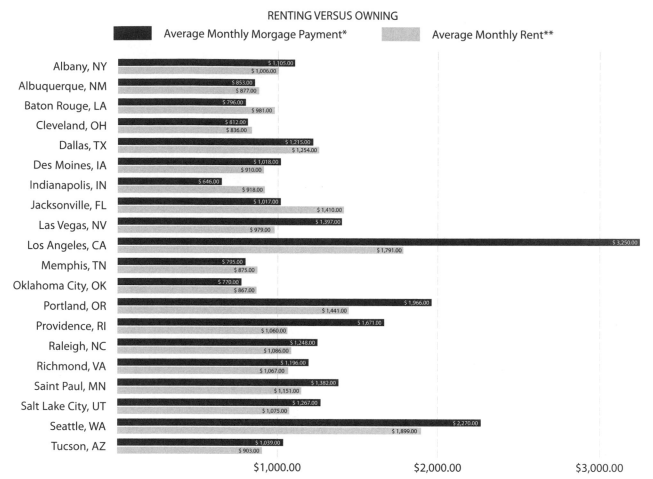

RENTING VERSUS OWNING

■ Average Monthly Morgage Payment*   ▨ Average Monthly Rent**

City	Mortgage	Rent
Albany, NY	$1,105.00	$1,006.00
Albuquerque, NM	$853.00	$877.00
Baton Rouge, LA	$796.00	$981.00
Cleveland, OH	$812.00	$836.00
Dallas, TX	$1,215.00	$1,254.00
Des Moines, IA	$1,018.00	$910.00
Indianapolis, IN	$646.00	$918.00
Jacksonville, FL	$1,017.00	$1,410.00
Las Vegas, NV	$1,397.00	$979.00
Los Angeles, CA	$3,250.00	$1,791.00
Memphis, TN	$795.00	$875.00
Oklahoma City, OK	$770.00	$867.00
Portland, OR	$1,966.00	$1,441.00
Providence, RI	$1,671.00	$1,060.00
Raleigh, NC	$1,248.00	$1,086.00
Richmond, VA	$1,196.00	$1,067.00
Saint Paul, MN	$1,382.00	$1,151.00
Salt Lake City, UT	$1,267.00	$1,075.00
Seattle, WA	$2,270.00	$1,899.00
Tucson, AZ	$1,039.00	$903.00

$1,000.00 $2,000.00 $3,000.00

* Average Monthly Mortgage Payment calculated using information from Federal Financial Institutions Examination Council Median Family Income (MFI) Report, 2018 and Kiplinger "Home Prices in the 100 Largest Metro Areas," January 2019.
** Average Monthly Rent for a two-bedroom unit using data from the U.S. Department of Housing and Urban Development, HUD Metropolitan Fair Market Rates Documentation System, FY 2019.

MONTHLY MORTGAGE PAYMENTS IF INTEREST IS: (factored at 30-year fixed rate and includes insurance and taxes)							
Loan Amount	3%	4%	5%	6%	7%	8%	9%
$60,000	$253	$287	$322	$360	$399	$440	$483
$80,000	$337	$382	$429	$480	$532	$587	$644
$100,000	$422	$477	$537	$600	$665	$734	$805
$125,000	$527	$597	$671	$749	$832	$917	$1006
$150,000	$632	$716	$805	$899	$998	$1,101	$1,207
$175,000	$738	$835	$939	$1,049	$1,164	$1,284	$1,408
$200,000	$843	$955	$1,074	$1,199	$1,331	$1,468	$1,609
$250,000	$1,054	$1,194	$1,342	$1,499	$1,663	$1,834	$2,012
$300,000	$1,265	$1,432	$1,610	$1,799	$1,996	$2,201	$2,414

FIRST-TIME HOMEBUYER AFFORDABILITY, 2018						
Starter Home Price	20% Down Payment	Loan Amount	Effective Interest Rate	Monthly Income	Qualifying Payment	Payment as a % of Income
$222,400	$44,480	$177,920	4.72%	$1,071	$51,408	25%

Source: National Association of Realtors®, First-Time Homebuyer Affordability, 2019.

Transportation

Before you choose the kind of transportation you'll want or need, think about where you said you'd like to live. In some cities, it's quite easy to walk or use public transportation. In some places, a vehicle is almost a necessity. Consider, too, your physical condition and your mechanical ability.

Do you want to get around by:

- ☐ Walking
- ☐ Bicycle
- ☐ Motorcycle
- ☐ Public transportation
- ☐ Your own car, previously owned
- ☐ Your own car, bought new every 7–8 years

- ☐ Your own car, bought new every 3–4 years
- ☐ Your own car, bought new every year
- ☐ Limousine/car service
- ☐ Other _____

If you want to own your own car:

What make? _____ Model? _____ Year? _____

How many miles per month do you plan to drive? _____

Monthly car payments	$ _____
Gasoline	$ _____
Maintenance and insurance	$ _____
Public transportation	$ _____
Transportation	$ _____ [2]

Enter at [2] on page 92.

If you think nobody cares if you're alive, try missing a couple of car payments.

—Earl Wilson

Keywords: transportation options [city], public transportation [city], cost of owning a car

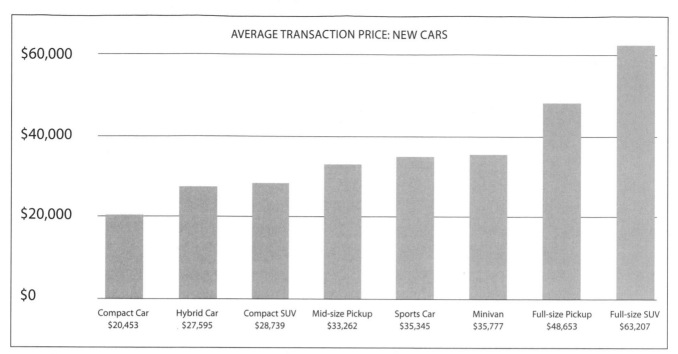

AVERAGE TRANSACTION PRICE: NEW CARS

Compact Car $20,453	Hybrid Car $27,595	Compact SUV $28,739	Mid-size Pickup $33,262	Sports Car $35,345	Minivan $35,777	Full-size Pickup $48,653	Full-size SUV $63,207

Source: *Kelley Blue Book*, Average New-Car Prices Up More Than 1 Percent Year-Over-Year for December 2018, Closing the Strongest Year of Growth Since 2013, According to *Kelley Blue Book*, KBB.com, January 3, 2019.

PASSENGER CAR OPERATING COSTS

	Variable Costs in Cents per Mile			Cost Per 10,000 Miles			
	GAS	MAINTENANCE + TIRES	VARIABLE TOTAL	VARIABLE COSTS	FIXED COSTS	TOTAL COST	TOTAL COST PER MILE
Hybrid	$0.0570	$0.0749	$0.1319	$1,319	$5,205	$6,524	$0.6524
Small SUV (FWD)	$0.0912	$0.0845	$0.1757	$1,757	$4,907	$6,664	$0.6664
Medium Sedan	$0.0918	$0.0858	$0.1776	$1,776	$5,944	$7,720	$0.7720
Minvan	$0.1187	$0.0823	$0.2010	$2,010	$6,360	$8,370	$0.8370
Medium SUV (4WD)	$0.1243	$0.0866	$0.2109	$2,109	$6,120	$8,229	$0.8229
1/2-Ton Crew-Cab Pickup	$0.1505	$0.0813	$0.2318	$2,318	$6,245	$8,563	$0.8563

* Fixed Costs include insurance, license, registration, taxes, depreciation, and finance charges.
Source: AAA (American Automobile Association), "Your Driving Costs," 2018 Edition.

Clothing

Your clothing budget depends on your talents, your tastes, and the time you want to devote to this part of your life. Perhaps you are one of those creative types who can whip up exciting outfits from plastic bags and old neckties. Maybe you always have and always will live in blue jeans. Bargain hunters, given enough time, can produce expensive designer wardrobes at discount store prices. Others wouldn't consider buying anything at less than full price. Some people, short on time, are willing to spend whatever is necessary to get what they need in a hurry.

Think about how much money you feel would be a reasonable amount to spend each year on clothing for yourself and each member of your family. How do you prefer to come by your clothes? Do you want or need an extensive wardrobe, or will just the basics do? Don't forget to make allotments for shoes, bathing suits, and other items that may not come immediately to mind. Then answer the questions below.

For clothing, I plan to:

☐ Sew for the family

☐ Purchase thrift store or "vintage" clothing

☐ Buy from discount or outlet stores

☐ Always buy on sale

☐ Buy from department stores and boutiques

☐ Buy designer fashions

☐ Other _____

I would like to have:

☐ A minimum wardrobe

☐ A moderate-size wardrobe

☐ An extensive wardrobe

☐ What I want, when I want it

Keywords: average clothing budget

List each member of your family and his or her projected clothing budget:

Family Member   Annual Budget

_____ $ _____

_____ $ _____

_____ $ _____

_____ $ _____

_____ $ _____

_____ $ _____

            Annual Family Total $ _____

Divide this figure by 12 to get your monthly clothing budget.

            Clothing $ _____   [3]

Enter at [3] on page 92.

Food

You've got bad eating habits if you use a grocery cart in 7-Eleven.

—Dennis Miller

Some years back, a TV commercial featured a well-known naturalist who asked that memorable question, "Ever eat a pine tree?" He went on to inform viewers that "Some parts are edible." Perhaps. But most of us have come to expect more sophisticated fare. Still, there's plenty of room for negotiation between grazing in the forest and living solely on steak and caviar. The government has defined four kinds of food plans, each of which supplies the necessary nutrients. The Thrifty Plan is based on low-cost foods (beans, rice), but these may be unappealing to some people and may take more time for preparation. The Moderate Plan offers a greater variety of foods. The Liberal Plan lets you buy whatever you want, regardless of the cost.

Would you like your diet to be based on:

☐ The Thrifty Plan ☐ The Moderate Plan

☐ The Low-Cost Plan ☐ The Liberal Plan

Do you have any special dietary habits that might increase your food budget (i.e., gourmet cooking is your hobby, you have a restricted diet)? The chart on page 85 may help you come up with an amount.

Food $ _____ [4]

Enter at [4] on page 92.

Sundries

Sundries are all those little things you pick up at the grocery or drug store: Shampoo, deodorant, toilet paper, cleaning supplies, and the like. How much would you plan to spend on these items each month?

Sundries $ _____ [5]

Enter at [5] on page 92.

Keywords: average food budget

The chart below is to help you come up with some estimated food costs. Pick the family size closest to the family profile you outlined on page 77 and then pick the type of food plan (thrifty, low-cost, moderate-cost, or liberal) you would prefer. If the sample family sizes don't match your profile, you can always add to your estimate using the individual costs.

COST OF FOOD AT HOME Per Month				
	Thrifty Plan	Low-Cost Plan	Moderate-Cost Plan	Liberal Plan
Family of 2:				
19-50 years of age	$387.90	$497.30	$614.90	$769.20
Family of 4:				
Couple & 2 Preschoolers	$566.30	$724.20	$893.00	$1,103.80
Couple & 2 School Age	$649.60	$852.70	$1,066.20	$1,294.00
INDIVIDUALS				
Child:				
1 year	$95.10	$127.80	$145.70	$177.10
2–3 years	$104.00	$134.20	$161.50	$195.80
4–5 years	$109.60	$137.90	$172.50	$208.70
6–8 years	$138.90	$192.00	$234.40	$276.90
9–11 years	$158.10	$208.60	$272.70	$317.90
Male: 19–50 years	$186.70	$242.10	$302.00	$369.50
Female: 19–50 years	$165.90	$210.00	$257.00	$329.80

Source: U.S. Department of Agriculture, USDA Food Plans: Cost of Food Report, March 2019.

Entertainment and Recreation

Although the following budget items are not necessary to sustain life, they do have an impact on your self-esteem and life satisfaction. Answer the following questions, remembering to consider your spouse and your children's needs as well.

Monthly Total

How many times/month will you eat at a restaurant? _____

What will your average bill be? $ _____

How much per month will be spent on meals out? $ _____

Would you like to entertain friends?

What would you spend per month? $ _____

Would you like to attend concerts, movies, plays, sports events, and the like?

What would you spend per month? $ _____

Will you download music or mobile apps? Subscribe to newspapers and magazines on your e-book reader?

How much a month would you like to spend? $ _____

Will you have hobbies or take part in sports that cost money?

Which ones? _____

How much will you need a month? $ _____

If you have children, what kinds of recreational/educational opportunities do you want for them? (Check their ages again.)

What? _____

How much will be spent per month? $ _____

One more consideration: Do you want to have special equipment related to entertainment or recreation? Would you like to have a laptop or tablet computer, MP3 player, gaming system, HDTV, musical instrument, boat, plane, country club or health club membership?

What do you want to spend on them per month? $ _____

Total entertainment $ _____ [6]

Enter at [6] on page 92.

Keywords: average spent entertainment per household, average spent eating out

Vacations

This is not so much a "whether or not" budget item as it is a "where and how often" expenditure. It's been shown that taking time off is an important part of maintaining good physical and mental health. How do you want to do it?

Do you want to take a vacation:

- ☐ Monthly
- ☐ Every six months
- ☐ Yearly

- ☐ Every two years
- ☐ Every three to five years
- ☐ Other _____

What kind of vacation would you like to be able to afford:

- ☐ Car trip to relatives
- ☐ Camping/hiking
- ☐ Day trips to local amusements
- ☐ A week at the seashore or mountain cabin
- ☐ Car trips to places of interest

- ☐ Plane trips to places of interest
- ☐ Foreign travel
- ☐ Cruises, travel packages, or exotic locations
- ☐ Other _____
- ☐ Other _____
- ☐ Other _____

What will you want to budget every year to meet your vacation objectives? $ _____

Divide that figure by 12 to come up with your monthly figure.

Vacation $ _____ [7]

Enter at [7] on page 92.

Keywords: average cost vacation

Child Care

If you are working while there are young children in the family (a reasonable assumption), you will need to consider your child care options. First, look back to see how many children you are planning to have and their ages.

Would you have:

☐ No need for child care

☐ A relative to care for them

☐ A cooperative arrangement with a relative or friend

☐ Care in a community-based center

☐ A private nursery school or day care center

☐ A sitter coming into your home

☐ Live-in help

How much will this cost per child, per month?

child one $ _____

child two $ _____

child three $ _____

Total child care costs $ _____ [8]
Enter at [8] on page 92.

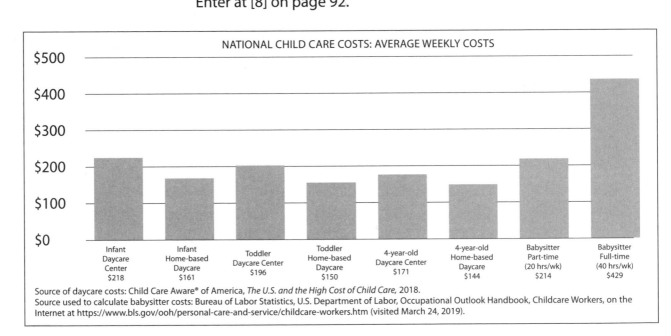

NATIONAL CHILD CARE COSTS: AVERAGE WEEKLY COSTS

Infant Daycare Center $218	Infant Home-based Daycare $161	Toddler Daycare Center $196	Toddler Home-based Daycare $150	4-year-old Daycare Center $171	4-year-old Home-based Daycare $144	Babysitter Part-time (20 hrs/wk) $214	Babysitter Full-time (40 hrs/wk) $429

Source of daycare costs: Child Care Aware® of America, *The U.S. and the High Cost of Child Care*, 2018.
Source used to calculate babysitter costs: Bureau of Labor Statistics, U.S. Department of Labor, Occupational Outlook Handbook, Childcare Workers, on the Internet at https://www.bls.gov/ooh/personal-care-and-service/childcare-workers.htm (visited March 24, 2019).

Dependant Care

If you indicated at the beginning of this exercise that you plan to care for a dependant other than your children (a parent or grandparent, for example), remember to add that into your monthly budget. What do you plan to spend on dependant care? $ _____

What if there is a divorce or separation in your future? Will you need to pay alimony or child support? How much? $ _____ Keep these costs in mind as you plan for monthly reserves.

Keywords: average childcare costs, average elder care costs, child support [state], alimony [state]

Health Care

Because an unforeseen accident or illness can play havoc with the most carefully planned budget, health insurance is a must. Many employers will subsidize your health insurance, but usually you will have to pay a portion of the cost. What kind of care do you want?

☐ Government-subsidized free clinics   ☐ Private physician and dentist

☐ Health Maintenance Organization care

See page 94 for some sample annual costs. Divide your projected annual costs by 12 months.

Health Care $ _____ [9]

Enter at [9] on page 92.

Furnishings

You probably need to purchase replacement equipment and items for your home, such as linens, appliances, furniture, and decorative items. What about computer or home entertainment equipment? Assume you have most of these items by this time.

Annual budget $ _____ divided by 12.

Furnishings $ _____ [10]

Enter at [10] on page 92.

Savings

This is an important part of any budget. There are predictable things to save for (a house, new furnishings, children's college, retirement) as well as things you'd rather not think about (losing your job, a major illness). It's not fun to spend money on a new roof or water heater, but sometimes it has to be done. And, it's a lot easier if you've planned for it. As a rule of thumb, every family should save at least six months' income in case of emergency.

What do you feel you should save each month for:

☐ Emergencies   ☐ Retirement

☐ Repairs, replacements, or major purchases   ☐ Income cushion

☐ Children's college

Savings $ _____ [11]

Enter at [11] on page 92.

Keywords: average spent health insurance, average spent home furnishings
percentage salary to savings

Miscellaneous

Are there things important to you that we haven't mentioned yet? Think about your values. Here are some possible additional expenses. Add your own if you need to.

What will be your monthly budget for holiday gifts and birthdays? $ _____

Will you have pets? If so, what kind? _____

How much per month will it cost to keep them? $ _____

Will you make contributions to social, political, or religious organizations?
If so, how much per month? $ _____

Do you want to send your children or grandchildren to private schools?   Yes   No   Undecided

How much will this cost per month? $ _____

Do you need an Internet connection, cable TV, cell phone, or other high-tech services?

How much will this cost per month? $ _____

Other costs, list: _____ $ _____

                       _____ $ _____

                       _____ $ _____

                                        Miscellaneous $ _____ [12]

Enter at [12] on page 92.

Keywords: average spent gifts, cost owning pet, cost private school, average spent cable and internet, average spent cell phone

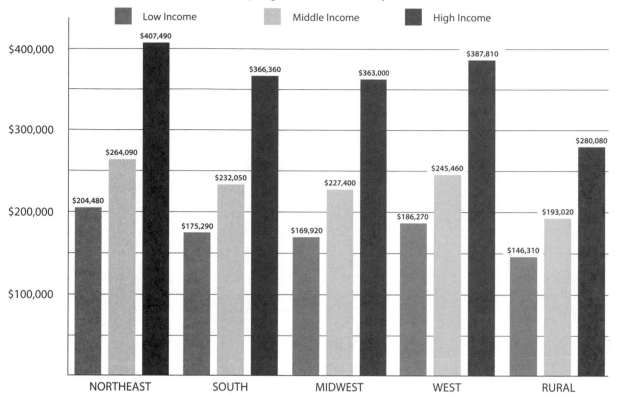

ESTIMATED COST OF RAISING A CHILD: BIRTH TO 17 YEARS OLD
By Region and Income Group

Low Income   Middle Income   High Income

	NORTHEAST	SOUTH	MIDWEST	WEST	RURAL
Low Income	$204,480	$175,290	$169,920	$186,270	$146,310
Middle Income	$264,090	$232,050	$227,400	$245,460	$193,020
High Income	$407,490	$366,360	$363,000	$387,810	$280,080

* Income groups are based on total annual pre-tax household income and are defined as: Low (less than $59,200); Middle ($59,200 to $107,400); High (more than $107,400).

Source: U.S. Department of Agriculture, Center for Nutrition Policy and Promotion, Expenditures on Children by Families, 2015. Released January 2017. Revised March 2017.

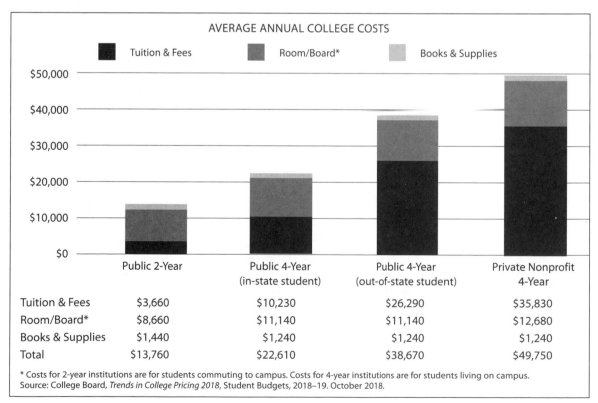

AVERAGE ANNUAL COLLEGE COSTS

Tuition & Fees   Room/Board*   Books & Supplies

	Public 2-Year	Public 4-Year (in-state student)	Public 4-Year (out-of-state student)	Private Nonprofit 4-Year
Tuition & Fees	$3,660	$10,230	$26,290	$35,830
Room/Board*	$8,660	$11,140	$11,140	$12,680
Books & Supplies	$1,440	$1,240	$1,240	$1,240
Total	$13,760	$22,610	$38,670	$49,750

* Costs for 2-year institutions are for students commuting to campus. Costs for 4-year institutions are for students living on campus.
Source: College Board, *Trends in College Pricing 2018*, Student Budgets, 2018–19. October 2018.

Keywords: average family expenditure

Your Lifestyle Budget Profile

Here's the moment of truth. Go through the exercise again and enter the monthly amounts you indicated in each category in the appropriate space below. Then add the column to come up with your total monthly budget, for the lifestyle you envision.

[1]	Housing	$	_____
[2]	Transportation	$	_____
[3]	Clothing	$	_____
[4]	Food	$	_____
[5]	Sundries	$	_____
[6]	Entertainment	$	_____
[7]	Vacations	$	_____
[8]	Child care	$	_____
[9]	Health care	$	_____
[10]	Furnishings	$	_____
[11]	Savings	$	_____
[12]	Miscellaneous	$	_____
	Total	$	_____

What Salary Will Support This Lifestyle?

The figure you have just computed is the total amount of money you will need to bring home in your paycheck. But you will need to earn more money than this figure because of deductions from your paycheck for Social Security, state, and federal taxes.

So before you begin looking for a career, you need to figure the gross pay (salary) needed to meet your budget requirements.

Taxing authorities use precise calculations to factor deductions. For the sake of this exercise, figure an average of 20% is withheld from your paycheck. What you have after taxes have been withheld is called net pay or takehome pay. This is the amount of money you have left to cover your expenses.

To find the monthly salary you will need to cover your expenses, divide your monthly expenses by 80 percent.

Expenses (or net pay) divided by 80% = Gross pay

$$\underline{\hspace{6cm}} \div 80\% = \underline{\hspace{6cm}}$$

Total from page 92   your required monthly salary

Multiply this figure by 12 (months) to get the annual salary figure required.

$$\underline{\hspace{6cm}} \times 12 = \underline{\hspace{6cm}}$$

your required monthly salary   your required annual salary

Keep this figure in mind as you start researching career possibilities. You might start by reading the employment section of classified advertisements in both your local newspaper and the newspaper of the closest large city or visit local online employment web sites. Do the jobs that meet your financial needs sound interesting?

AVERAGE ANNUAL HOUSEHOLD INCOME BY HOUSEHOLD SIZE

	Single Person	One Parent + at Least One Child Under 18	Married Couple Only	Married Couple with Children		
				Oldest Child Under 6	Oldest Child 6 to 17	Oldest Child 18 or Older
Income before taxes	$47,035	$46,039	$91,415	$98,257	$111,780	$115,319

Source: Bureau of Labor Statistics, U.S. Department of Labor, *Consumer Expenditure Survey 2017*, September 2018.

What Careers Support Your Lifestyle?

As you continue your life planning and career decision-making process, a key task is to find a career that will support the lifestyle you envision for yourself AND for which you think you will be qualified.

Keep your required annual salary figure from page 93 in mind as you start researching career possibilities in chapter six. You might start by browsing the jobs that are available in your area on a job search web site. Or, check out the employment listings in the classified section of both your local newspaper and a paper in the closest large city. There are also online classified services that accept listings for employment opportunities, the most famous of which is Craigslist.

Consult the *Occupational Outlook Handbook* * (OOH). Each job title listed has extensive earnings information. The Bureau of Labor Statistics has made the entire OOH available online in an easy-to-use format or you can find a copy at your local library or bookstore.

Using your favorite internet search engine, you can locate other online compensation and salary resources by using the keyword average "salary" and adding the job title of a specific career you want to investigate (e.g., "average salary" + "commercial diver").

To find those occupations that match your financial and lifestyle requirements, be prepared to spend some time exploring a variety of options. Make a list below of at least ten careers with average salaries that match your budget projections. For this activity, assume you are the sole "breadwinner" in your family.

CAREER TITLE AND AVERAGE SALARY   CAREER TITLE AND AVERAGE SALARY

_____   _____

_____   _____

_____   _____

_____   _____

_____   _____

* At the time of printing, the web address was http://www.bls.gov/ooh

Keywords: average salary [job title]

In Over Your Head?

As much as we would sometimes like to ignore them, numbers don't lie. You may be surprised at many of the costs associated with your budget. If your budget total seems unreasonably high, you will need to make some adjustments.

Go back and review your figures. Where could you make cuts most easily? Write your adjusted figures in a different color pen or pencil. These numbers should add up to the minimum amount of money you need to lead a lifestyle that would be acceptable to you.

Roberta, for example, decided that the several hundred dollars a month she could save by giving up her dream luxury car for a more modest vehicle wouldn't really be painful. It may be a bit depressing to adjust your dreams downward, but being a slave to your lifestyle isn't fun, either.

Bob and Barbara, like many people, found themselves "house poor." They dreamed of having a big new house in the best part of town. They built it, but the mortgage payments are so high that there's no money left for little pleasures like an occasional dinner and movie in town. Several years of living in anxiety because of their over-stretched budget has taken its toll on their health, their marriage, and their life satisfaction.

When Jason lost his job, he decided to get a roommate to share expenses. He found he could make ends meet by cutting out most recreational expenses and adjusting his eating habits: No steak for a while, lots of spaghetti.

Back to your budget. Did the figure you arrived at on page 92 seem higher than the salary you're likely to earn on your own? What amount do you think you could reasonably expect to earn? Write that figure on line b below.

Next, determine your net income (line a) if you earn that salary (see formula on page 93).

Now, reallocate your funds. Write the adjusted figures for your hard times budget below. The total should be a figure no larger than your *own* income. Don't count on your phantom spouse here.

HARD TIMES BUDGET

1. Housing $ _____

2. Transportation $ _____

3. Clothing $ _____

4. Food $ _____

5. Sundries $ _____

6. Entertainment $ _____

7. Vacations $ _____

8. Child care $ _____

9. Health care $ _____

10. Furnishings $ _____

11. Savings $ _____

12. Miscellaneous $ _____

a) Net Income $ _____
(total amount you have to spend)

b) Gross monthly salary $ _____
(amount you expect to earn)

Keywords: cutting personal spending

Some Sample Budgets

Phyllis, a single mother of two, teaches English at a high school in Southern California. Her sons are twelve and ten years old. The family lives in a small house in one of the older sections of town. It's a long drive to work for Phyllis, but new housing is very expensive. Besides, they like their old neighborhood. The boys attend a magnet school where they are getting an early chance to excel at languages and math. Every Friday night, the whole family goes out for pizza. Phyllis's hobby is photography, and she recently purchased a digital camera. Every summer, the family takes a two-week car trip to a place where Phyllis can take photos and the boys can enjoy and learn.

PHYLLIS'S BUDGET

1.	Housing	$	1,810
2.	Transportation	$	550
3.	Clothing	$	300
4.	Food	$	800
5.	Sundries	$	75
6.	Entertainment	$	290
7.	Vacations	$	175
8.	Child care	$	250
9.	Health care	$	375
10.	Furnishings	$	75
11.	Savings	$	250
12.	Miscellaneous	$	150
	Net Income	$	5,100

What is the gross monthly income required to come up with this net? $ _____

Source: Bureau of Labor Statistics, U.S. Department of Labor, *Occupational Employment Statistics,* May 2018.

97

Will has been in the army for three years. The pay's not great, but since he's single and doesn't have to pay for room or board, he has no complaints. Will loves to travel—that's one reason he enlisted. He saves part of every check for his travel fund, in order to take advantage of the special prices he can get while he's in the service. Last year he spent a month in Europe. This year he wants to go to Japan. Will recently opened another savings account to save money for a new car.

WILL'S BUDGET

1.	Housing	$ _____
2.	Transportation	$ _____
3.	Clothing	$ _____
4.	Food	$ _____
5.	Sundries	$ _____
6.	Entertainment	$ _____
7.	Vacations	$ _____
8.	Child care	$ _____
9.	Health care	$ _____
10.	Furnishings	$ _____
11.	Savings	$ _____
12.	Miscellaneous	$ _____
	Net Income	$ ____1,950____

What is the gross monthly income required to come up with this net? $ _____

Source: Defense Finance and Accounting Services, U.S. Department of Defense, *Enlisted Members (Active) Monthly Rates of Basic Pay,* March 2019.

Jeff and Francie and their two kids live in a new housing development in Indiana. Jeff works at a nearby factory, where he's been employed for 15 years. Francie works in the office at the plant. The twins are 14. They're bright kids, and Jeff and Francie want to send them to college. They were worried a few years ago when many people at the factory were laid off, but Jeff and Francie both kept their jobs. The children's college fund is intact and growing. When the family goes on vacation, their main concern is getting out of the city. Usually they go camping or rent a cabin on a lake. Francie says it seems like that's about the only time the whole family does anything together anymore — the boys are busy with part-time jobs and afterschool activities. She and Jeff have started going out alone a couple times a month, something they both enjoy.

JEFF & FRANCIE'S BUDGET

1.	Housing	$ _____
2.	Transportation	$ _____
3.	Clothing	$ _____
4.	Food	$ _____
5.	Sundries	$ _____
6.	Entertainment	$ _____
7.	Vacations	$ _____
8.	Child care	$ _____
9.	Health care	$ _____
10.	Furnishings	$ _____
11.	Savings	$ _____
12.	Miscellaneous	$ _____
	Net Income	$ 4,500

Total: $2,400/month take-home salary, Jeff
           $2,100/month take-home salary, Francie

What is the gross monthly income required to come up with this net? $ _____

Source: Bureau of Labor Statistics, U.S. Department of Labor, *Occupational Outlook Handbook*, 2019.

Carl is a psychologist and Ruth is a bank executive. They live with their small daughter in a cooperative apartment in New York City. Since their careers call for long and unpredictable hours at work, they have live-in help for the baby. They don't have a car—most of the time it's not necessary. They rent one when they need to. Vacations have been fewer since the baby was born, but the family would someday like a weekend cottage in the country. The full-time babysitter also makes it easier for Carl and Ruth to go out at night. They both love the theater and enjoy trying out new restaurants.

CARL & RUTH'S BUDGET

1.	Housing	$ _____
2.	Transportation	$ _____
3.	Clothing	$ _____
4.	Food	$ _____
5.	Sundries	$ _____
6.	Entertainment	$ _____
7.	Vacations	$ _____
8.	Child care	$ _____
9.	Health care	$ _____
10.	Furnishings	$ _____
11.	Savings	$ _____
12.	Miscellaneous	$ _____
	Net Income	$ _____13,500_____

Total: $6,500/month take-home salary, Carl
           $7,000/month take-home salary, RuthI

What is the gross monthly income required to come up with this net? $ _____

Source: Bureau of Labor Statistics, U.S. Department of Labor, *Occupational Employment Statistics,* May 2018.

Ben is a golf pro in Fort Lauderdale. Lynn is a nurse, but she's been home full-time since the birth of their first child. The family has a ranch house in the suburbs, with a big yard for the kids (now four and seven) and a garden for Lynn. They have two cars, neither of them new, but both kept in good condition by Ben. Outings are usually casual events like picnics at the beach. They like to have friends over for barbecue. Since Ben knows golf pros all over the country, vacation time means swapping homes with another family — a different part of the country each year. This year, they're all looking forward to a stay in Colorado.

BEN & LYNN'S BUDGET

1.	Housing	$ _____
2.	Transportation	$ _____
3.	Clothing	$ _____
4.	Food	$ _____
5.	Sundries	$ _____
6.	Entertainment	$ _____
7.	Vacations	$ _____
8.	Child care	$ _____
9.	Health care	$ _____
10.	Furnishings	$ _____
11.	Savings	$ _____
12.	Miscellaneous	$ _____
	Net Income	$ _____4,400_____

What is the gross monthly income required to come up with this net? $ _____

Source: PayScale. Head Golf Professional Salary. Web. 27 April 2019.

A Few Words about Poverty

Though the United States is one of the richest nations on earth, millions of its citizens today are living in poverty. Many of these people are homeless, living in shelters or on the street, often reduced to begging or going through garbage cans in order to eat. For many households, including a startling number of single parent families (see page 103), life offers chronic anxiety about paying their rent or buying the groceries they need. The societal and historical forces that have caused this situation must be changed, but that will take time.

How can you ensure that you will not be a future poverty statistic? There are no guarantees, but here are some things you might think about:

If you are a female, be aware of the fact that on average women earn only 80 cents for every dollar men earn. This pay gap is due in part to discrimination, including a "motherhood penalty" that can impact a woman's opportunities even after a maternity leave. Occupational segregation also contributes to pay inequity. This is where gender role stereotypes lead women into careers that, as a rule, are not high paying: retail, customer service, and office or administrative support, for example.

	10 LARGEST OCCUPATIONS FOR WOMEN WITH EARNINGS AND GENDER PAY RATIO	Women's Median Earnings	Men's Median Earnings	Gender Pay Ratio
1	Registered nurses	$65,612	$71,590	92%
2	Secretaries and administrative assistants	$38,470	$42,566	90%
3	Elementary and middle school teachers	$50,766	$55,197	92%
4	Customer service representatives	$32,893	$37,623	87%
5	First-line supervisors of retail sales workers	$35,217	$47,774	74%
6	Nursing, psychiatric, and home health aides	$26,816	$30,125	89%
7	Accountants and auditors	$60,280	$77,320	78%
8	Office clerks, general	$35,226	$39,160	90%
9	First-line supervisors of office and administrative support workers	$46,555	$57,466	81%
10	Bookkeeping, accounting, and auditing clerks	$39,939	$45,254	88%

Another factor is the way the culture reinforces gender role stereotypes in children. This can negatively impact girls as they grow older if they feel women's career options are limited, if they avoid taking certain classes they feel are the realm of males, or if they do not adequately prepare for a job because they believe they will never have to work outside the home.

One of the best things you can do to ensure your future, regardless of your gender, is to assume that you will have to support yourself and plan for that eventuality. Take math, science, and technology classes, and do as well in them as you can. Research careers that are in high demand and, if you have any skills and interests related to those fields, pursue them.

Source: American Association of University Women, *The Simple Truth about the Gender Pay Gap, Fall 2018 Edition.* 2018.

Could You Become a Poverty Statistic?

Approximately 39,700,000 people in the United States live below the poverty level. That is 12.3 percent of the total population.

9.3 percent of all families live below the poverty line.

According to the U.S. Census Bureau, there are more than 22 million single-parent families; 71 percent of those families are headed by women.

25.7 percent of all families headed by a woman with no husband present live below the poverty line.

In the United States, 17.1 percent of all children live below the poverty line.

Single-parent families maintained by men have median weekly earnings of $1,170.
Single-parent families maintained by women have median weekly earnings of $802.
Married couple families have median weekly earnings of $1,738.

What do you think contributes to poverty in this country?

_____

_____

_____

What might cause you to become one of these statistics?

_____

_____

How can you prevent that from happening?

_____

_____

_____

_____

Source: U.S. Census Bureau, Current Population Reports, *Income and Poverty in the United States: 2017*. September 2018.

Money Isn't Everything

Wealth and fame do not guarantee a rewarding life.

The price of anything is the amount of life you exchange for it.

—Henry David Thoreau

The only thing money gives you is the freedom of not worrying about money.

—Johnny Carson

On the other hand, it's quite possible to put more emphasis on money than it deserves: If only we were rich and famous, we think, we'd certainly be happy. But would we? Every day, it seems, there is news of one more celebrity getting divorced, being treated for drug addiction or alcoholism or emotional illness, or even committing suicide.

We won't attempt to say why this is so, but the stories do demonstrate that wealth and fame do not guarantee a rewarding life. The status symbols — the cars and houses and jewelry and so on — are very effective at making other people envious; however, they often mean little to their owners.

Studies have shown that people with a comfortable income are usually much happier than those living in poverty. However, excessive amounts of money do not seem to add significantly to life satisfaction.

Many people make conscious decisions to forego higher incomes in order to do something they think is more worthwhile, such as the military. Besides their service to our country, members of the armed forces value things such as annual paid vacation, education benefits, and travel.

A well-paid advertising executive who really wants to write short stories may be less satisfied with her life than a bus driver who loves his job. That is why it is so important to consider your values when making career decisions. Go back to the values exercise on page 35 and review which values are most important to you. Whatever course you take in your life must be compatible with them.

Every job has psychological and emotional costs. The trick is to find a balance: that is, a job that pays enough to support the kind of *physical* lifestyle you want, while not draining your *spirit* by forcing you to deny those values you hold most dear.

Consider the stories on the following pages. What values are being sacrificed in each case? We've used Bert's story as an example.

You will recall that our values categories are adventure, family, knowledge and truth, power, personal integrity and moral courage, money or wealth, friendship and companionship, recognition, independence and freedom, security, beauty or aesthetics, creativity, and helping others. Keep these in mind as you read each story.

Go back to the values exercise on page 35

Every job has psychological and emotional costs. The trick is to find a balance.

I'd rather be a failure at something I love than a success at something I hate.

—George Burns

It is neither wealth nor splendor, but tranquility and occupations, which give happiness.

—Thomas Jefferson

When you are doing the work you are meant to do it feels right and every day is a bonus, regardless of what you are getting paid.

—Oprah Winfrey

BERT'S STORY

I've wanted to be a missionary ever since I was a boy. Every year, people would come to our church from some distant country and show slides and talk about the work they were doing for the people there. I love to travel, and my religion has always been important to me. Right now, I'm stationed on an island in the South Pacific. We're building a new school and a much-needed hospital. It's taking longer than it should because sometimes the money just doesn't come through. It's difficult when your only support comes from people who are thousands of miles away. I have to remind myself to have faith and that, so far, things have always worked out. The people here are wonderful and they've taught me so much. I never thought I could be so thrilled about getting a bar of soap or a box of chocolate in the mail. Last time I was home I went into a supermarket and just stared at all the variety—the sheer number of things you can just pick up and buy. They even carry it to your car for you! But that was three years ago. I haven't seen my family since then. I'm not sure when I'll be sent somewhere else, and that makes it hard, but I think we've really accomplished something for the people on this island, and that makes it all worthwhile.

What are the sacrifices Bert must make?

Time away from his family, little access to material goods, dependence on others for support, not in control of his own future

Which values do those sacrifices reflect?

Family, money and wealth, security

What are his rewards?

Feeling like he's making a difference, being surrounded by people he respects

Which values do they reflect?

Personal integrity and moral courage, friendship and companionship, helping others

Do you share some of Bert's values?   Yes   No   Undecided

Are you willing to make similar sacrifices?   Yes   No   Undecided

If so, you may be happy with a career like Bert's.

LEON'S STORY

All I have to do to remind myself of the power I hold is to walk through the halls of this company. Five thousand employees, and they all know I could promote them or give them a raise—or fire them on the spot. I like the way everyone smiles and calls me "Sir" and goes out of the way to try to please me. I guess it sounds as though I'm just on a power trip, but I've worked hard to build this company and earn the respect of the people who work here. When I think of all the years of 60 or 80 hours a week in the office, all the kids' birthday parties I missed, the anniversaries I forgot. . . . Well, maybe it's no wonder that I don't get the same respect at home that I do at work. The kids are grown now, and I feel that I hardly know them. My wife has built a life of her own, and I'm not exactly indispensable to her. But I love the job. I plan to stay here as long as my health holds out—maybe until I'm 75.

What are the sacrifices Leon must make? _____

_____

Which values do these sacrifices reflect? _____

_____

What are Leon's rewards? _____

_____

Which values do they reflect? _____

_____

Do you share Leon's values?   Yes   No   Undecided

Are you willing to make the same sacrifices?   Yes   No   Undecided

If so, you might be happy with a similar career.

VINCENT'S STORY

Yesterday I sold my first painting. You might think that after all those years when no one was interested, selling one painting wouldn't mean very much. You would be wrong. It's not the recognition or the money I'm after. I see such incredible beauty in the world, and I only want to find a way to express it and to share it. I've had to take many jobs over the years—cab driver, hospital orderly, janitor—but I've never thought of myself as anything but an artist.

What are the sacrifices Vincent has made?

_____

_____

Which values do they reflect?

_____

_____

What are Vincent's rewards?

_____

_____

Which values do they reflect?

_____

_____

Do you share Vincent's values?   Yes   No   Undecided

Would you be ready to make similar sacrifices? Yes   No   Undecided

If so, you might be happy with a similar career.

108

SARA'S STORY

Being an environmental scientist is one of the most important jobs I can think of. After all, this is the only planet we have. I really love my job and I don't take the responsibility lightly. I had no social life in school because I was so serious about my studies. But, truthfully, I've always preferred books to parties. The thing is, I'm still studying. There's always something new to learn. I hardly ever see anyone away from work. I can't remember the last time I went shopping or played a round of golf. I've always wanted to have children, but that plan is on hold for now. Last week, though, we learned that fish have returned to a river I helped clean up and—well, you don't get a feeling like that from an afternoon of shopping. It's not easy, but I'm proud of what I do.

What sacrifices has Sara had to make? _____

_____

_____

What values categories would you put them under? _____

_____

_____

List Sara's rewards. _____

_____

_____

To which values categories do they belong? _____

_____

Do you and Sara have similar values?　　　Yes　　　No　　　Undecided

Would you be willing to make the same sacrifices?　　Yes　　　No　　　Undecided

If so, this might be a career for you to think about.

ROSE'S STORY

I've always had two goals: To have a good family life, and to be successful at a career. I love to travel. For a while I thought I might be a pilot, but that would mean being away from home a lot. I'm pretty good at math, too, and I'm a stickler for details, so I decided to become an accountant. I worked for a big firm for a few years, until Allen and I decided to start a family. Then I opened my own office at home. It's not as prestigious, but since I can control the number of clients I take on, I was able to scale the job down when the children were small and spend most of my time with them. Now that they're in school all day, I work full-time. I'm the boss, though, so I can arrange my schedule in order to be there for special events at school or when somebody's home sick. Allen has a good job, too, but it's important to me to know that I could support the family on my own if I had to.

What sacrifices has Rose made for her career? _____

_____

What values categories would you place them in? _____

_____

What are her rewards? _____

_____

What values do you think they mirror? _____

_____

Are your values similar to Rose's?   Yes   No   Undecided

Would you make the same sacrifices?   Yes   No   Undecided

If so, a career like hers might make you happy.

You Win Some, You Lose Some

Every job has its rewards and its sacrifices. How well a given career could work for you depends on your own values. It's important to recognize which values are compatible with a job and which are not. See how adept you are at recognizing which traits a job will call forth, and which it will deny. Review the values categories on pages 36 and 37. Then, for each of the following careers, list the values you think will be rewarded and those that will most likely be sacrificed.

Example: Career Military Officer

Rewards: <u>Adventure</u>

Sacrifices: <u>Freedom, money or wealth</u>

Computer programmer

Rewards: <u>Security, creativity</u>

Sacrifices: <u>Beauty and aesthetics, adventure</u>

Professional athlete

Rewards: <u>Recognition, power, adventure</u>

Sacrifices: <u>Freedom, security</u>

Fire fighter
Rewards: _____

Sacrifices: _____

Veterinarian
Rewards: _____

Sacrifices: _____

Fashion model
Rewards: _____

Sacrifices: _____

Radio announcer
Rewards: _____

Sacrifices: _____

Social worker
Rewards: _____

Sacrifices: _____

Mechanic
Rewards: _____

Sacrifices: _____

Farmer
Rewards: _____

Sacrifices: _____

Truck driver
Rewards: _____

Sacrifices: _____

Flight attendant
Rewards: _____

Sacrifices: _____

Homemaker
Rewards: _____

Sacrifices: _____

Garbage hauler
Rewards: _____

Sacrifices: _____

Accountant
Rewards: _____

Sacrifices: _____

Resort owner
Rewards: _____

Sacrifices: _____

Work may represent a sizable chunk of your life, but it has no claim on your free time.

After-Hours Rewards

Perhaps you found it difficult to determine which values the preceding jobs would not satisfy. There are several possible explanations, if you did. First of all, we generally look only at the rewards (financial and emotional) a given career has to offer. Personal and spiritual sacrifices are seldom mentioned, if they are even perceived. Also, some sacrifices don't become immediately apparent. In some cases, they may not appear at all. Anything from your individual employer to the economic situation of the world can affect the way you feel about your job.

As a result, many people end up in careers they've trained for, but that don't satisfy all their values. What can you do about that? Well, you can always change jobs, but sometimes there are powerful reasons to stay put. For example, a college professor who has invested many years in education may well hesitate before chucking it all to become a dancer just because teaching doesn't satisfy her creative side. Sometimes the job market is so bleak that anyone with any kind of job feels lucky. Or, if you have three children to support, you may have to pass on what could be your last chance to play minor league baseball because the wage is minimal.

Does that mean you're doomed to a lifetime of misery or, at best, of vague dissatisfaction? Not at all. Work may represent a sizeable chunk of your life, but it has no claim on your free time. Many people have found after-hours activities to fill in and make amends for those things that are lacking from 9 to 5.

Daniel is a garbage hauler. His top values are security and power. The job pays well, and it is certainly secure. ("One thing we know for sure," his boss is fond of saying, "there will always be garbage.") But power? Not much evidence of that. One day while Daniel was teaching his daughter how to throw a fastball, a neighbor stopped by, watched awhile, and suggested that Daniel might make a good Little League coach. He knew of a team that needed one. Daniel said, "Why not," and he's been having a great time leading his team to glory ever since.

Maria is an electrical engineer. Her top values are security, recognition, and aesthetics. Engineering met her need for security, but didn't satisfy her other requirements. She didn't want to give up her job, but she needed more satisfaction in her life. Maria decided to join a community theater group. She loves the atmosphere, she loves the plays, and most of all, she loves the applause.

Rodrigo is the executive director of a youth-service agency. Security and helping others are his top values. The job was great—he didn't want to leave it—but the pay was low and unlikely to improve. He couldn't save any money, and that made him feel insecure. When he received a small windfall from his grandmother, he decided to put it to work. He studied about investments and real estate, found some friends interested in a joint venture, and made some long-term plans. By investing wisely, Rodrigo was able to build an account for his retirement or for financial emergencies that might occur.

On each of the following lines, you'll find an occupation followed by a list of values. Circle those values you think would be met by the career. Then, on the line provided, state what this person might do to meet the other need.

Social worker: helping others   creativity   power _____

Assembly line worker: helping others   security   friendship _____

Carpenter: adventure   beauty and aesthetics   family _____

Sales representative: family   money   friendship _____

Homemaker: family   helping others   power _____

Museum guide: beauty and aesthetics   adventure   creativity _____

Professor: knowledge   creativity   recognition _____

Farmer: family   helping others   friendship _____

Psychologist: adventure   helping others   beauty and aesthetics _____

Accountant: power   money   creativity _____

Chemist: knowledge   creativity   recognition _____

Writer: creativity   helping others   friendship _____

Veterinarian: helping others   knowledge   power _____

Commitment

In high school, David, Michael, and Diane were inseparable. They agreed that music was the most important thing in the world. All were gifted musicians, and the trio could always be found in the music room at school, at the record store, or at the backstage entrance to Orchestra Hall. They loved all kinds of music—rock, jazz, classical, country, hip hop—and they vowed that, somehow, music would always be at the center of their lives.

After graduation, David attended a college with one of the best music programs in the country. Because of his excellent work there, he was awarded a fellowship to continue his studies in Europe. His dedication to his art eventually led to a job with one of the most prestigious orchestras in the U.S.

Diane took a different track. While in college, she began singing with a local rock group. She and one of the other musicians started writing songs together. The rest of the group eventually fell apart, but Diane and her partner formed and reformed the band, playing anywhere they could get a job, sometimes without pay. They spent years auditioning, posting demos on YouTube, trying to get noticed, and—most of all—working to improve their music. The band recently signed with an agent, and Diane hopes they will have a recording contract soon.

Michael didn't see much point in continuing his education after high school. Convinced that he would be the next country music superstar, he headed directly to Nashville and tried very hard—for about a week—to get discovered. Well, he thought, maybe he'd rather be a songwriter, anyway. He dashed off two sets of lyrics and sent them to his favorite singer. When there was no response, Michael got angry. "Who wants to be part of an arrogant industry like this, anyway?" he reassured himself as he tried to hitch a ride home. He'd be much happier working for his uncle's construction company, a place where he'd surely be appreciated.

As the above story demonstrates, ability alone will not make you successful. In the end, whether or not you *can* do something may be less important than how much you *want* to do it, how committed you are to achieving your goal.

Keywords: role commitment career success

Lots of people have dreams. However, like Michael, many people are unwilling to put in the necessary work to make their dreams come true. David and Diane did not succeed through luck, but through persistence and hard work. What kind of persistence would it take to realize *your* dream?

While most jobs require some kind of commitment toward training or education, the amount varies. You can probably get a beginning clerical position with only a high school business class. To be a psychiatrist, however, you have to go through college and medical school before you even *begin* your psychiatric training. That's quite a commitment — of time, energy, and money.

Similarly, some careers require continued commitment. It may be possible to be a casual or part-time sales clerk, but it is difficult to imagine an uncommitted professional tennis player or member of Congress.

Often, the financial dividends and independence make the investment of time and effort worthwhile. Professionals like doctors and lawyers are among the highest-paid people in our society. In most careers, the person who is most committed to the work — the one who has taken time to learn more or perform better — is the one likely to reach the top of the pay scale.

However, there are no guarantees. Dancers and musicians, for example, may train for many years and still never earn a living from their art. They "do it for love," realizing that the odds are against them.

Before choosing your career, it's important to consider the degree of commitment you feel comfortable with — both in training and on-the-job performance. Some people want their work to be a dominant force in their lives. For others, it is important to have plenty of time for family and other interests.

Again, there is no right or wrong answer. The choice is yours. The following exercise will give you a better idea of how an investment of time and/or money relates to future dividends.

An Investment in Education...

An investment in your future begins with education: the amount of time you are willing to devote to your training, the kinds of classes you are willing to take, and the amount of work you are willing to do in those classes. If you took math and science courses in high school (and did well in them), you will have more options concerning where you will go to college and what you will major in once you get there. Reading and writing skills are also essential in most career fields. College, of course, means more time committed, but in general, time devoted to education will pay off in the long run.

The following chart demonstrates the relationship between time commitment and financial reward.

JOB TITLE	MEDIAN ANNUAL EARNINGS	POST HIGH SCHOOL TRAINING/EDUCATION
Medical Transcriptionist	$34,770	1-year certificate or 2-year degree
Brickmason	$44,810	3- to 4-year apprenticeship including technical education & paid on-the-job training
Plumber	$53,910	4- to 5-year apprenticeship including technical education & paid on-the-job training
Court Reporter	$57,150	Certificate program lasting 2 to 5 years
Elementary School Teacher	$57,980	4-year degree + license or certification; some states require a master's degree after certification
Respiratory Therapist	$60,280	2- or 4-year degree + exam
Chiropractor	$71,410	at least 3 years of college + 4-year chiropractic degree
College Professor (full professor)	$78,470	6 to 10 years of college or more
School Psychologist	$79,010	6+ years of college + license or certification
Computer Programmer	$84,280	2- to 4-year degree; may earn certifications in specific programming languages
Computer Systems Analyst	$88,740	4-year degree or more
Chemical Engineer	$104,910	4-year degree or more
Attorney	$120,910	7 years of college + passage of bar exam
Air Traffic Controller	$124,540	2- or 4-year degree + exam
Dentist	$156,240	6 to 8 years of college + exam
Physician (family practice)	$208,000	8 years of college + 3 to 7 years internship & residency

Amounts reflect national median earnings, assuming full-time work.

Source: Bureau of Labor Statistics, U.S. Department of Labor, *Occupational Outlook Handbook,* 2019.

...Yields Dividends for a Lifetime

While it may not seem that $10,000 or $20,000 per year earning capacity is a big enough inducement to spend between three and 10 more years in school or in training, let's look at what that extra effort can mean over a lifetime.

The chart below shows more dramatically how each year of education affects future earnings.

How many years do you plan to work between the age of 18 and 65?

_____ years in workforce

Multiply the number of years you plan to be in the workforce with each of the annual salaries listed below to find out how much you would earn over the course of your working life.

$20,000 x _____ years in workforce = $ _____ lifetime earnings

$30,000 x _____ years in workforce = $ _____ lifetime earnings

$50,000 x _____ years in workforce = $ _____ lifetime earnings

$75,000 x _____ years in workforce = $ _____ lifetime earnings

$100,000 x _____ years in workforce = $ _____ lifetime earnings

What is the difference between a $20,000 and $30,000 annual salary over a lifetime? $ _____

What is the difference between a $20,000 and $50,000 annual salary over a lifetime? $ _____

What is the difference between a $20,000 and $75,000 annual salary over a lifetime? $ _____

What is the difference between a $20,000 and $100,000 annual salary over a lifetime? $ _____

What if you only earned minimum wage?

What is the current minimum wage (rate per hour) in your state or city? $ _____

How much can a person earn per year at that hourly rate? $ _____

What does that equal over your lifetime? $ _____

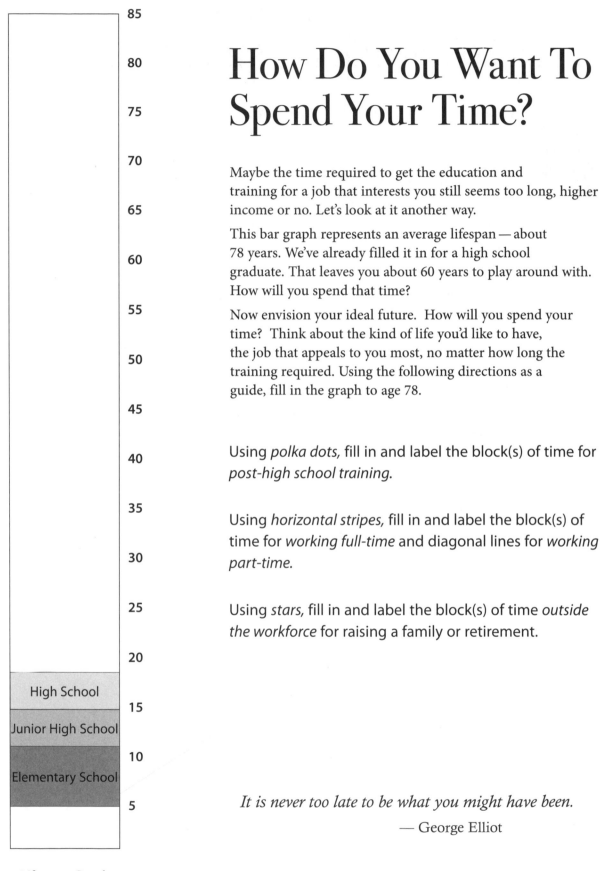

Lifespan Graph

How Do You Want To Spend Your Time?

Maybe the time required to get the education and training for a job that interests you still seems too long, higher income or no. Let's look at it another way.

This bar graph represents an average lifespan — about 78 years. We've already filled it in for a high school graduate. That leaves you about 60 years to play around with. How will you spend that time?

Now envision your ideal future. How will you spend your time? Think about the kind of life you'd like to have, the job that appeals to you most, no matter how long the training required. Using the following directions as a guide, fill in the graph to age 78.

Using *polka dots,* fill in and label the block(s) of time for *post-high school training.*

Using *horizontal stripes,* fill in and label the block(s) of time for *working full-time* and diagonal lines for *working part-time.*

Using *stars,* fill in and label the block(s) of time *outside the workforce* for raising a family or retirement.

It is never too late to be what you might have been.

— George Elliot

118

Use the information from your graph to answer the following questions.

How many years of post-high school training will you complete?

_____ years = a

How many years do you think you will work outside the home full-time?

_____ years = b

How many years do you think you will work outside the home part-time?

_____ years = c

Here are some interesting facts about your worklife.

How many hours might you work in your lifetime?

full-time   2,080 hours/year x _____ b = _____ f

part-time   1,000 hours/year x _____ c = _____ g

_____ f + _____ g = _____ hours you will work in your lifetime

That's a lot of time to be doing something that you do not find satisfying…that doesn't correspond to your values or passions…that doesn't meet your lifestyle desires.

Okay, let's look at it one more way.

For every year of post-high school education, you will work _____ years.

Hint: $\dfrac{b + c}{a}$ = _____ h

Next time you think, "I can't stay in school _____ more years! I didn't want to be a _____ anyway!" remember these figures. Education and training now are a small investment when you look at the long-range payoffs in life satisfaction. Hang in there…you'll be glad you did!

Ask Someone Who's Been There

The information in this book is necessarily more general than we would like. To get some specific answers to the questions *you* have, interview three people who are currently working. Use the following questions to help determine the rewards and sacrifices of each person's job.

NAME _____

OCCUPATION _____

HOW LONG IN THIS OCCUPATION? _____

How did you choose your occupation? _____
_____

Financially, does it let you live the way you prefer? _____
_____

If not, why not and what can you do about it? _____
_____

What rewards have you experienced? _____

        (Listen carefully here. Keep the different values categories in mind.)

    Values interpretation: _____

What sacrifices have you had to make for your career? _____

    Values interpretation: _____

What kind of commitment does this career take in terms of:

    Education _____

    Energy/endurance _____

    Stick-to-itiveness _____

If you had it to do over again, would you choose this career? _____

Why or why not? _____

Easier Said Than Done

As anyone who's ever vowed to lose weight or to save money knows, it's easier to *make* a commitment than it is to *keep* one. Long-term commitments are particularly hard to keep. In his book, *The Path of Least Resistance,* author Robert Fritz explains that, while it may be relatively easy to follow through at first, it is natural, over time, to fall back into comfortable old habits. Those who push on to meet their long-term goals or fulfill their dreams are usually those who have a clear vision of where they want to go or what they want to create.

By holding a picture in your mind of what it is you want, you will be better able to make the right decisions about your day-to-day actions. Should you study for the lit exam or go to the party? Well, what do you want? This is a key question, one you need to ask yourself often. It may be easier or more fun to go to the party. If you want to get into graduate school, however, you probably need to study for the test. Keeping your goal in mind will make it easier to decide.

> Kay wants to save money for college. Her friend wants Kay to go with her on a ski vacation.
>
> Jamal wants to do well at his weekend job. He feels like sleeping in on Saturday morning.
>
> Lee wants to be in the community play. The thought of auditioning for a part makes him anxious.
>
> Juanita wants to study art in France. Because of a scheduling problem, taking a French class would mean giving up her place on the tennis team.

	It's easier to…	…than…	But what I want is…	…therefore, I will…
Kay Jamal Lee Juanita You				

Complete this chart for Kay, Jamal, Lee, and Juanita.

What do you want? Look back to the goals you set in chapter 3 and fill in the chart above. Use this model to help make day-to-day decisions about realizing your dreams.

CHAPTER 4 CHECKPOINTS
What Cost this Lifestyle?
Every career choice involves sacrifices and rewards

You now have a strong understanding of the costs of any given lifestyle—financial costs, psychological costs, and the costs in terms of commitment to a given career. This knowledge will likely impact your career selection, so take the time to make sure you've mastered the concepts below.

☐ I completed a comprehensive budget for the lifestyle I aspire to once I complete my education/training.

☐ I realize just how many financial obligations I have to consider in my budget and understand the effect career choice will have on my lifestyle.

☐ I experienced the most common budgeting technique—taking a given income and deciding how it should be allocated.

☐ I discussed some causes of poverty and understand ways in which I might best avoid becoming a poverty statistic myself.

☐ I explored the myth that money will make me happy.

☐ I learned that there are sacrifices as well as rewards associated with every job and every lifestyle. I can now evaluate any career I am considering more objectively and determine whether or not that career would be a wise choice for me.

☐ I recognize the rewards and sacrifices of specific careers as they relate to my work values and realize that values not satisfied on the job can be met with appropriate after-hours activities.

☐ I recognize the long-term financial payoff of an investment in further education.

☐ I interviewed friends and acquaintances and gained specific information about the costs and rewards of various jobs.

☐ I realize that to meet long-term goals I will have to make short-term sacrifices, and I explored a systematic decision-making rubric that can help me attain my goals.

Keep pace with the drummer you hear,
however measured or far away.

—Henry David Thoreau

I never did a day's work in my life—
it was all fun.

—Thomas Alva Edison

CHAPTER FIVE
Your Ideal Career

There's more to consider than just the work

Gena was assigned to write a description of her ideal job for her career counselor..
"I don't want you to tell me what the job is," Ms. Brown had instructed. "Just tell me
where you'd like to work, who you'd like to work with, what you'd like to get from your
job — things like that." Gena sat down at her desk, turned on her computer, chewed
three sticks of gum, sent an e-mail message to her friend in Nova Scotia, updated her
Facebook status, and made several important phone calls. By 9 P.M. it was clear to
her that she had no idea what to write.

A clever woman, Gena decided to ask other people for their opinions, and they were
more than happy to tell her what to do.

"A good job would involve a lot of travel," her friend Paul said. "You don't want to get
stuck in some office all day, every day."

"It would have to be a job that lets you meet interesting people," her sister offered.

"I don't know about that," said her dad. "Be your own boss. That's the ticket."

"Do that and you'll never get a good night's sleep again," her grandfather
proclaimed. "What you want is a secure job with a solid company. Something you
know you can count on."

"If you want to have a family, it would help to have flexible hours," her mother said.

"Who cares about that?" asked her friend Susan. "I say go for the big bucks!"

Gena reviewed her notes at her desk. At first she didn't know what to make of such
an odd assortment of opinions. As she thought about them, though, they began to
make sense. A career, she realized, involves many things that have nothing at all to
do with the actual work, yet greatly affect how effective and satisfied a worker will be.

In a way, Gena decided, choosing a rewarding career is like building a successful softball team. Every
member of the team has an important role to play. Good pitching is essential, but without solid hitting
and defense, it won't get you into the play-offs. Likewise, a job that pays well but is unrewarding in other
respects won't make you happy.

What kinds of things need to be considered? Gena looked back at the answers she'd collected and listed
different categories. Traveling? That would involve the physical setting of a job, she decided. Working
with interesting people seemed to relate to working conditions. Her father's comment about being her
own boss, she felt, concerned relationships on the job. The security her grandfather urged on her related,
she knew, to his values. Her mother was right — she definitely had to consider how her job would affect
her family life. And, of course, there was the financial angle to consider.

Under each category, Gena listed the things that were most important to her. This was a good way to
begin narrowing her career choices, she decided. And, if she used her imagination, she could come up
with some new ideas, too. What jobs could she think of that would include as many elements from her
list as possible? This just might be fun, she thought.

Before you start investigating specific careers, it's a good idea to consider the general characteristics you favor in a job. They can provide an outline that will make your career research much easier. If you know you want to live in the city, for example, you can cross "forest ranger" right off your list of possible careers. Similarly, if you decide you want a job that lets you put family responsibilities first, you probably won't want to be a foreign correspondent for a network newscast.

On the following pages, you will find brief descriptions of particular categories of career considerations and lists of options involving each category. Check the box in front of any statement that appeals to you. Choose as many options as you like, but make sure they don't contradict each other. Feel free to add to the lists if we've overlooked something that appeals to you.

Physical Settings

By the setting of a job, we mean its geographic location as well as its specific working environment. Job satisfaction depends greatly on how you feel about where you work — and where your job forces you to live. You might love farming in the Midwest, for example. But if you have asthma or severe allergies, the humidity and pollen in the air could make your life miserable. Similarly, if you value beautiful surroundings, you probably won't want to work at a meat processing plant or a medical laboratory. And, if you can't stand to be indoors all day, a windowless inner office is not for you. Check the statements that appeal to you below.

- ☐ I would like to work in a city.
- ☐ I would like to work in the country.
- ☐ I would like to work in a small to medium-sized town.
- ☐ I would like to work in _____ (list a specific city or part of the country).
- ☐ I would like to work in another country such as _____ .
- ☐ I would like a job that might offer frequent transfers.
- ☐ I would like a job that will let me stay in one place.
- ☐ I would like a job that keeps me "on the road," traveling from place to place.
- ☐ I would like to work outdoors (list specifics if you can, i.e., in the woods, on a farm, at sea) _____ .
- ☐ I would like to work out of a car or truck most of the time.
- ☐ I would like to work in an office.
- ☐ I would like to work in my home.
- ☐ It's important to me that my work setting be pleasing to the eye.
- ☐ I would like to work in a garage or warehouse.
- ☐ I would like to work in a factory.
- ☐ I would like a job that involves both indoor and outdoor work.
- ☐ I would like to work in a science lab or hospital.
- ☐ I would like to work in a retail store.
- ☐ I would like to work in a restaurant.
- ☐ I would like to work on a construction site.
- ☐ I would like to work on a ship, plane, train, or bus.
- ☐ I would like to work in a hotel or resort.
- ☐ I would like to work in a museum or art gallery.
- ☐ I would like to work in an art or photography studio.
- ☐ I would like to work in a concert hall or theater.
- ☐ I would like to work in a school or library.
- ☐ I would like to work in a church, synagogue, temple, or mosque.
- ☐ I would like to work on the set of a movie or TV show.
- ☐ I would like to work in a TV, radio, or recording studio.
- ☐ I would like to work in _____ .

Working Conditions

Working conditions involve such things as what you like to work with and how you like to do your job. Consider your personality when you look at this list. Under what conditions do you feel most confident and at ease? What kinds of situations give you the most pleasure? How much structure do you like in your day? Do you like to be around people a lot, or are you just as happy being alone? Do you like to meet new people, or are you more comfortable sticking with the same circle of friends and acquaintances? Check the statements below that appeal to you.

☐ I would like a job that requires me to "dress for success" (dress up for a professional office).

☐ I would like a job that requires me to wear a uniform or costume.

☐ I would like a job that lets me dress any way I want.

☐ I would like a job that lets me work alone most of the time.

☐ I would like a job that lets me work with the same group of people.

☐ I would like a job that lets me work with many different clients.

☐ I would like a job that lets me work with ideas.

☐ I would like a job that lets me work with information.

☐ I would like a job that lets me work with computers.

☐ I would like a job that lets me work with numbers.

☐ I would like a job that lets me work with machines.

☐ I would like a job that lets me work with tools.

☐ I would like a job that lets me be creative.

☐ I would like a job that involves physical labor or activity.

☐ I would like a job with prescribed duties and procedures.

☐ I would like a job with strict deadlines.

☐ I would like a job with structured working hours.

☐ I would like a job with somewhat flexible hours.

☐ I would like a job that lets me structure my time any way I want.

☐ I would like a job that often calls for putting in extra hours.

☐ I wouldn't mind working nights or weekends.

☐ I would like a job that involves risk or danger.

☐ I would like a job that might take away my privacy.

☐ I would like a job that is intellectually challenging.

☐ I would like a job I could forget about when I'm not there.

☐ I would like to be able to work part-time when my children are young.

☐ I would like a job that involves a variety of tasks and duties.

☐ Other _____

Relationships at Work

For many people, the social aspect of a job is one of its most important parts. Advances in technology and high-speed Internet connections provide new opportunities to work from remote locations, connected to co-workers by computer. This would never work for some because of the isolation. What about you? How much social contact do you expect? Would you rather be the boss or employee? Would you like to work with specific types of people? Check the statements below that appeal to you. (Remember, telecommuters still work with people — by email, phone, fax, and occasionally face-to-face.)

- ☐ I would like to work alone.
- ☐ I would like to work in a group or on a team.
- ☐ I would like to work with a variety of people.
- ☐ I would like to be the boss.
- ☐ I would like to be supervised by others.
- ☐ I would like to work for myself.
- ☐ I would like to work with adults.
- ☐ I would like to work with children.
- ☐ I would like to work with people fighting an illness.
- ☐ I would like to work with people with disabilities.
- ☐ I would like to work with older people.
- ☐ I would like to work with creative people.
- ☐ I would like to work with people like me.
- ☐ I would like to work with people different from me.
- ☐ I would like to work with people who speak a different language.
- ☐ I would like to work with people from underprivileged backgrounds.
- ☐ I would like to teach people.
- ☐ I would like to entertain people.
- ☐ I would like to make people feel better.
- ☐ I would like to make people look better.
- ☐ I would like to help people get out of trouble.
- ☐ I would like to sell things to people.
- ☐ I would like to work with people who are incarcerated.
- ☐ I would like to give people guidance.
- ☐ I would like to run for elected office.
- ☐ I would expect to socialize with my co-workers.
- ☐ I would like to meet celebrities on my job.
- ☐ I would like to work in a competitive environment.
- ☐ I would like a job where everyone works together for the common good.
- ☐ I would like to serve the public.
- ☐ I would like to serve private clients.
- ☐ Other _____

Psychological Rewards of Working

The psychological rewards of working relate to your passions and your values. For many people, these mean much more than financial gain. Can you imagine that Mother Teresa would have given up her work with the poor to make a pitch on *Shark Tank*? Did Martin Luther King, Jr. ever wish he'd gone into real estate? Did LeBron James ever consider becoming an accountant? What do you expect to get from your job besides money? Check the statements below that appeal to you.

☐ I would like to be recognized in the community for the work I do.

☐ I would like a job where I am free to make my own decisions.

☐ I would like a job that furthers my mission in life.

☐ I would like a job that helps less fortunate members of the community.

☐ I would like a job that offers thrills and adventure.

☐ I would like a job that lets me put my family duties first.

☐ I would like a job in which I am continually learning something new.

☐ I would like a job that has high status in the community.

☐ I want to work with people I admire and respect.

☐ I would like a job that demands creativity and innovation.

☐ I would like to work for something I believe in, even if it is unpopular or puts me in danger.

☐ I would like a job that adds to the beauty in the world.

☐ I would like a job that adds to the safety of the world.

☐ I would like a position of power.

☐ I would like a job that gives me a lot of freedom.

☐ I want to feel secure that my job will be there as long as I want it.

☐ I would like to be applauded for my work.

☐ Other _____

Mixing Career and Family

While you are making career decisions, it is important to think about the kind of family life you want to have. Jobs that demand a great deal of travel or many evening and weekend hours might make it more challenging to have a close family life. On the other hand, if you want to have a large family, you need to think about careers that will financially support them. Today, 53 percent of U.S. civilian workers are men and 47 percent are women, so balancing career responsibilities with child care, care for aging parents, and household responsibilities is something everyone needs to be involved with. Since about half of all marriages end in divorce, also keep in mind that you cannot depend on the financial support of a spouse. Because nearly 81 percent of custodial parents are women, it is essential everyone prepares for careers with incomes that could support their families. Check the statements below that appeal to you.

☐ I want to be married.
☐ I want to have children.
☐ Family life is more important to me than my career.
☐ My career is more important to me than having a family.
☐ I would like both a rewarding career and a happy family life.
☐ I would like to stay home with my children when they are young.
☐ I would like my spouse to stay home with the children when they are young.
☐ I would like to work out of my house when my children are young.
☐ I would like a job with flexible hours so I can be available for my family.
☐ I would like to be able to afford to send my children to a daycare preschool.
☐ I would like to be able to afford to have a sitter come to the house.
☐ I would like to be able to afford to have live-in help with the children.
☐ I would like to be able to afford to have a housekeeper so I can spend more time with my family.
☐ I would expect my family to help out with household chores.
☐ Other _____

Having kids has been a fantastic thing for me. It's meant that I'm a little more balanced. In my twenties I worked massively, hardly took vacation at all. Now, I, with the help of my wife, I'm always making sure I've got a good balance of how I spend my time.

—Bill Gates

Financial Rewards

Financial rewards include not just *how much* money you make, but how you are paid, your benefits, job security, and so on. Check the statements below that appeal to you.

☐ I would like a job that pays at least $_____ per month. See page 93.

☐ I would like to be paid by the hour, with time and a half for overtime.

☐ I would like a monthly salary that doesn't vary with the number of hours I work.

☐ I would like to work on a commission basis.

☐ I would like a job that would be secure even in times of recession.

☐ I'm willing to accept a lower salary if the potential for either financial or psychological rewards is good.

☐ Money isn't important to me — I just need enough to get by.

☐ I want a job with good benefits (e.g., health insurance, pension plan, paid vacations, etc.).

☐ I'd like my salary to be based on my job performance.

☐ I'd like a job with scheduled pay increases.

☐ I'd like to be paid for the things I create or produce (e.g., paintings, articles, cookies, etc.).

☐ I'd like a job that offers bonuses or other incentives.

☐ I'm willing to start with a very low salary as long as there is an opportunity to work towards a very high salary.

☐ Other _____

Job Skills

This final category should help you fill out your general career outline. What are the skills you would most like to use on your job? Check back to chapter two and record your findings below.

My physical skills include: _____ _____

_____ _____ _____

My intellectual and creative skills include: _____

_____ _____ _____

My social skills include: _____ _____

_____ _____ _____

The skills I would like to acquire are:

_____ _____ _____

_____ _____ _____

_____ _____ _____

You will need to expand this list when you come up with a specific career goal.

You probably checked a number of statements in each category. Read them all again to get a *very* broad picture of your career desires. It's unlikely that any job could meet all these requirements, so go back and choose the one or two statements from each category that mean the most to you. Circle the boxes in front of those statements. Then enter them on the next page. Keep these in mind as you begin shortening your list of possible careers.

Gena's chart looked like this:

The physical setting I want to work in is: <u>pleasing to the eye or an art museum or gallery.</u>

The working conditions I would most enjoy include: <u>a job that lets me work with many different clients and that lets me be creative.</u>

I would like my work relationships to be: <u>with creative people. I would also like to serve the public.</u>

The psychological reward most important to me is: <u>I must be continually learning something new.</u>

My goals for mixing career and family include: <u>having both a rewarding career and a happy family life, and being able to work out of my house while my children are young.</u>

Financially, I would like: <u>my salary to be based on my job performance.</u>

The skills I have or would most like to acquire include: <u>writing, doing research, and public speaking.</u>

It's unlikely that any job can meet all your requirements. Choose those that mean the most to you.

My Ideal Job

The physical setting I want to work in is: _____

The working conditions I would most enjoy include: _____

_____

I would like my work relationships to be: _____

_____

The psychological reward most important to me is: _____

_____

My goals for mixing career and family include: _____

_____

Financially, I would like: _____

_____

The skills I have or would most like to acquire include: _____

_____

Do your answers support any of the career choices you had in mind? Do they rule out any of them? Do they suggest new possibilities?

Gena found that her answers both narrowed and expanded her list of potential careers. She'd been thinking seriously about a career in business, possibly because both of her parents worked for large corporations. However, that kind of job probably would not provide the kind of flexibility she'd like to have when her children are young. Besides, she wasn't sure she'd meet the most creative people working in business. Some of her answers, though, opened up new avenues of thought. She had always been interested in the arts, and her writing and researching skills could be used in a job that would let her keep on learning. Perhaps she could write about the arts or work in the public relations department of an art museum? With experience like that, she thought, she might be able to stay home and do freelance writing projects during the time she was home with her children.

Job Characteristics

Another important point to remember is that workers today have many more options than they did 20 or 30 years ago. Technological advances have created hundreds of new jobs. Changes in society have brought about changes in the workplace: flexible hours, job sharing, telecommuting, and composite careers, for example, were unheard of in the not-too-distant past. And, more than ever before, people are going into business for themselves, creating their own careers and/or businesses.

Some people are enticed by these new possibilities. Others prefer to work in more traditional modes. The new ways of working will probably give you more freedom, but they usually also involve more risks and offer less security. They require a higher anxiety tolerance. Traditional jobs offer more security and are likely to be more comfortable for those with lower anxiety tolerance. Which category appeals to you? Before you choose, make sure you know what these terms mean.

CONSIDER YOUR OPTIONS

Full-time job: A job calling for 35 to 40 hours or more of work each week.

Part-time job: A job at which you work less than 35 hours per week.

Structured hours: Strictly prescribed — and probably monitored — work hours. For example, from 8 A.M. to 5 P.M., Monday through Friday. In some jobs, employers must insist that you be on the job at a particular time. For example, if you work in a store that opens at 9 A.M., your boss is not going to take your request to show up sometime between 9 and 10:30 very seriously. If you are the anchor for the 10 P.M. news, you better be at your desk when the cameras start rolling.

Flexible hours: Work hours that provide more leeway. On some jobs, for example, you might be able to work any eight hours between 7 A.M. and 7 P.M. Many jobs offer a flexible starting time, but require all workers to be on the job during the busiest hours of the day. Self-employed people can be free to set their hours any way they like.

Composite careers: Having two or three jobs at the same time. For example, many college instructors are also researchers or writers. You might be a contractor and a cabinet maker, or a lecturer and consultant. Many people combine more secure or higher-paying jobs with higher risk or lower-paying jobs. They probably get more satisfaction from the riskier career, but their other job provides more security. This is one way to "have your cake and eat it, too."

Working for salary: Being paid by the hour or the month.

135

Working on a freelance or commission basis: Freelancers are paid by the job. Salespeople and agents are paid commissions, usually a percentage of their sales. For example, if a real estate broker receives a commission of 6 percent, he or she would earn $6,000 for listing and selling a $100,000 condominium.

Telecommuting: This option appeals to many, because it combines the security of working for an established company with the flexibility of completing your work at home. Rather than traveling daily to a company site, you work from another location. Telecommuting also expands a person's employment opportunities; they aren't limited to finding employment in their own community. They may live in Saint George, Utah while the company they work for is based in Santa Barbara, California—or even Buenos Aires, Argentina.

Home-based business: Technology has also made it easier to start—and maintain—your own business. With a great idea or service and some basic equipment (computer with Internet connection, fax machine, printer), a one-person, home-based office can be efficient and productive. Sophisticated software programs and the power of the Internet make being your own bookkeeper, office manager, graphic artist, marketing expert, and shipper feasible for those willing to embrace the technology learning curve.

Lifetime career: Having the same job, or same kind of job, throughout your working life.

Sequential careers: Having a series of different careers throughout your working life.

Anxiety: Worry or fear about future uncertainties. Anxiety isn't all bad, however. In fact, up to a certain point, it will help you do a better job. For example, if you are anxious about tomorrow's history test, you are more likely to prepare for it and you may perform better than if you'd had no anxiety. (Why study if you're not worried?) If you are *too* anxious, however, your performance will suffer. You'll be too nervous to do a good job.

Anxiety tolerance: How well you can deal with fears and uncertainties. Some people like the feeling that "anything could happen," or are confident that they can deal with whatever problems come along. These people have high anxiety tolerance. Those with low anxiety tolerance find the worry and fear hard to deal with. It's hard to escape anxiety, however, so learning to tolerate the discomfort is important. Remember that these fears are normal. Everyone has them. Learning to act in spite of them is a mark of maturity.

On the chart below, circle one job characteristic on each line that appeals most to you.

Column 1	Column 2
Full-time	Part-time
Structured hours	Flexible hours
Employee	Employer
Salaried	Freelance, commission
Company site	Telecommuting or home-based business
Single career	Composite careers
Lifetime career	Sequential careers

Did you circle more characteristics in column 1 or in column 2? _____

Column 1 represents careers with fewer risks, higher security, and less freedom. These careers also allow for a lower level of anxiety tolerance.

Column 2 represents careers with more risks, lower security, and more freedom. Careers like these usually call for fairly high anxiety tolerance.

Do your choices feel right for you?	**Yes**	**No**	**Undecided**
Do you consider yourself a risk taker?	**Yes**	**No**	**Undecided**
Do you often worry about future events or situations?	**Yes**	**No**	**Undecided**

Refer to this chart as you make your career decisions and explore different job titles. Would you be more comfortable in a job offering security or one providing more freedom? While these characteristics are at opposite ends of the scale, one is not better than the other. It's entirely a matter of what feels right for you.

Fears are normal; learning
to act in spite of them is a
mark of maturity.

Employee or Employer?

Another consideration, also based on your personality, is whether you would find it more rewarding to be an *employer* or an *employee*. Employers, as they relate to the following exercise, are defined as people who own their business, whatever its size. In other words, these people are *entrepreneurs*. They usually have more freedom and control over their time. However, they may often need to take major risks, both personal and financial. Is this an option that appeals to you?

ENTREPRENEURIAL CHECKLIST

Select the answer that best describes, or comes closest to, your feelings.

Willing to risk capital:
- ☐ 1. As long as I feel that there is a good chance of success, I'll go for it.
- ☐ 2. I'm willing to invest some capital, but I always leave a sizable cushion, just in case.
- ☐ 3. I have never really felt comfortable risking money or time on things I'm not absolutely sure of.

Independence:
- ☐ 1. Most of all, I want to be my own boss; it's my major goal.
- ☐ 2. I don't mind working for other people, but I'd rather be on my own.
- ☐ 3. Being on my own really scares me. I'd rather have the security of being an employee, and let someone else worry about the problems.

Flexibility:
- ☐ 1. I adapt to change quickly and decisively.
- ☐ 2. I move, but it takes time and careful consideration.
- ☐ 3. I would rather see things stay the same; I get uptight when change occurs.

Self-confidence:
- ☐ 1. I am very confident in myself and know that I can handle most situations.
- ☐ 2. I am confident most of the time, particularly when I know the ground rules.
- ☐ 3. I'm not in control of my destiny; other people really control my future.

Attitude toward people:
- ☐ 1. I am naturally drawn to people; I like them, and they like me.
- ☐ 2. I find most people enjoyable, and most people are attracted to me.
- ☐ 3. I like things more than people and don't have many friends.

Knowledge of the particular business:
- ☐ 1. I know the business that I've been thinking about well and will enjoy it.
- ☐ 2. I'm reasonably confident I can learn the business, and it appears that I will enjoy it.
- ☐ 3. I am not familiar with this type of business, nor do I know whether I will enjoy it.

Keywords: realities entrepreneurship

Ability to start from scratch:

☐ 1. I enjoy the challenge of building something from scratch on my own; I'm a self-starter.

☐ 2. If given basic guidelines, I can do a good job.

☐ 3. I really prefer to have the entire job laid out, then I'll do it well.

Commitment:

☐ 1. I have a high drive and commitment and won't stop until the project is done.

☐ 2. I seem to have a higher level of perseverance when things are going well.

☐ 3. I start many projects, but rarely find time to finish them.

Common sense:

☐ 1. I consider myself realistic and "street wise" when it comes to business.

☐ 2. Most business situations make sense, but there are areas where I feel out of step.

☐ 3. I am inexperienced and impractical in business matters.

Willingness to accept failure:

☐ 1. "Nothing ventured, nothing gained" is my motto.

☐ 2. I want to succeed, but if I fail, I will accept it.

☐ 3. I want to avoid failure, and won't take a risk if it doesn't look like a sure thing.

Health:

☐ 1. I have excellent health and feel good, both physically and mentally.

☐ 2. I get sick on occasion, but it doesn't last long.

☐ 3. I have problems with my health; illness always seems to get in my way.

Work habits:

☐ 1. I plan before I start and then work my plan; I'm well-organized.

☐ 2. I find that I'm organized most of the time; but on occasion, I do get out of control.

☐ 3. I take things as they come, and sometimes get priorities confused.

To total your score, add up all the checked numbers. A number one has the weight of one, a number two scores a two, and a three equals three. If your total score is between 12 and 16, you are a good candidate and should consider starting your own business at some time.

This checklist is for self-evaluation of your personal characteristics, to see if you will have a better-than-average chance of success as an entrepreneur. The material may touch on some tender personal areas; you'll have to be honest with yourself. Be careful to avoid self-deception; don't brush the negative under the rug.

Take enough time to evaluate the criteria and information, and try to relate some actual experiences from your past. Determine how you will handle things when it gets tough. If you can count on anything, you can count on the fact that owning your own business operation is going to be challenging.

This short personal appraisal is by no means an evaluation of whether you are qualified to be an entrepreneur. It is simply a way of focusing on your personal attributes, and it may help you decide on taking that major step. You may want to ask a few of your close friends or relatives to evaluate you, perhaps more objectively than you can do it for yourself.

Reprinted with permission: *How to Start, Expand and Sell a Business, a Complete Guidebook for Entrepreneurs* by James C. Comiskey.

Professionalism: It's not the job you do, it's how you do the job.

—Anonymous

What About Status?

As an American, you are probably well acquainted with the concept of status. It usually comes attached to a brand name, though those names may vary widely from place to place. It's often expensive, and it's more important to some people than it is to others.

Basically, the same rules apply to the perceived status of different careers. Certain job titles, like certain brands of jeans, offer more prestige. What is considered a high-status job may vary in different groups or circles, however. For example, a philosopher might have high status in intellectual circles but hardly any among business-oriented groups.

Sometimes higher status is assigned to people in professions that require more education: doctors, lawyers, college professors, and so on. Sometimes it relates to the respect society bestows on groups like the clergy. The arts, too, seem to have a certain prestige. A few jobs — in the military or the diplomatic corps, for example — come with assigned ranks so there can be no mistakes about status. In fields like sales, prestige is related to what you sell. Someone in estate jewelry, for example, will have higher status than someone who sells parts from junked cars.

Interestingly, though, status does not necessarily relate to income. That junk dealer could earn much more than the jewelry salesperson — or the doctor, for that matter. Some jobs that require just a year or two of technical training offer higher pay than many careers calling for a college degree. Plumbers and electricians, for example, have a higher average salary than teachers and librarians. In other words, just like the "right" kind of shoes, status can be expensive.

That's why you need to give some thought to your own values as you consider your job choices. In itself, status is neither good nor bad. Because some people place so much importance on it, however, it is easy to confuse your own feelings with those of your friends or associates. Peer pressure can be strong, but remember that your friends will not be working at your chosen career. You will.

What does status mean to you? Whose opinions matter to you most? What values does status reflect? Can you explain why, today, a rock star has more status than a teacher or a politician? Consider these questions and then, to help clarify your thoughts, indicate whether you agree or disagree with the statements on the next page.

It is important to me to have a job with high status.

        Agree   Disagree

I am willing to invest the time it takes to train for a job with high status.

        Agree   Disagree

It is more important to me that a job has status than that it pays well.

        Agree   Disagree

I don't think I could be happy at a job that others might look down on.

        Agree   Disagree

CHAPTER 5 CHECKPOINTS
Your Ideal Career
There's more to consider than just the work

You have now taken a look at the general characteristics you hope to find in a job. This will eventually help you to identify your ideal career. Before moving forward, confirm that you've achieved each of the goals below.

☐ I completed a series of questionnaires and identified the specific working conditions and job characteristics that most appeal to me.

☐ I considered the job characteristics that are most important to me and I'm thinking creatively about jobs that meet those requirements.

☐ I analyzed which skills I'd most like to use in my ideal job.

☐ I considered a variety of formats for structured or unstructured employment and gauged my level of anxiety tolerance in relation to working.

☐ I evaluated whether my attitudes, characteristics, and skills are more in line with the role of employer or of employee.

☐ I started to sort out my feelings about status as it relates to job selection.

*Choose a job you love, and you will never
have to work a day in your life.*
—Confucius

Every calling is great when greatly pursued.
—Oliver Wendell Holmes, Jr.

CHAPTER SIX
Career Research
Reading about careers isn't enough

Section Two:
WHAT DO I WANT?

Marta had a dream. She didn't know exactly where she was, but it was warm and far away. And it was beautiful. There were lots of people around, but everyone seemed to be doing his or her own thing. They were all wearing shorts and T-shirts, and they worked diligently with what appeared to be tiny tools or instruments. Periodically, someone would shout excitedly, and everyone else would cheer. This went on until a brilliant sunset brought on the night. Marta woke up feeling content, but puzzled. When she shared her dream with her friend, Jennifer, she said, "I wonder what it was all about. I'd like to go back there, wherever it was."

"Sounds like some kind of archaeological dig to me," Jennifer replied.

"What's that?"

"You know. It's like looking for bones or tools or any kind of remnant of past civilizations. Archaeologists go out and recover these things, and then they study them and help put together a picture of what life was like at a certain time in a certain place."

"Oh, yeah? That sounds like something I might like to do."

Now that you've considered some of the general characteristics you'd like in a job, it's time to get more specific. As you work through this chapter, you will identify several jobs that might meet your requirements and then set out to learn as much about them as you can.

Perhaps you've already thought of some careers you'd like to know more about. If not, now's the time to start. Can you, like Marta, picture an ideal job? In addition to the work itself, think about the settings and the situations it might involve. Would you find them pleasing day-in and day-out, year after year? Take some time to daydream about your future career. Shut your eyes for a few minutes and consider different possibilities. Wait until one feels right and you, too, feel content.

144

Career Clusters

In order to select a career you'll be happy with, you should have some knowledge of the many jobs available. There are thousands of them, and we can't list them all here. The U.S. Department of Labor makes things a little easier by organizing jobs into Career Clusters, which you'll find on the Occupational Information Network, otherwise known as O*NET Online.

The jobs in each category have certain things in common. By investigating the family groups that appeal to you most, you may come up with quite a number of possible careers. We've listed the 16 major groups along with a few jobs in each category.

Review the Career Clusters (in bold), and place a check mark in the box next to those areas that sound interesting to you.

☐ *Agriculture, Food, and Natural Resources*

Agricultural Inspectors, Animal Breeders, Commercial Fishers, Conservation Scientists, Construction and Well Drillers, Environmental Engineers, Farm Workers and Laborers, Fish and Game Wardens, Foresters, Food Scientists, Gas and Oil Drillers, Landscapers and Groundskeepers, Logging Workers, Mining Engineers, Nursery Workers, Park Naturalists, Water Treatment Plant Operators, Zoologists

☐ *Architecture and Construction*

Architects, Bricklayers and Stonemasons, Cabinetmakers, Carpenters, Crane and Tower Operators, Construction Managers, Drafters, Electricians, Energy Auditors, Glaziers, Line Installers and Repairers, Mechanic and Repairer Helpers, Meter Readers, Painters, Pipelayers, Structural Metal Workers, Surveyors

☐ *Arts, Audio/Video Technology, and Communications*

Actors, Animators and Multi-media Artists, Announcers, Art Directors, Camera Operators, Choreographers, Costume and Wardrobe Specialists, Curators, Dancers, Film and Video Editors, Fine Artists, Graphic Designers, Interior Designers, Movie Projectionists, Musicians, News Reporters, Photographers, Producers and Directors, Sound Engineering Technicians, Writers and Authors

☐ *Business, Management, and Administration*

Accountants and Auditors, Agents and Business Managers, Billing Clerks, Budget Analysts, Business Executives, Employee Training Specialists, Human Resource Managers, Management Analysts, Meeting and Convention Planners, Office Managers, Operations Research Analysts, Public Relations Specialists, Receptionists, Secretaries, Shipping and Receiving Clerks, Supply Chain Managers, Tax Preparers

☐ *Education and Training*

Adult and Vocational Education Teachers, Coaches and Scouts, College Professors, Education Administrators, Elementary and Secondary School Teachers, Fitness Trainers and Aerobics Instructors, Instructional Coordinators, Librarians, Preschool and Kindergarten Teachers, Principals, Public Health Educators, School Counselors, Special Education Teachers, Teacher Assistants, Tutors

☐ *Finance*

Actuaries, Bank Tellers, Bill and Account Collectors, Brokerage Clerks, Compliance Officers and Inspectors, Credit Checkers and Authorizers, Economists, Financial Analysts, Financial Counselors, Insurance Adjusters and Examiners, Insurance Underwriters, Loan Officers, New Accounts Clerks, Securities Salespeople, Title Examiners and Searchers

☐ *Government and Public Administration*

City and Regional Planning Aides, Climate Change Analysts, Command and Control Center Officers, Court Clerks, Detectives and Criminal Investigators, Equal Opportunity Representatives, Government Programs Eligibility Interviewers, Government Property Inspectors and Investigators, Infantry Officers, Legislators, Municipal Clerks, Postal Service Mail Carriers, Radar and Sonar Technicians, Tax Examiners, Transportation Inspectors, Urban and Regional Planners

☐ *Health Science*

Anesthesiologists, Athletic Trainers, Biomedical Engineers, Chiropractors, Dentists, Dieticians, Emergency Medical Technicians, Family and General Practitioners, Forensic Science Technicians, Health Services Administrators, Massage Therapists, Medical Laboratory Technicians, Optometrists, Pharmacists, Psychiatrists, Registered Nurses, Speech Pathologists and Audiologists, Surgeons, Veterinarians

continued . . .

☐ Hospitality and Tourism

Baggage Porters and Bellhops, Bartenders, Buspersons, Casino Gaming Workers, Chefs and Cooks, Concierges, Dishwashers, Food Preparation Workers, Hotel Desk Clerks, Janitors and Housekeepers, Reservation and Ticket Agents, Restaurant Hosts and Hostesses, Tour Guides, Travel Agents, Umpires and Referees, Waiters and Waitresses

☐ Human Services

Child Care Workers, Clergy, Funeral Directors, Hairstylists and Cosmetologists, Laundry and Dry-Cleaning Workers, Manicurists and Pedicurists, Mental Health Counselors, Personal and Home Care Aides, Physical Therapists, Residential Advisors, Skin Care Specialists, Social and Community Service Managers, Social Workers, Sociologists, Tailors

☐ Information Technology

Business Intelligence Analysts, Computer Engineers, Computer Programmers, Computer Security Specialists, Computer Support Specialists, Computer Systems Analysts, Data Communications Analysts, Database Administrators, Information Technology Project Managers, Network and Computer Systems Administrators, Software Quality Assurance Engineers and Testers, Telecommunications Specialists, Video Game Designers, Web Developers

☐ Law, Public Safety, Corrections, and Security

Animal Control Workers, Arbitrators and Mediators, Bailiffs, Corrections Officers, Crossing Guards, Dispatchers, Fire Fighters, Judges and Hearing Officers, Lawyers, Paralegals, Life Guards and Ski Patrollers, Police Patrol Officers, Probation Officers, Security Guards, Sheriffs

☐ Manufacturing

Appliance Installers and Repairers, Buyers and Purchasing Agents, Electric Motor Repairers, Forklift Operators, Furniture Finishers, Glass Blowers, Industrial Designers, Industrial Production Managers, Jewelers, Machinists, Packers and Packagers, Precision Assemblers, Quality Control Inspectors, Welders and Solderers, Woodworking Machine Operators

☐ Marketing, Sales, and Service

Advertising Managers, Cashiers, Counter and Rental Clerks, Customer Service Representatives, Floral Designers, Merchandise Displayers and Window Trimmers, Market Research Analysts, Models, Online Merchants, Real Estate Agents and Brokers, Retail Salespeople, Sales Representatives, Service Station Attendants, Stock Clerks, Wholesale and Retail Buyers

☐ Science, Technology, Engineering, and Mathematics

Aerospace Engineers, Anthropologists, Archaeologists, Astronomers, Biologists, Chemists, Civil Engineers, Electrical and Electronics Drafters, Engineering Managers, Energy Engineers, Hydrologists, Mapping Technicians, Meteorologists, Mechanical Engineers, Science Technicians, Statisticians

☐ Transportation, Distribution, and Logistics

Air Traffic Controllers, Airline Pilots, Ambulance Drivers, Automobile Mechanics, Bus Drivers, Crane Operators, Deckhands, Flight Attendants, Freight Inspectors, Locomotive Engineers, Parking Lot Attendants, Sailors, Taxi Drivers, Traffic Technicians, Transportation Security Agents, Truck Drivers

Which two groups sound the most appealing to you? Write them below.

_____   _____

Organizing occupations in career clusters is just one way of classifying different types of jobs. As you browse the Internet or look through your library's career section, you'll find others. You'll also find web sites and books about careers in specific fields, such as finance, high-tech careers, jobs of the future, careers in the arts, and so on.

You'll want to go to O*NET Online's Code Connector.* Linked to major occupational groups they call Job Families, you'll find comprehensive lists of careers within each category. This will help you develop a broad picture of careers you might find exciting and satisfying.

* At the time of this printing, the web address was http://www.onetcodeconnector.org

Bring In Your Identity

The occupational groups known as career clusters are based on broad industries with commonalities such as interests, values, and skill sets. Turn back to your **Personal Profile** chart on page 27 to review your values and passions. Now go over the groups again. Below, list a couple of careers that appeal to you most, or that seem to complement your values and passions.

_____   _____   _____

_____   _____   _____

Next take another look at your strengths and skills. Can you think of any careers within your chosen interest group(s) that also seem to fit in with these aspects of your personality? List other possible careers on the following lines.

_____   _____   _____

_____   _____   _____

What about your lifestyle budget? (See page 94.) That's an important piece to this puzzle. Don't forget the characteristics of your ideal job on pages 134 and 137. You'll want to take your financial requirements and ideal working conditions into consideration as you proceed to the next step — in-depth research regarding specific careers and job titles.

When Letitia looked back at her bull's eye chart, she saw that her highest values were power, helping others, and personal integrity and moral courage. Looking again at her list of passions, politics and social justice seemed to be the ones that she most wanted to be a part of her career. As she reviewed the occupational groups, she decided that Community and Social Services and Legal were most appropriate for her.

Letitia scored high in both the dominating and influencing areas on her personal strengths test. Writing, researching, and persuading are among her skills. Therefore, she decided that becoming a lawyer was a wise choice for her. Two other careers she hadn't thought about also looked appealing—counseling and government administration. Letitia added them to her list of jobs on which to do more research.

Career Research

"Tell me and I forget. Show me and I remember. Involve me and I understand."

This sage advice should guide your career research process as you include all three steps.

Career research begins with a library investigation or an internet search. While this is an essential part of your project, too many people make a career choice after completing only this first step. Stopping your research at this point is a little like marrying someone you've been told about, but have only just met. The information you gather will not be truly meaningful until you combine it with observation and experience.

Choosing a career (like choosing a marriage partner) is one of the most important decisions you will ever make. If you take the time and energy necessary to do this job right by completing all three steps in the process, you're bound to have a happier, more fulfilling life.

Remember that the choices you are making now are tentative. You may change your mind many times before settling on your future course. The career choice you make now is meant to be used for the rest of the book, not necessarily for the rest of your life. The process you are learning, however, can be useful over a lifetime, no matter how many career changes you make.

STEP ONE

READ AND RESEARCH
LIBRARY RESEARCH

You may find it useful to first visit your campus or community library or Career Information Center. Most of the information you will need can be located there. Look for books in the career category or interest areas you find most interesting (agriculture, science, business, and so on).

Stop by the reference desk of your library and take a look at the U.S. Department of Labor's *Occupational Outlook Handbook* (OOH). It's revised every two years, so you'll have up-to-date information about the job: what workers do on the job, working conditions, the training and education needed, earnings, and expected job prospects.

If you haven't already done so, now is the time in your *process* to go online. The career research tools available on the internet far exceed those found in traditional print resources. At this point in your decision-making process you've discovered your unique traits and dreams, qualities that only you can determine. Using these personal insights as a guide, start mining government databases dedicated to helping you sort through the hundreds of career opportunities available. You'll use this information to help you complete the **Career Interest Surveys** on pages 150 to 156.

Keywords: career research, [industry or occupation] career

ONLINE RESEARCH

Start your Internet research with America's Career InfoNet (http://www.acinet.org). You'll find a collection of electronic tools offering unique solutions to what can be an overwhelming task. The most extensive career library online, this powerful resource will help you determine occupational requirements, identify wage and employment trends, and discover the skills required for your selected careers. You'll find information on the general job market outlook for different education levels, state-by-state labor market statistics, and short video profiles of nearly 550 jobs. Pour yourself a tall glass of your favorite beverage, turn off your cell phone, ask friends and family not to interrupt you — and search away.

Once you've found a list of career titles that intrigue you, visit the online version of the *Occupational Outlook Handbook* (OOH)* found on the Bureau of Labor Statistics' web site. Look up the job titles on your list and you'll get extensive descriptions on each. The OOH information might also include links to industry associations related to that career that you can use to expand your research.

You'll find information on employment and wage estimates for over 800 occupations on the Occupational Employment Statistics (OES) website.** You'll also find O*NET Online*** helpful when searching for occupations that utilize your particular skills, as discussed on pages 145 and 146.

Many magazines and newspapers archive articles on their websites. A keyword search on any Internet search engine will uncover specialized information. Just remember: articles may become quickly outdated, so don't bother looking for information that was published more than a year or two ago.

It's also helpful to check your newspaper's online classified ads or Craigslist. If remaining in your town or city is important, this is a critical consideration. You'll get a feeling for the quantity and kinds of jobs currently available in your area. To expand your search to other areas, browse the listings on web sites such as Monster.com, CareerBuilder.com, or Indeed.com.

CARL'S STORY

Carl spent a great deal of time thinking about what he wanted to do, but he was still uncertain. One day he went to a bookstore and began reading his way to his future. He went from section to section—travel, psychology, architecture—paging through books to see how he felt, what held his interest, what he wanted to know more about. When he reached the business section, he started to feel at home. He was fascinated by everything he read, and he wanted to know much more. Based on this excursion, Carl investigated business careers more seriously. His interest held. Today, he is a successful and satisfied owner of a securities brokerage house.

* At the time of this printing, the web address was http://www.bls.gov/oco
** At the time of this printing, the web address was http://stats.bls.gov/oes
*** At the time of this printing, the web address was http://www.onetonline.org/

Career Interest Survey

Now it's time to choose three careers that appeal to you most so you can begin learning as much about them as you can. Review the careers chosen on page 147. It will be helpful if you can interview people working in these fields. Separate worksheets are provided for each job title.

JOB TITLE _____

1. What specific tasks would I perform on this job? (For example, a sales clerk would answer questions, tidy displays, unpack merchandise, ring up sales, make change, and so on.)

_____

_____

2. What is the job environment likely to be? Is this compatible with the setting I said I wanted on *page 126?*

_____

_____

3. What would be the rewards of working at this job? Are they the same as the ones I listed on *page 129?*

_____

_____

4. I would find this job particularly satisfying because: (Review your passions, values, interests, and life goals for guidance.) *See page 27.*

_____

_____

5. Is this job compatible with my work behavioral style? If so, in what ways? *Review pages 38–43.*

_____

_____

6. How much training or education would I need? Review your options (college, technical school, apprenticeship, work experience, etc.). *See pages 340–341.* What commitment am I willing to make? *Review pages 114–120.*

_____

_____

7. Does this job require specific physical attributes or abilities (strength or health requirements, 20/20 vision, and so on)? If so, what are they? Do I meet them?

_____

_____

8. What could I expect to earn as a beginner in this field? _____

   What is the average mid-career salary? _____

9. Does this meet my salary requirements? *See pages 93 and 131.*   Yes   No

   _____

10. Will there be many job openings when I am ready to go to work? How might societal, economic, and technological changes impact this career? *Online resources will be helpful.*

   _____

   _____

11. What aptitudes, strengths, and skills does this job call for? Are they transferable to another career if I change my mind or this job title becomes obsolete? *See page 132.*

   _____

   _____

12. What can I do today to begin preparing for this job?

   _____

   _____

13. What classes must I take in high school to qualify for this job?

   _____

   _____

14. Where in this town or state could I find a job in this field?

   _____

   _____

15. How does this career mesh with my family plans? Is it consistent with my desired lifestyle? *See page 130.* Does it offer opportunities for flexible hours or part-time work? Is the income high enough so I could maintain my family on it alone if necessary? Could I afford the kind of day care I'd like for my children?

   _____

   _____

   _____

16. Are there opportunities for self-employment in this field (business owner, freelance work, consulting, and the like)?

   _____

   _____

Create a timeline outlining how this career has changed over the last 10 years and predicting how it might change in the next 10 years. *Start with online resources.*

JOB TITLE _____

1. What specific tasks would I perform on this job? (For example, a sales clerk would answer questions, tidy displays, unpack merchandise, ring up sales, make change, and so on.)

_____

_____

2. What is the job environment likely to be? Is this compatible with the setting I said I wanted on *page 126?*

_____

_____

3. What would be the rewards of working at this job? Are they the same as the ones I listed on *page 129?*

_____

_____

4. I would find this job particularly satisfying because: (Review your passions, values, interests, and life goals for guidance.) *See page 27.*

_____

_____

5. Is this job compatible with my work behavioral style? If so, in what ways? *Review pages 38–43.*

_____

_____

6. How much training or education would I need? Review your options (college, technical school, apprenticeship, work experience, etc.). *See pages 340–341.* What commitment am I willing to make? *Review pages 114–120.*

_____

_____

7. Does this job require specific physical attributes or abilities (strength or health requirements, 20/20 vision, and so on)? If so, what are they? Do I meet them?

_____

_____

8. What could I expect to earn as a beginner in this field? _____

   What is the average mid-career salary? _____

9. Does this meet my salary requirements? *See pages 93 and 131.*   Yes   No

_____

10. Will there be many job openings when I am ready to go to work? How might societal, economic, and technological changes impact this career? *Online resources will be helpful.*

_____

_____

11. What aptitudes, strengths, and skills does this job call for? Are they transferable to another career if I change my mind or this job title becomes obsolete? *See page 132.*

_____

_____

12. What can I do today to begin preparing for this job?

_____

_____

13. What classes must I take in high school to qualify for this job?

_____

_____

14. Where in this town or state could I find a job in this field?

_____

_____

15. How does this career mesh with my family plans? Is it consistent with my desired lifestyle? *See page 130.* Does it offer opportunities for flexible hours or part-time work? Is the income high enough so I could maintain my family on it alone if necessary? Could I afford the kind of day care I'd like for my children?

_____

_____

_____

16. Are there opportunities for self-employment in this field (business owner, freelance work, consulting, and the like)?

_____

_____

Create a timeline outlining how this career has changed over the last 10 years and predicting how it might change in the next 10 years. *Start with online resources.*

JOB TITLE _____

1. What specific tasks would I perform on this job? (For example, a sales clerk would answer questions, tidy displays, unpack merchandise, ring up sales, make change, and so on.)

_____

_____

2. What is the job environment likely to be? Is this compatible with the setting I said I wanted on *page 126?*

_____

_____

3. What would be the rewards of working at this job? Are they the same as the ones I listed on *page 129?*

_____

_____

4. I would find this job particularly satisfying because: (Review your passions, values, interests, and life goals for guidance.) *See page 27.*

_____

_____

5. Is this job compatible with my work behavioral style? If so, in what ways? *Review pages 38–43.*

_____

_____

6. How much training or education would I need? Review your options (college, technical school, apprenticeship, work experience, etc.). *See pages 340–341.* What commitment am I willing to make? *Review pages 114–120.*

_____

_____

7. Does this job require specific physical attributes or abilities (strength or health requirements, 20/20 vision, and so on)? If so, what are they? Do I meet them?

_____

_____

8. What could I expect to earn as a beginner in this field? _____

   What is the average mid-career salary? _____

9. Does this meet my salary requirements? *See pages 93 and 131.*   Yes   No

_____

10. Will there be many job openings when I am ready to go to work? How might societal, economic, and technological changes impact this career? *Online resources will be helpful.*

_____

_____

11. What aptitudes, strengths, and skills does this job call for? Are they transferable to another career if I change my mind or this job title becomes obsolete? *See page 132.*

_____

_____

12. What can I do today to begin preparing for this job?

_____

_____

13. What classes must I take in high school to qualify for this job?

_____

_____

14. Where in this town or state could I find a job in this field?

_____

_____

15. How does this career mesh with my family plans? Is it consistent with my desired lifestyle? *See page 130.* Does it offer opportunities for flexible hours or part-time work? Is the income high enough so I could maintain my family on it alone if necessary? Could I afford the kind of day care I'd like for my children?

_____

_____

_____

16. Are there opportunities for self-employment in this field (business owner, freelance work, consulting, and the like)?

_____

_____

Create a timeline outlining how this career has changed over the last 10 years and predicting how it might change in the next 10 years. *Start with online resources.*

STEP TWO

SHOW ME AND I REMEMBER

The popularity of how-to videos is evidence that this statement is true. Books about exercise, cooking, or playing tennis are often less expensive and provide more information than videos do. But somehow seeing Roger Federer hit a perfect serve or *Top Chef* contestants whip up a chicken pot pie makes a more lasting impression.

As you completed your three **Career Interest Surveys**, one of your choices probably emerged as the favorite. If two or more of the jobs still hold strong appeal for you, choose the one you are least familiar with for this part of your research. If you discovered that none of the careers you investigated meet your requirements, make some new choices and go through the research and survey process once more. Again, remember that this is a tentative decision, a trial choice. Don't feel you are obligated to stick with this career simply because you are choosing it now.

When you have completed your survey and interviewed someone now working in the field of your choice, you are ready to begin step two.

SEEING IN THE MIND'S EYE

Picture yourself on the job. What would a typical working day be like? Use the information you gathered in step one to answer the following questions. Sit down, close your eyes, and actually see yourself going through the day. Pay particular attention to your feelings. Concern yourself with more than just the work. How would you feel in the morning, as you got ready to leave home? What would you do at lunch? How would you feel at the end of the day? How would you spend your evening?

IMAGINING A TYPICAL DAY

If your working hours would be something other than 9:00 A.M. to 5:00 P.M., adjust the following schedule accordingly.

7:00 A.M. Getting ready for work. What would you wear? How do you feel about going to work? Are you looking forward to the day? _____

_____

8:00 A.M. Traveling to work. How would you get there? How far would you travel? Would you work at home? _____

_____

9:00 A.M. Walking into work. Describe the setting. Who else is there? What kind of greeting do you get from them? _____

_____

9:00 A.M. to 12:00 noon What would you be doing during this time? If this is a typical day, what tasks and responsibilities would you carry out?

_____

10:00 A.M. _____

11:00 A.M. _____

Noon. Where would you have lunch, and with whom? Would you socialize with co-workers? Clients?

_____

_____

1:00 P.M. to 5:00 P.M. As the day goes on, see yourself handling some special problems or challenges that might arise in this field. What are they? How do you deal with them?

_____

1:00 P.M. _____

2:00 P.M. _____

3:00 P.M. _____

4:00 P.M. _____

5:00 P.M. _____

6:00 P.M. Going home. How do you feel at the end of the day? What might you be thinking about?

_____

_____

7:00 P.M. and on. How would you spend a typical evening? Would you need to bring work home? Would you be with your family? Your friends? Are there hobbies or volunteer activities you would want to pursue?

_____

_____

To him that watches, everything is revealed.
—Italian Proverb

The Shadow Program

How difficult was it for you to see yourself on the job? Chances are, despite all your research, some of the questions were hard to answer. This exercise is meant to help you get the kind of information not likely to be found in books.

The shadow program actually lets you spend a day watching someone perform the job you want to have. First, of course, you have to get that person's permission. Write a business letter to the person of your choice, explaining what you want to do: You want to follow this person around for a day. You want to stand in the back of the room. You do not want to get in the way. You do not expect this person to spend much time with you or answer your questions during work hours. You would, however, like to have some time at lunch or after work to ask questions about the things you've seen. (Be sure to bring a notebook and pen so you can record your impressions and jot down any questions that occur to you during the day.)

Your letter should be neatly typed — and checked carefully for errors. Keep it short and to the point, but be sure to state why it is important that you observe someone doing this job. State that you will call on a given day to get the person's response and set up an appointment if he or she is willing to take part in this program. Don't forget to send a handwritten thank you note soon after your day as a shadow.

Keywords: job shadow career, job shadow tips, job shadow thank you

Your letter might look something like the one below.

1426 Washington Street
Kansas City, MO 64113
April 6, 2018

Ms. Keiko Yamamoto
ABC Advertising
1100 Walnut Drive
Kansas City, MO 64105

Dear Ms. Yamamoto:

I am investigating the field of advertising copywriting as a way to use both
my degree in journalism and my creative energy. It has been recommended to
me that I spend a day watching someone in this position as they go about their
workday. Socorro Hernandez suggested I contact you.

Would you be willing to let me spend a day observing you, enabling me to learn
more about what this career entails? As your "shadow" I would remain quietly in
the background as you go about your daily tasks. I know that you are a busy
person, and I would not expect you to take time out from your usual schedule.
I would, however, appreciate it if you could take half an hour to answer my
questions at the end of the day.

Although I've done thorough research on copywriting, I feel a day on the job —
even in the background — would tell me so much more than I can learn from
books. I will call you on Monday, April 16, to get your response. If you are
willing to help me, perhaps we can schedule a day that would be convenient for
you to have me around.

Thank you for your time and consideration.

Yours truly,

Donna Garibaldi

Donna Garibaldi
(123) 555-6789 home
(123) 234-5677 cell
donna.garibaldi@eventon.net
www.donnagaribaldi.com

P.S. If your calendar permits, I would like to take you to lunch that day to show
my appreciation.

STEP THREE

INVOLVE ME AND I UNDERSTAND

One of the best ways to decide whether or not your career choice is a good one is to get a job in that field. You won't actually be working at your dream job, of course. But, by putting yourself in a position to watch other people do that kind of work, you can get an accurate picture of what it's like.

Your goal then is to get an entry-level job that puts you in contact with people in your chosen career. Not all jobs in your chosen field will do that. For example, delivering newspapers won't tell you very much about what it's like to be a reporter, but answering phones at the newspaper office might be enlightening.

It's fairly easy to come up with entry-level jobs for some careers. Future doctors or nurses, for example, can be candy stripers at the local hospital. Future chefs or restaurateurs might be able to bus dishes at the best restaurant in town.

What if you want to be a buyer for a department store or a lawyer? If a related entry-level job doesn't come immediately to mind, take some time to think things through. Where do the people in your career field work? An office? A courthouse? A garage? What other kinds of jobs do people do in these settings? Can you do any of those jobs?

Practice your skill at recognizing entry-level jobs by thinking of possible positions for people interested in the following careers. In column A, list jobs that will expose you to the work of each career.

Example: Mechanic = gas jockey, auto parts sales or cashier

CAREER	COLUMN A PAID	COLUMN B VOLUNTEER
Attorney		
Social Worker		
Accountant		
Veterinarian		
Police Officer		
Retail Salesperson		
Classical Musician		
Politician		
Hairstylist		
Office Manager		

HINT: If all else fails, most businesses will allow you to come in for a few hours each week and run errands. Author Mindy Bingham's brother did this for a law firm while he was in high school; he owns that same law firm today.

Keywords: entry level [industry] jobs

Experience is the teacher of all things.

—Julius Caesar

Keep the following points in mind as you go about your entry-level job:

1. It may not be fun or interesting. Although it's hard to stick with a job that's boring — or even nasty — keep your goal in mind. Remember that you won't have to do this forever.

2. It may not pay well; it may not pay at all. The point of this job is to learn, not necessarily to earn. If you need to volunteer your services in order to get where you want to be, do so. Many charities and social service agencies in your community will have volunteer opportunities relating to specific career fields. For example, if you're interested in a law career, you may be able to volunteer for the legal aid society. In column B on the preceding page, list volunteer jobs you could do that would put you in contact with an interesting career possibility.

CRITIQUE YOUR EXPERIENCE

The more you can "experience" actual work responsibilities and settings through opportunities like simulations, shadowing, internships, and entry-level or volunteer work, the better able you'll be to analyze whether a specific occupation is an option for you. After each work encounter, you'll want to write a critique using the following questions to stimulate your thoughts.

Once you have a job in your chosen area of interest, observe what is going on around you. Pay attention to your feelings. Do you like the setting? Do you feel comfortable? Is what is happening exciting? Does the pace of the day match your personality? Is the level of responsibility comfortable or threatening? Does the work hold your interest, or could this be boring after a short time? Do you like the people you work with? How do they seem to feel about their jobs? Are they bored? Challenged? Overworked? About how many hours a week do they work? Do they take work home with them? Are they expected to take part in after-work activities (sports, entertaining clients, and the like)? Do they travel? How often and for how long?

Your answers to questions like these should tell you whether to go ahead with your career plans or if you need to make new ones. Answer them honestly, and don't feel bad if you decide to make a change. It's much easier to do so now than it will be after you've invested years in training.

The Chemistry Test

When the Newcomers' Club decided to hold a dinner dance to raise money for the homeless, officers Jacob, Coretta, George, and Joan drew lots to decide who would be in charge of what. As a result, Coretta was designated to make centerpieces, George became the treasurer, Jacob was delegated to selling tickets, and Joan was chair of the entire event.

Things did not go well. Jacob sent the tickets back three times before they were printed to his satisfaction. And the thought of asking people he didn't know well to buy them made him feel quite ill at ease.

Joan needed to be sure that everyone was in agreement before she made any decisions. As a result, meetings went on for hours and everyone was frustrated.

Coretta preferred to take her own course rather than follow the directions on assembling the centerpieces. Details like that just didn't interest her. None of the decorations came out looking the same, though Coretta tried to tell everyone that they were more interesting this way.

George was into creative bookkeeping. He didn't like solitary activities like this, but when he tried to keep the books while carrying on a conversation with a friend, he made a number of mistakes.

With everything in chaos, the group was about ready to cancel the event altogether. Then they remembered what they had learned about work behavior styles and their own personal styles in a presentation to their club. Assessing their strengths, they found that each had a preferred behavior style:

> Coretta — dominance
>
> George — influencing
>
> Joan — steadiness
>
> Jacob — compliance

They reassigned the duties, this time choosing the person who was best suited to each job. Since Coretta liked to be in charge and make decisions, she became the chair. George, the influencer, was a natural to take over ticket sales. Joan liked working with explicit instructions so she loved being in charge of the decorations. And Jacob, as treasurer, made sure every cent was accounted for. Accuracy was extremely important to him.

As the committee's story shows, your work behavior style affects the way you perform — and the way you feel about — a job. Turn back to page 43 and review the four classic work styles. Everyone has to be able to use each of the styles to some extent, but one of them is probably the most comfortable for you. Which one?

TEAM BUILDING

Match the four people described below with the job for which his or her chemistry test would "qualify" them in each of the work environments listed. If you were in charge of the businesses, how would you assign these employees to build the most effective team?

Ellen's preferred behavior style is dominance. She is a high-energy individual who likes to be in charge of what she is doing. She is decisive and always looks for the most efficient way to do things. She likes to solve problems, is comfortable with change, and is very goal directed.

Robert's style is influencing. He is a creative person who likes flexibility in his work environment. He is gregarious and likes to work with people. Robert's enthusiasm can be contagious. He is good at persuading people to act. He likes varied tasks and will take calculated risks.

Michiko is most comfortable with steadiness. She likes to work with other people, particularly in a supportive role. A patient and considerate person, Michiko likes tasks with well-defined procedures. A steady worker, she follows her project through from beginning to end. She is a listener and a doer.

Romero's preferred style is compliance. He is extremely detail oriented and is likely to question the decisions of others. He wants to know the facts behind the issues. A conscientious worker, he is precise in any task he undertakes and wants to make sure it is done accurately.

MATCHING WORK STYLES TO JOBS

How would you assign the jobs below to these four individuals?

For example, in a book publishing company, jobs would be assigned like this:

BOOK PUBLISHING
Publisher: *Ellen*
Sales rep: *Robert*
Book designer: *Michiko*
Editor: *Romero*

CONSTRUCTION

Draftsperson _____

Contractor _____

Architect _____

Carpenter _____

HOSPITAL

Minister/priest/rabbi _____ _____ _____

Administrator _____

Lab technician _____

Physician _____

FACTORY

Cafeteria chef _____

Assembly line worker _____

Foreman _____

Quality control inspector _____

SCHOOL

Secretary _____

Principal _____

Attendance clerk _____

Counselor _____

BANK

Loan officer _____

Bank teller _____

Manager _____ _____

Accountant _____

RESEARCH LAB

Project manager _____

Fundraiser _____

Scientist _____

Computer programmer _____ _____

Even within career categories, certain specialties may be more suited to one behavior style than to the others. Can you identify which personality type would likely be happiest in each of the jobs below? Review the definitions of behavioral style on page 43. Then, although this is not an exact science, see what makes sense to you. Be prepared to defend your choices in discussion.

WRITER

Freelance magazine writer: *dominance*

Copywriter for advertising agency: *influencing*

Reporter for local newspaper: *steadiness*

Technical writer for science textbooks: *compliance*

PHYSICIAN

Anesthesiologist _____

Surgeon _____

Chief of physicians at local hospital _____

Teacher at medical school _____

TEACHER

Teacher in public school system _____

Private tutor or coach _____

Professor of accounting at university level _____

Trainer for major corporation _____

CHEF

Head chef in a large restaurant — tastes everything! _____

Catering company owner _____

Teacher of adult education cooking classes _____

Associate chef in a restaurant _____

Answers:

Dominance: Freelance magazine writer, chief of physicians, private tutor or coach, catering company owner

  People in these jobs are all self-directed. They are in charge.

Influencing: Copywriter, teacher at medical school, trainer for major corporation, teacher of adult education cooking classes

  People in these careers work closely with others and are involved with teaching or influencing them.

Steadiness: Reporter for local newspaper, anesthesiologist, teacher in public school system, associate chef in restaurant

  These workers like a highly-defined set of procedures. They enjoy supportive, predictable roles.

Compliance: Technical writer for science textbooks, surgeon, professor of accounting at university level, head chef in large restaurant

  People in these jobs are precise and exacting and concerned about quality control.

Which career seems to be your favorite choice at this point in time? What work behavior style do you think would be prominent in someone happy with this job?

_____

Why? _____

_____

Does this match your personal work style? Review your answers on page 42.

                        Yes   No   Perhaps

In what ways?

_____

_____

To gain a better understanding of your own style, consider taking the complete DiSC *Personal Profile System®* test. By taking the complete assessment, you'll discover particulars about yourself that will help you match your traits with specific careers and tasks.

Has your research led you to a tentative career choice? If not, the next chapter offers a model you can use to help make this — or any — decision.

Information on personality styles is adapted from the widely-used DiSC™ Dimensions of Behavior model and the *Personal Profile System®* assessment instrument, ™copyright 1972, Carlson Learning Company. Used with permission of Carlson Learning Company, Minneapolis, Minnesota.

CHAPTER 6 CHECKPOINTS
Career Research
Reading about careers isn't enough

You have now explored a valuable three-step process for learning about and deciding on a career. You have started to narrow down career choices that might suit you best. Before you make that decision in the next chapter, confirm each of the following statements.

☐ I understand the 16 career clusters and the types of jobs in each.

☐ I reviewed and considered my personality traits, financial requirements, ideal working conditions, and projected lifestyle as I begin narrowing down my optimal careers.

☐ I learned library and online research skills and put them to use in evaluating information about potential careers.

☐ I completed at least three **Career Interest Surveys** for careers that appeal to me.

☐ I visualized what it would be like to spend a typical day at the job of my choice.

☐ I practiced writing a business letter and conducting an interview.

☐ I saw first-hand what it might be like to spend a day at my chosen career either through job shadowing or volunteering.

☐ I can identify jobs within an industry that match my work behavioral style.

☐ I identified a specific job I consider a good match for my personality and work behavioral style.

The indispensible first step to getting the things
you want out of life is this: decide what you want.
—Ben Stein

Choice, not chance, determines destiny.
—Anonymous

CHAPTER SEVEN
Decision Making
How to choose what's best for you

Section Two:
WHAT DO I WANT?

Quint was starting his junior year of college, and, as people never seemed to tire of telling him, it was time to make some decisions about his future. Quint wondered why he should bother. Everyone else seemed to know exactly what he should do.

His parents wanted Quint to go to law school, preferably his mother's alma mater back East. His girlfriend, Sheila, wanted to get married. Mr. Lear, his baseball coach, thought Quint could probably get a contract with a minor league team if he did well in his remaining time at college. His two best friends wanted Quint to go into business with them. It would be great working together and being their own bosses, they said.

But what did he want? Quint wasn't sure, and he didn't really like to think about it. He wished the whole subject would just go away.

Your life is defined by the choices you make.

—Mindy Bingham

Learning to make decisions can be difficult. You grow up learning to please your parents or your teachers. Then, suddenly, you're supposed to know how to please yourself. When did that become the issue?

Actually, it's always been the issue. Most people are probably better at making decisions than they realize. When, for example, was the last time you took someone else's advice on what TV show to watch or what to wear?

Because making these decisions is so easy, you may not be aware of the process behind them. Using it is almost automatic. By becoming aware of the steps involved, you can apply this process to decisions in almost every area of your life.

Let's take apart one of these easy decisions — what to wear today, for example. The first thing you probably do is think about your image or what you would like your image to be. Your goal, then, is to dress in a way that will enhance this image. The logical next step is to consider your choices — the clothes you have or your budget for buying anything new. You can immediately rule out certain items, like the shirt Aunt Grace sent you from her last vacation, which, apparently, was to the planet Mars. And the boots you were wearing when you took that walk through the cow pasture at night.

Before you make your decision, you will also probably think about what *other* people wear — especially the people who fit your goal image. Finally, you evaluate your choices and consider which of your outfits comes closest to meeting your goal, and that's your decision.

Some decisions are harder to make, but the process is the same. On the following pages, you will learn a decision-making model that, with practice, can become as automatic as getting dressed in the morning.

Identifying Choices

Joyce decided she wanted to be a doctor the day her little sister was hit by a car. She saw how the staff at the emergency room calmly went about saving Kim's life, as though they did this sort of thing every day. "Of course," Joyce thought later, "they do!" She couldn't imagine a more wonderful job.

She also wants to buy a car. There's no room for this in her budget, so Joyce needs to come up with some additional money. She could get a night job at the local fast food restaurant (it's about the only employer with work in her town), but she worries about the effect on her grades. If they fall, she won't be able to get into the medical school she wants to attend. She also thinks that it might be a good idea to volunteer at the hospital in order to get some experience, but she clearly can't do this and hold down a paying job as well.

List Joyce's goals below.

1. _____

2. _____

Which would you say is her long-term goal? Which is her short-term goal?

It's important to differentiate between the two. Short-term goals are those things that seem essential to your happiness *right now*. Because achieving them can result in immediate gratification, it's tempting to focus on them. Long-term goals, after all, might take *years* to fulfill. Shouldn't you be allowed some happiness in the meantime?

Of course you should, and you will have happiness. But, make sure it's not at the expense of your future. In 10 years, what will mean more to you — an impressive wardrobe or a rewarding career? An aging car or a comfortable income? If you consider your long-term goals first, decision making will become much easier.

What is Joyce's long-term goal? _____

What are the options she must choose from now that will affect her long-term goal?

1. _____

2. _____

3. _____

Gathering Information

Once you've determined what your choices are, you need to find out as much as you can about each option in order to make an informed decision. This is a term that usually refers to a decision based on facts and/or thought. The more information you have about your choices, the better your decision is likely to be.

Before Joyce decides to take a job in the fast-food restaurant, for example, she needs to find out:

1. How much the job would pay per hour
2. How many hours a week she could work
3. What the down payment and monthly payments would be on the kind of car she wants to buy
4. How much she would need to spend each month on insurance, maintenance, and gas for the car

Without this information, Joyce might decide to take the job only to find that she still can't afford to buy a car. Considering that she may have jeopardized her future by taking time away from her studies, this would have been a bad decision for Joyce.

Take another look at Joyce's choices:

1. To take a job in a fast food restaurant
2. To volunteer at the hospital
3. To spend her time studying and maintaining her grades

Before she can choose the best alternative, she needs to know:

1. What grades she needs to get into the the medical school of her choice
2. Which classes she must take in order to major in pre-med
3. The availability of and requirements for financial aid or scholarships at this college
4. How much she could expect to earn on the job

Can you list some other information that would be helpful to Joyce as she weighs her alternatives?

1. _____

2. _____

3. _____

4. _____

Evaluating Choices

When you've listed your alternatives and learned as much as you can about each of them, you are ready to evaluate your choices. A good way to do this is to list the pros and cons of each choice. You must also judge how likely each alternative is to be successful or get you what you want.

As you may have noticed, this process calls for a certain amount of guesswork. It is also possible to "load the deck" in favor of the choice you would like to think is most appropriate for you. It is in your best interest, however, to be as honest as you can while making your evaluations. This *is* the time, though, to consider your *feelings* about your choices. Taking into account the information you've gathered, does your intuition tell you that one course is most suitable for you now? (Many people are inclined to base decisions on their hunches *before* they've investigated the facts. If you're going to use your intuition, it's important to use it in *light of,* not *in spite of,* what you know.)

No matter how thorough and honest you are, though, it is not always clear which choice you should make. Each alternative will have its pros and cons, and there are no guarantees that any course you take will be successful. By keeping your goals and values firmly in mind, however, you can be confident of making good decisions most of the time.

Joyce began evaluating her choices on the chart below.

In the spaces remaining on the chart, evaluate Joyce's other choice — not to work at all so she can concentrate on her studies.

Identify your choices	Evaluate your choices		
	Pros	Cons	Probability of success
Working at fast food restaurant	Earn money to buy car	Not related to medicine — therefore no relevant experience	Since I am smart and reliable, I should be able to get this job
Volunteer at the hospital	First medical job for resume	Less study time — may lower grades	Since I am smart and reliable, I should be able to get this job
Not work at all	_____ _____	_____ _____	_____ _____

JESSICA'S STORY

Jessica needs to decide whether to take a math class next quarter and, if so, which one. She could take calculus, but she knows it's hard. Getting a good grade would mean less time for socializing with friends in the evening. Geometry would be easier. She always got A's and B's in high school math, so it should be a cinch. She could even get by with no math class at all. She doesn't like math that much, but her counselor, Ms. Briscoe, reminded her that math isn't important for what it lets you become; it's important for what it keeps you from becoming. She said that, without math, Jessica was cutting her options for future careers by 75 percent. Did she really want to do that?

Use the chart below to identify Jessica's choices and evaluate each one.

Identify your choices	Evaluate your choices		
	Pros	Cons	Probability of success
1. _____	_____	_____	_____
_____	_____	_____	_____
2. _____	_____	_____	_____
_____	_____	_____	_____
3. _____	_____	_____	_____
_____	_____	_____	_____
4. _____	_____	_____	_____
_____	_____	_____	_____

If you were Jessica, what would you do? _____

_____

_____

JOHN'S STORY

John is bored with school. He doesn't see how any of his classes relate to real life. Besides, he's probably going to fail English. Why not just drop out and go to work, he wonders. He's confident he could get a job in highway construction. He does enjoy the time he spends in the school's computer lab, however. The new computer with the graphic design software is especially intriguing. He's done some good work on it. The community college counselor told John that, if he brought his grades up, he could get a degree in this field. He's heard of a program at the local technical college, too. Or maybe he should join the army. The recruiter promises John could get specialized training there.

Use the chart below to identify John's choices and evaluate each one.

Identify your choices	Evaluate your choices		
	Pros	Cons	Probability of success
1. _____ _____	_____ _____	_____ _____	_____ _____
2. _____ _____	_____ _____	_____ _____	_____ _____
3. _____ _____	_____ _____	_____ _____	_____ _____
4. _____ _____	_____ _____	_____ _____	_____ _____

If you were John, what would you do? _____

_____

_____

Decision-Making Model

The decision-making model you've just learned should work well in most instances. When you are making decisions about long-term goals, however, you will also want to take your resources, wants, and needs into consideration. This will let you see "the big picture" and should help motivate you to follow through with the actions that will help you achieve your goals.

The comprehensive decision-making model includes these steps:

1. **Define your goal.**
2. **State the decision to be made.**
3. **Analyze your resources.**
4. **Analyze your wants and needs.**
5. **Identify your choices.**
6. **Gather information.**
7. **Evaluate your choices.**
8. **Make your decision.**

Note: You've already done much of this work. In chapter 2, page 27, you analyzed your personal resources. You analyzed your wants and needs in chapters 3–5. And, in chapter 6, you identified your choices and gathered information on pages 150–155.

GLORIA'S CHART

Goal: Become a computer repair technician

Decision to be made: How and if to get the training I need

Resources: Basic knowledge of computers
> Good with hands
> Like working with computers
> Love detail work
> Love to take things apart and put things together

Wants and needs: Value security — there will always be computers to repair
> Want to work for myself someday to have flexibility for raising family
> Want to be able to support family on one income if necessary

Gather information: Review my **Career Interest Survey** for computer repair technician

Identify your choices	Evaluate your choices		
	Pros	Cons	Probability of success
1. Go to trade school	—certifiable training, best guarantee of a job	—costs time and money	—should have no trouble getting into this program or doing this work
2. Learn on the job	—earn while I learn, use my skills	—probably low pay during training, no certificate, therefore lower pay in the long run	—may have to compete for opening, but can probably do the work
3. Become a waitress	—no training necessary, possibly higher immediate earnings	—not what I want to do forever, little security, doesn't make use of my skills	—should be able to get a a job in this field

What choice would you make if you were Gloria? _____

_____

Gloria decided to take a two-year apprenticeship and save some of her earnings to pay for trade school and a certification.

DECISON-MAKING RUBRIC

Complete the chart below for yourself. Identify and evaluate four possible career choices.

Goal: To identify a career that I will find satisfying.

Decision to be made: Which career would I find most satisfying?

My resources: _____

_____

_____

_____

My wants and needs: _____

_____

_____

_____

Gather information: _____

Identify your choices	Evaluate your choices		
	Pros	Cons	Probability of success
1. _____ _____	_____ _____	_____ _____	_____ _____
2. _____ _____	_____ _____	_____ _____	_____ _____
3. _____ _____	_____ _____	_____ _____	_____ _____
4. _____ _____	_____ _____	_____ _____	_____ _____

Make a choice _____

How realistic is this choice? _____

Make a Decision

Making a decision is often difficult, but there's no way around it. You can stall and fret and change your mind. Sooner or later, though, *not* making a decision is making a choice. If you can't decide what to have for lunch, you are choosing not to eat. If you can't decide who to ask to the party, you are choosing to go alone — or not to go at all.

Decisions can — and often should — be changed. Many people fear making them because they think that mistakes are not permissible, that there's only one correct course of action. However, people don't make decisions simply to be right. Executives, for example, are paid to make decisions so that work can proceed. They make the best decisions they can, but sometimes the decisions need to be changed. The point is, it's necessary to take action, and that's what making a decision allows you to do.

Basically, there are two styles of decision avoidance. Some people just can't bear to think about their choices at all and they let things happen by default. This is a passive behavior pattern. The other extreme is more aggressive. People with this behavior pattern suffer from "paralysis by analysis." They insist on examining every option and collecting every bit of information. Then, afraid they may have overlooked something, they never quite get around to making a decision.

What is your decision-making (or avoiding) style? Check the places along the scale below that you think best represent your personality. If the words in the left-hand column describe your behavior, you may tend to avoid making decisions. On the other hand, if your behavior is better described by the words on the right, you may tend to make decisions too quickly. There is no right or wrong spot on the scale. But, by being aware of your tendencies, you may be better able to use them in your best interest.

passive	_____	_____	_____	_____	_____	_____	_____	aggressive
contemplative	_____	_____	_____	_____	_____	_____	_____	impulsive
controlled	_____	_____	_____	_____	_____	_____	_____	free
rational	_____	_____	_____	_____	_____	_____	_____	emotional
easily influenced	_____	_____	_____	_____	_____	_____	_____	self-directed
delaying	_____	_____	_____	_____	_____	_____	_____	expediting
cautious	_____	_____	_____	_____	_____	_____	_____	risk-taking
structured	_____	_____	_____	_____	_____	_____	_____	creative
agonizing	_____	_____	_____	_____	_____	_____	_____	relaxed

By using the **Decision-Making Rubric** — being as honest with yourself as possible — you may not always make the best decision. But you are probably not going to make the worst one, either. Letting others make your decisions, or making them by default, is giving up control of your life and your future. This is not the way to find satisfaction.

Evaluate your options, use your best judgment, take a deep breath, and make up your mind.

Keeping Your Options Open

It may seem that you are limiting your options when you make a decision. Sometimes you are. Deciding to quit school or to have a baby alone can really put a crimp in your social life and your financial future.

Since making decisions is inevitable, however, keeping your options open is one more factor to consider when you make your plans. Should you apply for a job you might like even if you're not sure you want it? Which decision would give you the most flexibility?

Remember that few decisions are irreversible or fatal. You *can* change your mind. And the better you get at making decisions, the better you'll be able to judge when it's time to make a change.

Flexibility is an important attribute that shows every sign of being even more important in the future (more on this later). As the world changes, or as your own values, wants, and needs evolve, you will need to make adjustments — new decisions. With practice, you'll become secure in the knowledge that you've done it before and you can do it again.

You've made a decision. It's time to make your plans.

The rest of this book helps you learn *How To Get What You Want*.

It is our choices that show what we truly are, far more than our abilities.

—J.K. Rowling

CHAPTER 7 CHECKPOINTS
Decision-making
How to choose what's best for you

Congratulations! You have arrived at a preliminary career decision that you will use as you develop your **10-year Plan**. Just as importantly, you understand that this career decision can be changed as you continue to learn more about yourself and the world around you. Before you start exploring how to obtain your chosen career, make sure you've mastered the following tasks.

- ☐ I clarified the difference between long- and short-term goals, and I recognize the importance of considering my plans for the future when making daily decisions.

- ☐ I understand that before evaluating different options I need to identify factors surrounding each option and, with those facts in mind, determine the probable outcomes of each option.

- ☐ I learned how to evaluate the pros, cons, and likelihood of success of different choices.

- ☐ I completed a systematic **Decision-Making Rubric** to determine the career that most closely matches my goals and needs.

- ☐ I understand that my own resources, wants, and needs should be factored when making major life decisions, and I know how I can use the decision-making rubric for those choices.

- ☐ I evaluated the strengths and weaknesses of my decision-making strategies.

- ☐ I practiced identifying jobs within an industry that match my work behavioral style.

I always view problems as opportunities in work clothes.

—Henry J. Kaiser

Efforts and courage are not enough without purpose and direction.

—John F. Kennedy

If you want to be happy, set a goal that commands your thoughts, liberates your energy, and inspires your hopes.

—Andrew Carnegie

CHAPTER EIGHT

Setting Goals and Solving Problems

Skills for successful living

Section Three:
HOW DO I GET IT?

You can't build a reputation on what you're going to do.

—Henry Ford

Getting what you want differs from *deciding* what you want in one very important way: *It requires action.* It's easier to fantasize your future than it is to build it, but you must build it all the same. The remaining chapters in this book will teach you some processes that should be of help. *You* will need to come up with the energy, motivation, and confidence to get your plans off the ground, however.

HUBERT'S STORY

More than anything in the world, Hubert wanted to complete the college education he'd abandoned when he ran out of money several years earlier. His employer was willing to pay Hubert's night school tuition and, with a degree, Hubert would get a hefty raise in pay and also be eligible for promotion to a management position.

But there never seemed to be time to take the necessary classes. This fall, for example, he'd promised to coach a neighborhood football team. Winter quarter was out. He and his wife, Hannah, liked to spend their weekends skiing, and there wouldn't be time enough to study. Hubert's friends depended on him to pitch for their softball team in the spring. And, during the summer, there was just too much work to do on the house and in the yard.

Sometimes Hubert got discouraged, but it wasn't really his fault. Could he help it if his friends depended on him? He certainly wasn't about to disappoint his wife or the kids on the football team. The more he thought about it, the more he became convinced that his employer was to blame. Why did he have to have a college degree in order to be promoted? And why did he have to go to class on his own time? It would make more sense for his boss to give him a year off — with pay, of course — and let him complete his degree that way. "Sure, that's the solution. I'll talk to Ms. Romero about it tomorrow," Hubert told himself as he grabbed his softball mitt and walked out the door.

Tools For Solving Problems

Whether he admits it or not, Hubert has a problem, and the prospects of his solving it are not good. If he doesn't change his ways, Hubert's life is likely to be plagued with unsolved problems.

Yours needn't be, however. Problem solving takes time and effort. It takes self-discipline, a quality with which Hubert is not well acquainted. But, it can be done. In his book, *The Road Less Traveled*, author M. Scott Peck lists four techniques that, used together, should be helpful. Dr. Peck points out that using his techniques is not easy or painless. He says, in fact, that they will cause you a certain amount of suffering. However, the pain is temporary, and it can lead to rewards that make it seem insignificant.

The first tool or technique, according to Dr. Peck, is **delaying gratification**. This means doing without the double fudge brownie you'd like to have now for the sake of the satisfaction you'll feel next month, when you've lost five pounds. For Hubert, making the effort to get his degree would mean giving up time he'd like to spend with his friends or family. But, if he gets the raise and promotion as a result, he might feel his sacrifices were worthwhile.

Delaying gratification is difficult because the rewards of living only for the moment are more tangible. You can taste that brownie. The pounds you thought you wanted to lose seem much more abstract, however. And, when temptation strikes, long-term goals can easily be forgotten or postponed.

As you learn to delay gratification — put off the temporary joys of today in favor of lasting rewards in the future — you will be acquiring an important tool in solving problems.

The second technique in Dr. Peck's problem-solving prescription is **accepting responsibility**. Hubert was willing to blame his friends, his wife, even his employer, for his inability to go back to school. Passing the blame is not effective in solving problems. When the problem is yours, so is the responsibility to solve it.

This is a difficult fact to accept. Sometimes other people do things that upset you or disrupt your plans. If Hubert's friends didn't want him to play softball, for example, he might find it easier to get to class. But it is Hubert who wants to earn a college degree, and it is Hubert's responsibility to take the classes he needs to do that. His friends are his friends. They are not his keepers. If Hubert could accept responsibility for his actions — and his problem — he would say no to his friends and do the thing which, in the long run, will help him achieve his goals.

The *good* news on this point is that taking responsibility also gives you the opportunity to choose. And, just as you are responsible for becoming the person *you* want to be, you are *not* responsible for becoming the person anyone else wants you to be. Pressure from home or from friends can be intimidating. It's natural to want to please the people you care about. But, if they want you to do something you feel is not truly you or not something you want to become, you can "just say no" with a clear conscience.

Dedication to truth or reality is the third problem-solving technique you need to master. Wishful thinking has not been shown to be an effective way to solve problems. It *is* popular, however. That is why we still see ads proclaiming that you can "lose weight painlessly overnight," or "make a million dollars at home in your spare time."

As long as Hubert clings to the belief that his company's regulations do not apply to him, he has no motivation to try to meet them. He should remember that his employer has a procedure to follow, and she will apply it to him as well as to everyone else who works for her. "The truth isn't always pretty," as they say, but you cannot solve a problem by denying it exists.

Finally, problem solving requires **balancing**, which leads to *flexibility*. According to Dr. Peck, balancing is "the type of discipline required to discipline discipline." In other words, there are times when you *shouldn't* delay gratification. It's important to know how to live joyously in the moment — as long as you aren't being self-destructive by doing so.

And, even though it is important to recognize truth or reality, it is not always appropriate to act on that truth. You may be angry with an employer who assigns extra work on weekends, for example. But throwing a tantrum is not going to change the situation or improve your standing in the office.

In short, balancing requires judgment. Although you may be too young to always know the correct action to take in a given circumstance, you *can* learn to think things through before you act, and make an honest effort to take the most effective or least destructive course.

> *"I must do something" will always solve more*
> *problems than "Something must be done."*
>
> — Anonymous

Keywords: delaying gratification, accepting responsibility

Crystal and Sterling got married the same month they graduated from college. Both wanted to go to graduate school. Money was a problem, so they decided to work for a few years, putting as much of their earnings as possible into a savings account. One Saturday afternoon, just for fun, they went through a model home at a new development in the area. They were hooked. Crystal and Sterling agreed that this was their dream home. It was big and beautiful and brand new and, best of all, they had enough money in their savings account to make the down payment. Buying the house would mean postponing graduate school, maybe forever. Both Crystal and Sterling would have to remain at their present jobs, which were not entirely satisfying, in order to make the monthly house payments. They wouldn't be able to have a child in the foreseeable future. There would be no dinners out, no vacations. They probably couldn't even furnish the house.

Who is responsible for solving Crystal and Sterling's problem?

_____

If they buy the house, what sacrifices might they have to make?

_____

_____

If they wait and go back to school what sacrifices will they have to make?

_____

_____

What facts should Crystal and Sterling consider before they make their decision?

_____

_____

What wishful thinking might come into play as they make their decision? How likely is that to happen?

_____

_____

If you were Sterling and Crystal, what would you do? _____

_____

Setting Goals and Objectives

Remember Marta's story, back on page 144?

After talking with her friend Jennifer, Marta decided she would like to know more about archaeology. Do archaeologists spend more of their time in the field or in the office? Who do they work for? How much education would she need? Where is most of the field work being done these days? Is it really hot there? Rainy? Would there be snakes?

These were all things she wanted to know before registering for the classes she would take next year. That gave her two months to do her research. Marta developed an action plan: She set her goal and then listed objectives for getting the information she needed.

Marta's action plan looked like this:

Goal: To answer my questions about archaeology by March 1.

Objective 1: Read at least one book or four articles on archaeology by January 20.

Objective 2: Search the Internet for information and discussion groups by January 25.

Objective 3A: Call the university and the Natural History Museum by January 31 to see if there are any archaeologists on staff.

Objective 3B: If so, interview a working archaeologist by February 14.

Objective 4: Research climate and reptile life at the three most appealing field sites by February 21.

Marta's action plan consists of setting goals and objectives. If she follows her plan, it is likely to get her the information she needs by the time she needs it.

Think of goals and objectives as a kind of recipe for getting what you want. The goal is the end product you want to achieve within a certain amount of time: Let's say chocolate chip cookies (30 minutes). The objectives are the ingredients and the methods you use to make them. Once you know what the goal is (cookies), it's relatively easy to focus on the objectives (find the semi-sweet chips, never mind the onions).

Like ingredients, objectives are measurable (2 eggs, 3 cups of flour). And, like a recipe, they give you a time-frame in which to work (bake for 12 minutes at 350 degrees).

The more specific your goals and objectives, the more helpful they will be. Consider the recipe once again. What if, instead of chocolate chip cookies, it was called "chewy, sweet things with brown parts inside?" Would you still have a pretty good idea of what you were making? Would you even be tempted to try? And, what if the recipe called for "a bunch of eggs" and "some sugar," and directed you to "bake until sometime in the future?" What are your chances of ending up with something even your brother, the walking waste disposal, wouldn't eat?

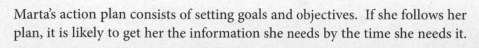

Let's go over the definitions again, this time without the cookies.

A goal is a statement that specifies what you want to achieve or do within a certain amount of time. An objective is an action that will help you meet your goal — and measure your success. An objective tells you what will be different when you've accomplished it, by how much or how many, and by when.

Take a look at Marta's first objective:

To read at least one book or four articles on archaeology by January 20.

What will be different when Marta achieves this objective? We've underlined that part of her statement.

By how much or how many? The triangles point out the numbers.

By when? Notice the circled date.

Using these same symbols, go back to page 186 and diagram Marta's other objectives.

Now write and diagram some objectives of your own. Choose two goals from the following list and write three objectives for each.

To buy a new car in six months.

To save for a trip to _____ next year.

Learn how to make _____ within six months.

Get a job as _____ this summer.

To be accepted at _____ next year.

(school)

Goal: _____

Objectives:

1. _____

2. _____

3. _____

Goal: _____

Objectives:

1. _____

2. _____

3. _____

YOUR LIFESTYLE GOALS

Now write some goals and objectives of your own. Turn back to page 63 and choose three statements about your desired lifestyle. Write a goal and three objectives for each one. Focus on three goals you can meet in the coming year that would help you achieve a more satisfying future. Diagram the objectives to make sure they include all necessary components.

One of Maria's lifestyle goals was:

To have a career that is flexible enough to accommodate raising a family.

Her objectives:

1. Over the next two months, to interview five professional women who are successfully mixing career and family.

2. By the end of the semester, to research and identify eight careers that are flexible and yet offer the economic security required for a family.

3. By the end of the semester, to visit my counselor and make sure I am taking the necessary courses to prepare me for careers meeting my requirements.

Your lifestyle goal: _____

    Objectives:

        1. _____

        2. _____

        3. _____

Your lifestyle goal: _____

    Objectives:

        1. _____

        2. _____

        3. _____

Your lifestyle goal: _____

    Objectives:

        1. _____

        2. _____

        3. _____

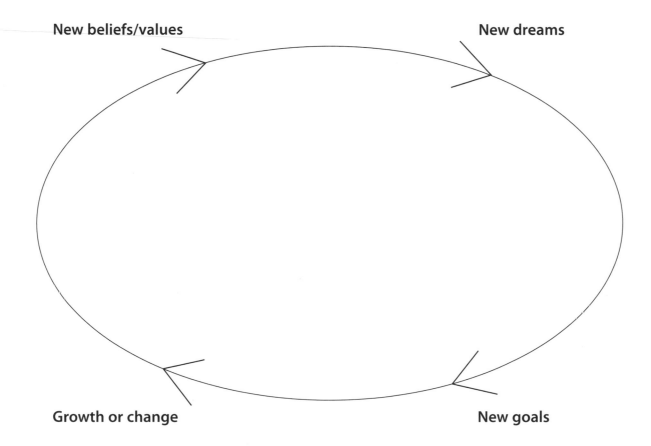

New beliefs/values

New dreams

Growth or change

New goals

NEW GOALS AS WE GROW

Along with our careers, our lifestyles are determined largely by our values, opportunities, and desires — all things that tend to change over the course of a lifetime. When we set goals, we do so in an attempt to satisfy our present values. In reaching those goals, however, our minds are stretched, our limits are extended — and we change. We are constantly testing ourselves and our abilities. In the process, we often find that we have found new values and set new goals, and so the process repeats itself. As our values change, our goals change. Reaching new goals leads to recognizing new values, and so on.

Keep in mind that life is an ever-changing and ever-growing process. The most satisfied people among us are those who actively set and reach new goals throughout their lives. If you can master this process, you are likely to have a rewarding future.

CHAPTER 8 CHECKPOINTS
Setting Goals and Solving Problems
Skills for successful living

You have made great progress in making the plans, learning the skills, and acquiring the tools you will need to realize your dreams. Solving problems and setting goals are two of the most important skills for developing any action plan. Check out the objectives below to ensure that you've met them.

☐ I learned how to apply problem-solving techniques that involve delaying gratification, accepting responsibility, and striking a balance between pleasure and discipline.

☐ I learned the process for writing quantitative goals and objectives.

☐ I learned to write quantitative goals and objectives of my own including those that relate to my lifestyle goals.

☐ I understand the cycle of growth and I'm aware of opportunities to expand my goals as I develop new values and ideas for my future.

I have learned that success is to be measured not so much by the position that one has reached in life as by the obstacles which one has overcome while trying to succeed.
—Booker T. Washington

Nothing in life is to be feared. It is only to be understood.
—Marie Curie

CHAPTER NINE

Avoiding Detours and Roadblocks

The road to success is dotted with many tempting parking places

Section Three:
HOW DO I GET IT?

Carlos attended a high school where most of the students were from wealthy families. Although Carlos's parents earned a comfortable living, they couldn't give him the cars or vacations his friends took for granted. They were proud when Carlos was accepted for admission at a well-known liberal arts college, but they told him he would have to help pay his own expenses. Carlos angrily told his parents that none of his friends had to do that. He wouldn't go to college at all if he had to work, too. It would be too hard, and, besides, it just wasn't fair.

No one in Liz's family had ever graduated from high school, much less gone to college. So after high school she went to work at a department store. She'd always dreamed of becoming a teacher, but that wasn't realistic, she decided. What made her think she was any better than her family and friends? It wouldn't be fair to leave them behind.

Karla liked to think about being a mechanical engineer, but she knew she'd never be one. She didn't know any women who were mechanical engineers. And, besides, she'd have to take all that math. It would be too hard.

Christy was one of many children in a poor family. He had cerebral palsy and didn't even begin to speak until he was 11 or 12. The only part of his body he could use was his left foot. He learned to type and paint with it, and eventually became recognized as both a writer and artist.

There are two important things you should know about life: it's not easy, and it isn't always fair.

The way you choose to respond to these facts will greatly affect your successes and life satisfaction. The first three stories are made up, but illustrate some common attitudes. The fourth story is true. Christy Brown was an Irish painter and writer. He accepted his condition as a challenge and set out to see what he could do with his life.

There are many people like Christy Brown, people whose attitudes take them far beyond what others would expect them to achieve. There are also many people like Carlos, Liz, and Karla, who let their attitudes limit their opportunities.

It's easy to find reasons to complain. It's easy to give up on a dream without trying harder to achieve it. But it's impossible to find satisfaction in a life that's based on negative feelings and behaviors.

Ironically, realizing that life is hard—for everyone—somehow makes it easier to overcome the obstacles and achieve your aspirations.

This chapter should help you recognize some of the most common detours and roadblocks to success so you can avoid them.

I think a hero is an ordinary individual who finds strength to persevere and endure in spite of overwhelming obstacles.

—Christopher Reeve

I Can't Do It Because...

People can be extremely creative when thinking of excuses for not doing something. That's not surprising when the action to be avoided is undesirable. What is puzzling, though, is how often we make excuses for not doing the things we most want to do!

You may believe that your excuse is valid, but somewhere, someone with the same problem or affliction is busy living your dream. Are you just going to sit there and let that happen? Why?

The responsibility of stating who you want to be and how you are going to get there can be very frightening. However, not doing so is generally much worse and can lead to a life of considerable dissatisfaction and unhappiness.

Lessons often come dressed up as detours or roadblocks, and sometimes as full blown crises. The secret to getting ahead is to be open to the lessons.

—Oprah Winfrey

It is impossible to live without failing at something unless you've lived so cautiously that you might have well not lived at all, in which case you've failed by default.

—J.K. Rowling

Keywords: role excuses success

Ninety-nine percent of the failures come from people who have the habit of making excuses.

—George Washington Carver

What's Your Excuse?

We've listed some pretty convincing excuses below. Check any that apply to you.

- ☐ I'm a woman
- ☐ I'm a man
- ☐ I'm black
- ☐ I'm white
- ☐ I'm Hispanic
- ☐ I'm Asian
- ☐ I come from a different culture
- ☐ I'm rich
- ☐ I'm poor
- ☐ I'm too smart
- ☐ I'm not smart enough
- ☐ I'm too ugly
- ☐ I'm too fat
- ☐ I'm too thin
- ☐ I'm too short
- ☐ I'm too tall
- ☐ I'm blind
- ☐ I have impaired vision
- ☐ I'm deaf
- ☐ I have a hearing loss
- ☐ I can't speak
- ☐ I have a speech impediment
- ☐ I'm a paraplegic
- ☐ I'm a quadriplegic

- ☐ I'm physically disfigured
- ☐ I've lost a limb
- ☐ I have a debilitating disease
- ☐ I've been treated for emotional problems
- ☐ I've been persecuted for my beliefs
- ☐ I've had a serious illness
- ☐ I'm shy
- ☐ I'm adopted
- ☐ I'm an orphan
- ☐ I come from a single-parent home
- ☐ I've been abused
- ☐ I've been in trouble with the law
- ☐ I'm chemically dependent
- ☐ I'm homeless
- ☐ I have to take care of a parent or sibling
- ☐ I have a baby
- ☐ My family won't let me
- ☐ My family expects too much of me
- ☐ No one believes in me
- ☐ People have convinced me I can't
- ☐ I can't do it because…
- ☐ Other _____

How valid are your excuses? Turn the page.

They Did It in Spite of . . .

. . . Physical Challenges

Jim Abbott, born with only one hand, pitched for the California Angels, New York Yankees, Chicago White Sox, and Milwaukee Brewers over the course of ten seasons in Major League Baseball.

Despite her deafness, **Marlee Matlin** has acted on stage, in film, and in television. She won an Oscar and a Golden Globe Award for her debut film role, and has Emmy, Golden Globe, and Screen Actors Guild award nominations for a variety of other performances.

Stephen Hawking, former Lucasian Professor of Mathematics at Cambridge University, had ALS or Lou Gehrig's disease. Considered the most brilliant theoretical physicist since Einstein, when ALS left him unable to walk or speak, he communicated through a computer attached to his wheelchair.

Winston Churchill, one of the greatest orators in the twentieth century, had a serious speech impediment.

President Franklin Roosevelt had polio and was unable to walk.

Ludwig Von Beethoven was totally deaf when he composed some of his greatest music.

U.S. Army Second Lieutenant Melissa Stockwell lost her left leg to a roadside bomb while deployed in Iraq. After being medically retired with a Purple Heart and a Bronze Star, she focused on sports. She swam in the 2008 Beijing Paralympics, is a three-time paratriathlon world champion, and earned a bronze medal at the 2016 Rio Paralympics.

Award-winning actor **Michael J. Fox** was diagnosed with early-onset Parkinson's disease in 1991. He has remained in demand as an actor but devotes much of his time to a foundation he started to improve therapies and find a cure for Parkinson's disease.

Mario Lemieux, Hockey Hall of Famer, Olympic Gold Medalist, and winner of two Stanley Cups, was diagnosed in 1993 with Hodgkin's lymphoma. The day of his final radiation treatment, he scored a goal and an assist in a game against the Philadelphia Flyers.

At age 13, **Bethany Hamilton** lost her left arm when she was attacked by a 14-foot tiger shark. Unwilling to give up her dream of surfing professionally, she was back in the water a month after the attack and, just over a year later, won her first national title.

. . . Discrimination or Oppression

Nelson Mandela remained the recognized leader of South African blacks despite spending more than 27 years as a political prisoner; he was elected President after his release.

Dith Pran escaped from a Khmer Rouge death camp in Cambodia and made his way to the United States where he became a photographer for *The New York Times*.

Indira Gandhi of India and **Benazir Bhutto** of Pakistan became heads of state in two of the most male-dominated countries in the world. Tragically, both women were assassinated.

In 1968, women accounted for less than 10 percent of students entering MD, JD, and MBA programs. Today, women account for 51 percent of MD and JD students. However, women still only earn 36 percent of MBA degrees and about 20 percent of bachelor's degrees in computer science and engineering.

A total of 114 Justices have served on the U.S. Supreme Court. Only four of those Justices have been women—**Sandra Day O'Connor**, **Ruth Bader Ginsburg**, **Sonia Sotomayor**, and **Elena Kagan**.

... Personal or Family Problems

Eleanor Roosevelt, painfully shy, orphaned, and considered unattractive, became not only First Lady of the United States, but a writer, speaker, political leader, and one of the most admired women in the world.

Albert Einstein was considered mentally dull as a youth.

Abraham Lincoln suffered bouts of severe depression throughout his life.

Olympic Gold Medalist **Greg Louganis's** dyslexia went unrecognized when he was a child. Because he stammered and was slower to learn, his classmates called him retarded. He was also adopted.

Joseph Fernandez, former Chancellor of the New York City public school system, was a member of a street gang and a high school dropout.

A recently divorced, single mom, **J.K. Rowling** was doing part-time clerical work and receiving welfare to make ends meet while completing her first *Harry Potter* novel. Her manuscript was rejected by 12 publishers before it finally got the green light. She is now the world's wealthiest novelist.

Mary Groda-Lewis was an elementary school dropout, street fighter, and juvenile offender. She had a stroke while giving birth and almost died, but she eventually received a high school equivalency degree and went to college. Determined to be a doctor, she was rejected by 15 medical schools before being accepted by Albany Medical College. She graduated from medical school at age 35.

Romano Banuelos, the thirty-seventh Treasurer of the United States, came to this country at age 16, when she was abandoned by her husband. She had seven dollars, two children, and no training. She did not speak English. Her first job was washing dishes, but with hard work and determination, she went on to become the manager of the largest Mexican wholesale food business in the world.

Amy Purdy contracted bacterial meningitis at age 19 and lost her spleen, both kidneys, and both legs below the knee. She is now a top-ranked female adaptive snowboarder, a three-time world cup gold medalist, and second-place *Dancing with the Stars* finisher.

You can't change the circumstances of your birth, your family, or your past experiences, but like many of the people on these pages, you can choose the way you let these things affect your life. You can concentrate on the things you cannot do. Many limitations are, after all, very real. Or, you can make the most of the choices remaining to you. All of your opportunities lie in those areas that you can change, those places where you can act. Why waste energy on the rest? An old saying puts it well: "Give me the strength to change those things I can, the serenity to accept what can't be changed, and the wisdom to know the difference."

Do you know of any people in your own community who have overcome handicaps or adversities in their lives? If so, add their names below. These people are all heroes, and they can be inspiring role models.

It takes courage to be who you really are. It also takes a lot of effort.

Taking Responsibility

As you learned in chapter 8, you are responsible for directing your own life and solving your own problems. Trying to give that responsibility away (which is what you do when you make excuses) can get in the way of having the life you want. After all, if something isn't your problem, how can you solve it? Since it isn't anyone else's problem either, if it doesn't get solved, it becomes a roadblock to your success.

The way to remove the roadblock is to take responsibility for it. Once you do that, you can usually think of ways to get around it or move it out of the way. For example, if you can't speak French because it's too hard, there's not much hope of ever learning French. But, when you say instead that you can't learn French because you haven't put in the effort, a remedy comes readily to hand. If you can't go to college or vocational school because you can't afford it, there's not much hope of getting the training you need. But if you can't go to college because you're not willing to work your way through or seek out financial aid, a number of solutions seem possible.

Can you think of any excuses you've made recently that made it seem something or someone else was responsible for your predicament? Write them below.

1. _____

2. _____

3. _____

Now analyze your own role in those situations and rewrite the statements, this time taking responsibility for the problem.

1. _____

2. _____

3. _____

STARTLING STATEMENT QUIZ

Circle the answer you think most accurately completes each of the following statements.

1. 46 percent of U.S. workers consider themselves underemployed. Of those who identified as underemployed, _____ percent reported they were working in jobs that did not use their education/training.
   a. 17
   b. 31
   c. 54
   d. 76

2. In 2017, _____ percent of all children lived in poverty.
   a. 7.2
   b. 13.6
   c. 17.1
   d. 24.8

3. In 2017, _____ percent of families headed by a female (with no husband present) lived below the poverty line.
   a. 11.4
   b. 19.2
   c. 25.7
   d. 39.1

4. In March 2019, the overall unemployment rate for persons age 25 and over was 3.8 percent. For high school dropouts age 25 and over, the rate was _____ percent.
   a. 4.3
   b. 5.1
   c. 5.9
   d. 7.2

5. In March 2019, average hourly earnings were _____
   a. $18.15
   b. $27.70
   c. $34.59
   d. $40.66

6. At the end of 2018, the median weekly earnings for full-time workers, 25 years and over, with a bachelor's degree or more were _____ for women and _____ for men.
   a. $994 and $1,348
   b. $1,155 and $1,541
   c. $1,257 and $1,707
   d. $1,410 and $1,929

7. At the end of 2018, the median weekly earnings for full-time workers, 25 years and over, who were high school graduates but with no college were _____ women and _____ for men.
   a. $622 and $835
   b. $767 and $947
   c. $853 and $1,019
   d. $965 and $1,104

8. Between January 2015 and December 2017, _____ percent of long-tenured displaced workers cited plant or company closings or moves as the reason for their job loss.
   a. 9
   b. 16
   c. 25
   d. 37

9. The average life expectancy for alcoholics is _____ years shorter than that of non-alcoholics.
   a. 5–7
   b. 8–10
   c. 10–12
   d. 12–15

10. In 2016, there were 35.7 million hospital stays in the United States; the mean cost per stay was _____ .
    a. $6,900
    b. $8,200
    c. $9,600
    d. $11,700

11. In 2016, _____ percent of households age 55 and older had no retirement savings.
    a. 60
    b. 48
    c. 36
    d. 24

12. While the average retirement age among Americans is 63, nearly _____ percent feel they will be 70 or older before they are able to retire.
    a. 25
    b. 20
    c. 15
    d. 10

ANSWERS

1. d. 76 percent of workers who identified as underemployed reported they were working in jobs that did not use their education/training.[1]

2. c. It is difficult to believe that close to 1 in every 5 children growing up in our country today live below the poverty line.[2] This is partly due to insufficient career planning by their parent(s).

3. c. Among female-headed households, 25.7 percent had earnings below the poverty line.[3] The poverty rate for all segments of the population was 12.3, which means that female-headed households were a little more than twice as likely to be poor. Why and what can be done to combat this reality?

4. c. The unemployment rate for high school dropouts age 25 and over was 5.6 percent, almost twice as high as the overall unemployment rate.[4] It is interesting to note that the unemployment rate for those age 25 and over with an associate's degree was 3.4 and 2.0 percent for those with a bachelor's degree.

5. b. Average hourly earnings in March 2019 were $27.70, which equals annual earnings of $57,616 (for 2,080 hours of work).[5] How does that compare to minimum wage and to your annual gross earnings requirements from chapter 4? Do you need to earn more than an average wage?

6. b. At the end of 2018, median weekly earnings for full-time workers with a bachelor's degree or more were $1,155 for women and $1,541 for men.[6] What might be some of the reasons for the substantial difference in the earnings of women and men?

7. a. At the end of 2018, median weekly earnings for full-time workers who graduated from high school but had no college were $622 for women and $835 for men.[7] This is a lot less than what college graduates can expect to earn, and the gap is growing wider as more jobs require a skilled background.

8. d. 37 percent of long-tenured displaced workers (those who had their job over 3 years) reported they lost their job when the plant or company they worked at closed or moved.[8] Another 37 percent cited that their position or shift was eliminated, and an additional 26 percent reported insufficient work as the reason. Global competition and advancing technology drive this trend. As it continues, workers with advanced or specialized skills will be better able to compete for jobs.

9. c. Alcoholism can shorten a person's life by 10–12 years.[9] Alcoholics may suffer from liver disease or heart disease, are at a higher risk for diabetes, lung disease, and stroke, and die from injury or violence at a higher rate. Taking care of your health and well-being will also impact your work life. Employers look for workers with healthy habits.

10. d. In 2016, the mean cost per hospital stay was $11,700.[10] Quality health insurance is something you may need to make room for in your budget, even if an employer subsidizes it. It is also important to have enough in retirement savings to supplement the increased medical costs that often accompany aging. The mean cost of a hospital stay for those 18 to 44 years was only $8,600, while the cost for those 65 to 84 was $14,500.

11. b. According to the Government Accountability Office (GAO), 48 percent of households age 55 and older had no retirement savings in 2016.[11] An earlier GAO report from 2015 indicated the following for households with some retirement savings: median savings of $104,000 for households age 55 to 64 and $148,000 for households age 65 to 74.[12] Those savings equate to an annuity of about $310 and $649 per month, respectively. Is it any wonder that… (see below)

12. a. Nearly 25 percent of Americans feel they will be 70 or older before they can retire.[13] An additional 5 percent feel certain they will never be able to retire. This feeling cuts across all age groups, with 25 percent, 28 percent, and 33 percent of workers under 30, in their 30s, and in their 40s, respectively, all indicating it is unlikely they will be able to retire before 70. Much of this pessimism is tied to insufficient retirement savings, since Social Security is only designed to provide about 40 percent of pre-retirement income.

See page 366 for sources used.

Detours and Roadblocks

When you consider the fact that many crucial life decisions are made very early in life, it's not surprising that things don't always turn out as well as we'd like. What may appear to be the easiest or most appealing path to an adolescent does not necessarily lead to a satisfying life for an adult. Fortunately, decisions can be changed and adjustments made at any point in life.

Of course, it isn't easy to change course. You may have lost some of the confidence and self-esteem that can keep a person going during tough times. Perhaps you've taken on family responsibilities, as well. There are sure to be days (or even years) when you'll be tempted to give up or give in to the easy way out, the temporary solution.

Hold on! You can delay their resolution, but in the long run problems cannot be escaped or ignored. They can only be solved. Short-term relief can lead to long-term regret.

Dana and Miko's lives seemed to be on the same course. Both had married right after high school graduation. Both had children. Now, eight years later, both were getting divorced and would have to support themselves and their children. Dana decided the best way for her to do that would be to get the technical training necessary to become an electrician. It would get tough, she knew, but it would let her make a good life for herself and her daughter. Miko started training, too, but quit after two weeks. It was just too hard, she said.

Who acted impulsively? In what way?

_____

_____

Try to imagine what the future holds for Dana and Miko. Describe their lives 15 years later in the space below.

Dana's life:

_____

_____

_____

_____

_____

Miko's life:

_____

_____

_____

_____

_____

Josie and Juan and their neighbors, Judy and Joe, worked as machine operators at the local fabric mill. Over dinner one evening they decided that they would all have to train for better jobs if either family was to thrive during tough economic times. At the same time, they would need to hold on to their current jobs just to make ends meet. After one semester of juggling work, school, and family responsibilities, Joe and Judy gave up. Josie and Juan stuck to their plan and gradually adjusted to the new way of life. After eight years, they joyfully completed their education and found jobs as a high school teacher and coach and a certified public accountant. Life became more rewarding, both financially and emotionally.

Which couple acted impulsively? In what way? _____

_____

_____

What could life be like for these two couples in 15 years? Visualize their futures and describe them below.

Josie and Juan's life: _____

_____

_____

_____

_____

Judy and Joe's life: _____

_____

_____

_____

_____

Sam and Janice became friends and business partners at the age of eight, when they had a lemonade stand together and argued for three days about who would be "the boss." Both were business majors in college, but Janice found the math classes too challenging and eventually left school without a degree. Sam went on to earn a master's degree in Business Administration. He lost touch with Janice until years later, when she was hired to be a teller at a bank where he was vice president.

Who acted impulsively? In what way? _____

_____

_____

_____

Describe what you think Sam and Janice's lives might be like 15 years from now.

Sam's life: _____

_____

_____

_____

_____

_____

_____

Janice's life: _____

_____

_____

_____

_____

_____

_____

Is It Worth Staying in School?

You decide. Go back to pages 150–151. What careers did you say you might like? List them below.

_____

Do any of these careers require further training or education? If so, imagine that you quit
school before completion. Could you qualify for any of these jobs without a degree or required
certification?

Yes   **No**

If so, which ones? _____

If not, you need another plan. Review your **Personal Profile** chart on page 27, your preferred
lifestyle on page 63, your lifestyle budget requirements on page 93 or your hardship budget on page
96, and your ideal career portrait and priorities on page 134.

Now go through the career search process on pages 150–151 once more. This time, though, make
sure that a diploma beyond high school isn't required for the jobs you are investigating.

List three careers that meet your personal requirements but do not further education or training.

_____

Compare these jobs with the ones you listed at the top of the page. How are they different? Which
careers do you think would be more satisfying? Why?

_____

_____

_____

Imagine your life 15 years from now. What do you think it would be like if you take a job from
your second list, the one that doesn't require education or training beyond high school? Which
would you find more satisfying—a career from the first or second list?

_____

_____

_____

The Economics of Bad Habits

Bad habits (smoking, drinking, drugs, etc.) will affect your physical and mental health and, thus, your ability to achieve. They are, therefore, another roadblock to success.

You have probably heard most of the common arguments for staying away from harmful substances. Most people usually hesitate to start a harmful habit because of the physical danger involved, but have you ever considered the economics of your habit? If you haven't taken up any of these habits, the following exercise might motivate you to stay away from them. If you already use a harmful substance, it might motivate you to put some energy into giving it up.

Complete the chart below, using the following information:

You are 18 years old when you begin smoking and you continue to smoke a pack a day for the rest of your life. If you live to be 78, the average life expectancy in the U.S. (your chances of reaching this age are lower because of your habit, by the way), and a pack of cigarettes continues to cost $7.04,* how much will your habit cost every year? Every 10 years? How much over your lifetime? Can you think of any other ways you might like to spend this money?

	One pack/day	Other use for money
Cost/year	$	
Cost/10 years	$	
Cost/60 years	$	

* NOTE: $7.04 was the average price of a pack of cigarettes in the United States in March 2019. Various state and local taxes cause this figure to vary greatly across the country. If you use smoking as your bad habit for the activity on page 209, you'll want to use the cost in your own area.

You will spend about $2,570 a year. That comes to $25,700 over 10 years, or $154,200 over 60 years.

Let's take our experiment one step further: If, between the ages of 18 and 65, you annually put $2,570 in a retirement account earning 8 percent interest,* that account would be worth $1,171,041.

If you deposited your smoking money monthly instead of annually ($214 per month = $2,570 divided by 12 months), your account earning 8 percent interest* would be worth $1,347,389 when you turn 65.

In other words, if you save the money you might have spent smoking, you would be able to retire with a guaranteed annual interest income (at 8 percent) of

$93,683 per year if you made annual deposits, or

$107,791 per year if you deposited your money monthly.

Some habits are much more expensive than cigarettes. Before you get involved with them, use the same equation to determine how much they would cost you over a lifetime.

Habit _____

Cost/day _____ Cost/week _____

Other use for money

Cost/year	$	
Cost/10 years	$	
Cost/60 years	$	

* NOTE: Over the last two decades, interest rates on investment accounts have fluctuated between 14% and 1%. We have chosen 8% as an average. You can find the current interest rates for a variety of available investment options on the Internet. You'll also find many useful online calculators for factoring retirement savings.

If You've Decided to Give Up Your Dream

Evie always wanted to be a journalist. She did very well in college. Her teachers encouraged her in her plans. Then, two quarters before graduation, Evie quit college and married her high school sweetheart. She told everyone she'd changed her mind about journalism, that this was what she really wanted. Deep in her heart, though, she wasn't sure why she decided to give up her dream.

Keith wanted to be a social worker, but his parents always assumed he would take over the family business. He tried to talk with them about his plans, but they just didn't understand. The business they had worked so hard to build could not last without his help, they said. Keith decided he owed it to his family to obey their wishes.

Carlotta changed her mind about becoming a research scientist when she took a look at the class requirements. How could she ever pass all those math tests? She might as well forget the whole idea, she told herself.

Sometimes there are good reasons to give up your dream. If your eyesight doesn't meet FAA standards, for example, you may as well forget about being a pilot. If the factory that has employed several generations of workers in your town closes its doors, you need an alternate plan. Or, if you come across an intriguing idea you hadn't thought of before, you owe it to yourself to give this new dream serious consideration.

Often, however, people give up too soon or for the wrong reasons. Usually, if they look more closely, these people find that they are acting out of fear.

Fear can take many forms. It can feel like obligation. It can feel like loss of interest. It can even feel like falling in love. Are you giving up on your dream because of fear? Consider the possibility carefully, especially if one or more of the categories on the following pages applies to you.

210

In a study of high school valedictorians, researchers at the University of Illinois found that, during their college careers, the young women in the group tended to scale back the ambitions they had on the day they graduated from high school. It wasn't because of their grades. In fact, the females were getting consistently better grades than the males in the group. So why were they changing their plans while the males remained more dedicated to their goals? There are several possible answers.

The study found that by their sophomore year in college, many of the female valedictorians were weighing whether ambitious career plans would fit with motherhood. Occupational segregation based on gender role stereotypes can feed the fear that success at work makes women less likely to have the time or energy to marry or have children, which leads women into career paths that may offer lower pay and less flexibility.

This fear, however, is largely unfounded. Today, 71.5 percent of mothers with children under age 18 are part of the workforce. Increasingly, women are not just working to supplement the family's income. In fact, 42 percent of mothers with children under age 18 are their families' primary or sole breadwinner.

Balancing a career with marriage and children can be challenging regardless of gender, but scaling back career plans will not necessarily make you a better parent. People who prepare for a more demanding career usually earn more and have more flexibility in their work lives—and these things help them be the kind of parent they want to be.

Sources: Karen D. Arnold, *Lives of Promise: What Becomes of High School Valedictorians: A Fourteen-year Study of Achievement and Life Choices,* 1995.

Bureau of Labor Statistics, U.S. Department of Labor, *Employment Characteristics of Families—2018.* April 2019.

Let's explore this concept further. Do you think the workers in each of the careers below are mostly male or mostly female? In the first column, beside each job title, write an F is you believe more females work in this field, an M if you think more males do.

Now go back and circle the careers that would probably offer the most flexible hours. In other words, which workers could most easily decide to take time off in the afternoon to attend a son or daughter's basketball game? Some careers are decidedly more flexible than others.

_____ Cashier		_____ Securities sales agent
_____ Child care worker		_____ Chiropractor
_____ Janitor		_____ Nurse (RN)
_____ Receptionist		_____ Architect
_____ Auto body repairer		_____ Computer programmer
_____ Plumber		_____ Chemical engineer
_____ Elementary school teacher		_____ Air traffic controller

Keywords: most flexible careers

Cashier	$21,030	Securities sales agent	$64,120
Child care worker	$23,240	Chiropractor	$71,410
Janitor	$26,110	Nurse (RN)	$71,730
Receptionist	$29,140	Architect	$79,380
Auto body repairer	$41,330	Computer programmer	$84,280
Plumber	$53,910	Chemical engineer	$104,910
Elementary school teacher	$57,980	Air traffic controller	$124,540

Amounts reflect national median earnings, assuming full-time work.
Source: Bureau of Labor Statistics, U.S. Department of Labor, *Occupational Outlook Handbook,* 2019.

Along the bottom of the following graph, first list the careers that are held mostly by women, beginning on the left-hand bottom column. We've already included the child care worker and receptionist as examples. Next add the jobs held mostly by men. Now, star the flexible careers, jobs in which workers can choose their own hours. We've used the chiropractor as an example.

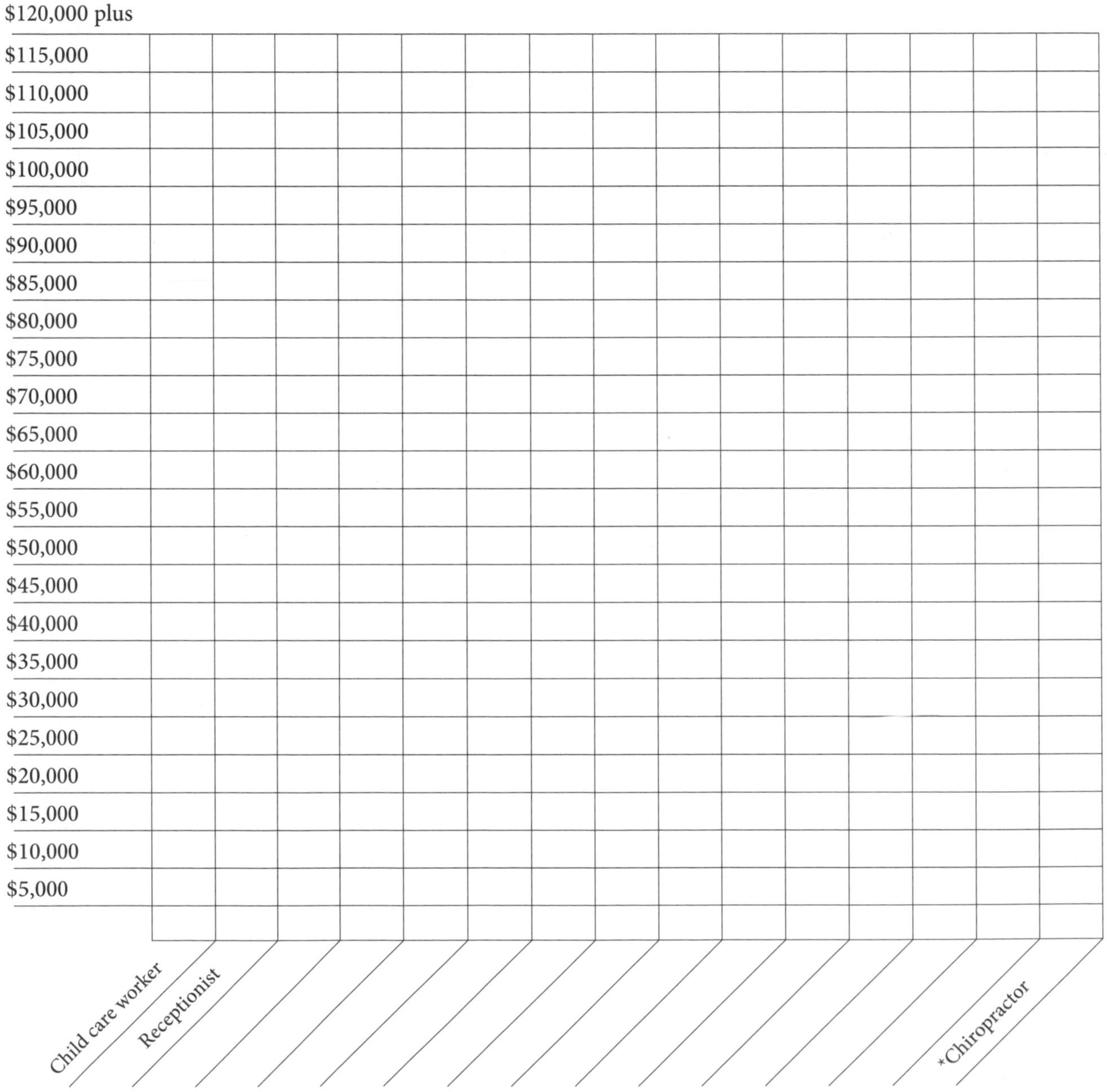

$120,000 plus
$115,000
$110,000
$105,000
$100,000
$95,000
$90,000
$85,000
$80,000
$75,000
$70,000
$65,000
$60,000
$55,000
$50,000
$45,000
$40,000
$35,000
$30,000
$25,000
$20,000
$15,000
$10,000
$5,000

Child care worker   Receptionist   *Chiropractor

Now use a pencil to chart the annual average salaries of the flexible careers. Use a pen to chart the annual average salaries of the non-flexible careers. (Note: The salaries we've used come from Department of Labor sources. Individuals might be able to earn a higher salary by working freelance or starting their own small businesses.)

Suppose a woman with three children suddenly found herself the sole support of her family. Decide what a family this size in your community needs a year to live in minimal comfort.

$ _____ per year

Now, draw a double line across the chart at this dollar level.

Which careers from the list would be most suitable for parenting? That is, which would provide both flexibility and an adequate salary? List those careers below. (Hint: These careers are graphed in pencil, above the double line.)

_____

_____

Which of the careers on your list require either a college or vocational degree or some other type of special training? Circle them.

Do more men or women currently hold these jobs?

More men   More women

Role models are important, and in many careers women still have fewer of them than men. Consequently, it may be more difficult for young women to visualize themselves being successful as engineers, contractors, or computer specialists. As graduation draws near, panic may set in. It may suddenly seem appealing to be a receptionist rather than an engineer, a teacher rather than a computer programmer. However, an impulsive change in direction could be costly for your future family.

REMEMBER: The higher you go on the career ladder, the more flexibility you will have for parenting. When you earn a higher wage, you may be able to afford to work less than full time. Highly trained professionals also usually have more freedom to set their own hours.

A final note: Regardless of gender, your plans should not depend on the financial support of a spouse. You should work to prepare for a career that provides an income that could support a family if needed. When both partners in a household are capable of supporting the family financially, you both have more freedom to enrich your lives. For example, either partner might go back to school at some point or take time out to stay home with children. You have more freedom to change careers or to save more for retirement. Or, if one of you is unable to work for any reason, it increases the chances that your family will be okay.

If You're "The First In The Family"
Or If Your Family Does Not Support Your Dream

Families are great, but they don't always understand. Why would a son want to be a teacher when, for generations, the eldest male has taken over the family business? When no one else in the family has felt a need to attend college, why does the daughter now want a degree? What could make the wife and mother who's always taken care of the family suddenly feel the need to get a job? Why does the husband and father with what appears to be a perfectly acceptable career want to do something else?

These attitudes are common and understandable. After all, any change in the status quo can seem threatening to the rest of the family. What will happen to them, individually and as a group? It would all be much easier if things could just stay the way they are.

For their sake, and for your own, make every attempt to convince your family that you are not rejecting them, you are merely doing what you need to do for your own life satisfaction. If you cannot make them understand, if you don't get their support, you may be tempted to give in and give up on your dream. Don't do it. In the end, it is your life — and you are ultimately responsible for your own happiness. If you cannot get the support you need at home, try to get it elsewhere. Friends can be helpful, or see page 334 about locating mentors.

If You Don't Think You Deserve It

No one can make you feel inferior without your consent.

— Eleanor Roosevelt

Remember the message center exercise on pages 50-53? What kinds of messages have you been getting about your future prospects? If any of them are negative ("You'll never amount to anything") or limiting ("remember your place"), you may have to fight periods of self-doubt and low self-esteem. At these times, it may seem like a good idea to give up and prove that the messengers are right: you are a failure and you don't deserve to succeed. A better idea is to acknowledge the messages, thank them for their input, and get on about your business.

Some people send themselves messages about their own worthiness. With so many poor, homeless, and starving people in the world, they reason, they have no right to pursue an economically rewarding career. Of course, it is important to be concerned about other people's needs. But, in fact, you can't solve many problems by becoming a victim yourself. Remember that when you do achieve your goal, you will be in a better position to help others or to work for social change.

Keywords: family support career choice, feeling worthy success

Before You Give Up

Can you think of a dream or ambition you had in the past that you have abandoned? Something you wanted to do or accomplish? Perhaps you dreamed of singing a solo in your church choir or learning to speak French. Maybe, while watching "Law & Order," reruns you've dreamed of becoming a district attorney.

Think of a dream that you have given up or are considering giving up? (If you haven't given your dreams much thought, now is the time to start thinking about them seriously. Try to write them down when they come to mind.)

Before you decide to give up something you once thought you wanted badly, answer the following questions.

What was your old dream? _____

How long did you hold it? _____

When did you decide to give up your dream? _____

Why? _____

What is your new dream? _____

Why does it appeal to you now? _____

Is there hard evidence to support your decision to give up your dream (you can't carry a tune, you've flunked out of school, you've run out of money, etc.)?

_____

If so, is this just an obstacle, or have you really reached the end of the road?

_____

If there is no hard evidence, have you discussed your decision with your teachers or your advisor? What do they think?

_____

If you've come up against an obstacle, would you hang on to your dream if the obstacle would simply disappear (the math requirement is lifted, you win the sweepstakes)?

_____

If you've decided to give up your dream because of some rational obstacle (money, grades), think of every possible way to overcome your problem. List them below. Are any of them workable?

_____

_____

If your reasons for giving up your dream are weak, your decision may be based on fear or anxiety. In the story on page 210, for example, Carlotta decided not to become a research scientist because she is anxious about math. She didn't fail at math. Her fear kept her from even trying to get through it.

Try not to let this happen to you. The truth is, everyone has anxieties. Trying to avoid situations that might make you feel uncomfortable can put unnecessary constraints on your life. The best thing to do is to learn how to tolerate the feelings that come with being ill at ease. If you can experience the anxiety (go to the party, get on the airplane), you will gradually overcome it.

By avoiding the thing that made her anxious, Carlotta deprived herself of that opportunity. What if she had signed up for a math class instead? Is there anything she could have done to lessen her anxiety?

She might have tried visualization. This is a technique that allows you to think about the thing you fear in great detail over a period of time. As you do this, you become less sensitive to the object of your fear and more confident about your abilities to deal with the situation.

Always remember, it's simply not an adventure worth telling if there aren't any dragons.

—Sarah Ban Breathnack

Keywords: visualize and overcome fear

Conquering Your Fears

If you, like Carlotta, suffer from math anxiety, try this exercise. Start by relaxing. It's important to feel at ease. Visualize yourself entering the classroom and taking a seat. See yourself listening to the lecture and understanding what is being said. Allow yourself to experience your feelings when the first test is announced. Then think about a time when you were up against something you were sure you couldn't do but, with hard work and concentration, did successfully. Now see yourself studying for the test. Visualize taking your seat on exam day, picking up your pencil, reading the questions, and completing every problem.

If you repeat this exercise daily for several weeks, you should begin to feel more comfortable with the subject. When that happens, you will become more confident, and that should help you perform better in the real class, as well. (You can't just see yourself studying, however. You have to actually *do* it!)

Write a guided visualization below that might help you conquer a fear you currently have. Try to see yourself actually doing whatever it is that makes you anxious and write the process below.

_____

_____

_____

_____

_____

_____

_____

_____

_____

_____

One Step at a Time

At first, Sally was delighted to be offered a full scholarship at a prestigious law school. But then the anxiety set in: The law school was way across the country, and she had always lived in the town where she grew up. She'd never even been on an airplane (that was another fear). What if the other students didn't like her? After all, her family had no money or social standing, while many of her classmates would be wealthy socialites. She was tempted to turn down the scholarship. But she knew the education she could get there would help prepare her for her dream — becoming a civil rights lawyer and, perhaps, eventually, a Supreme Court justice.

Sally's college advisor, Mr. Chan, had a suggestion: "Why don't you make a list of five or six things that frighten you?" he said. Sally thought about the assignment overnight, then wrote down her concerns:

> Fear of flying
>
> Fear of living so far from home
>
> Fear of being an outsider because of my background
>
> Fear of public speaking
>
> Fear of confronting a friend who betrayed a confidence
>
> Fear of failing my driver's test

"Okay," said Mr. Chan when she returned the next day. "Now rearrange your list. Put the item that concerns you least at the top and work your way down toward the situation that causes you the most anxiety."

That was easy enough, Sally decided:

> 1. Fear of confronting my friend
>
> 2. Fear of failing my driver's test
>
> 3. Fear of feeling like an outsider
>
> 4. Fear of public speaking
>
> 5. Fear of flying
>
> 6. Fear of living away from home

"Now what am I supposed to do?" she asked.

"Many people find they can overcome their fears by taking them on one at a time, from easiest to most difficult," said Mr. Chan. "So your job is to take care of the first item on your list as soon as possible. Then do the second, and so on.

"It's sort of like a baby learning to walk. First you learn to creep, next you crawl, and then you stand up. Finally, you're ready to take the big step, but the earlier trials have helped you gain the skills and confidence you need to succeed."

That night, Sally couldn't get to sleep. How could she confront her friend? It made her head ache and her stomach queasy. She didn't like the feeling at all, but she did talk to Lynn the next morning. Afterwards, Sally was relieved — and very pleased with herself. She had done it! She'd faced her fear and kept her friendship intact as well!

Feeling more confident now, she made an appointment to take her driver's test two weeks later. She reviewed the manual, visualized passing the test, and got her best friend to promise she'd practice driving with Sally for at least five hours before the exam. When Sally passed, she started to feel as though she could continue mastering her anxieties and gained a new sense of personal strength.

Next on her list, Sally had to learn that she could feel at ease with, and be accepted by, people from different backgrounds. She was invited to the dean's reception for outstanding students, though she hadn't planned to go. Now, however, it seemed like a good opportunity. Sally decided to put aside her usual shyness and talk with everyone in the room. She felt self-conscious at first, but before long she was more comfortable and found herself behaving more confidently.

The next step, however, seemed more of a problem. For Sally, speaking with people one-on-one was quite different from addressing a crowd. Since this was a more difficult situation, she made another visit to Mr. Chan.

219

"Sometimes we have to break things down even further," he said. "These challenges can't be bridged all at once. It takes time to overcome them. I suggest you come up with a step-by-step plan that will lead you to speaking in public, say, within two months.

"Try visualizing yourself in the situation, thinking through the various steps. Practice this three times a day while you're relaxed until you are comfortable with the feeling."

Sally decided her first step would be to volunteer an answer in math class every day for a week. She practiced visualizing raising her hand and speaking until she felt ready to try it. It was uncomfortable the first day, but within a week it seemed more natural.

That gave her the courage to register for a speech class beginning the following month. Until it started, Sally kept volunteering answers in her other classes. At least once a day, she also visualized doing well in the speech class.

After the first day of speech class, when everyone had left the room, Sally went up on stage and stood behind the lectern. She pretended to adjust the microphone, and looked out over the auditorium. Her imaginary audience applauded her wildly.

Finally, the day came. Sally was well prepared for her speech. The class didn't respond as she had hoped but, when she thought things through, Sally decided she had done what she wanted to do. She could feel good about herself. And, the next time she got up to speak, the class did respond to her noticeable improvement.

By this time, Sally was beginning to get a sense of herself as one who could achieve her other needs as long as she was willing to face her fear and work through her discomfort. She began looking forward to her flight as one more in a series of heroic adventures...a challenge that she could conquer. She also began to feel she would be able to deal with the problems she would encounter in her new life at college. There would be times when she'd be homesick, she knew, and she would certainly be frightened or nervous about the many new situations coming her way. But she also was learning she could tolerate discomfort and, if she faced it squarely, it would eventually diminish so she could get on with her goal: Getting the best education she could, and realizing her dream.

YOUR COURAGE ACTION PLAN

Like Sally, you may be facing a number of situations that make you uncomfortable or afraid. Some of them may even tempt you to give up your dream. List five fears you have or situations you are avoiding.

1. _____

2. _____

3. _____

4. _____

5. _____

Which of these do you think would be easiest for you to overcome? Which would be hardest? List your fears again, starting with the situation that causes you the least anxiety and working toward the item that makes you feel most uncomfortable.

1. _____

2. _____

3. _____

4. _____

5. _____

Think of a plan you could use to confront the first two items on your list. Write your plan below.

_____

_____

_____

Once you put your plans into action, record your feelings and experiences in the space provided.

_____

_____

_____

YORIK'S STORY

Yorik was born in Yerp, a tiny country on the Yorta Sea. Yerp is a beautiful place, and the Yerpese are generally a very happy people. Their main industry is raising yaks — wooly, horned cattle — for the production of yak yarn and yak yogurt.

Yorik, unfortunately, is allergic to yaks and everything yakish. As such, his future in Yerp is limited. He is an ambitious young man, however, and decides that, if he is ever going to realize his dreams (and maybe even stop sneezing) — he would have to leave Yerp. So, one day, he kisses his parents good-bye and gets on a boat to America.

Yorik arrives in the United States alone and with little money. He doesn't know anyone here. He has little education, and just a limited knowledge of English. But he is healthy (at last!) and ambitious, determined to make a good life for himself. He thinks he should be able to accomplish his goals within ten years.

What advice would you give Yorik? His career and lifestyle goal is listed below with a sample of his first year objectives. As Yorik's career counselor, write a **10-year Plan** that you think would help him achieve his goals. Include objectives for education or training, living arrangements, employment, and finances. (Do you remember the components of an objective? The diagrams we've used as an example should refresh your memory.)

Yorik's goal: At the end of ten years, to speak English fluently, hold a satisfying job that I have trained for, own a home, and have $10,000 in savings.

Year one:

Education or training: To take English classes twice a week all year long.

Living arrangements: To rent a small, inexpensive apartment and, within two weeks, find two roommates.

Employment: Within 30 days, to find a full-time job I qualify for that pays at least $10 an hour.

Finances: To save $3,000 for education or training within two years.

Write your **10-year Plan** for Yorik:

Year one:

Education and training: _____

Living arrangements: _____

Employment: _____

Finances: _____

Year three:

Education and training: _____

Living arrangements: _____

Employment: _____

Finances: _____

Year five:

Education and training: _____

Living arrangements: _____

Employment: _____

Finances: _____

Year eight:

Education and training: _____

Living arrangements: _____

Employment: _____

Finances: _____

Year ten:

Education and training: _____

Living arrangements: _____

Employment: _____

Finances: _____

How did Yorik delay gratification in the plan you just described? _____

_____

How might he have acted impulsively? _____

_____

Did he take responsibility for himself?   Yes   No

What excuses might a less determined person have made? _____

_____

What anxieties might he have had to overcome? _____

223

Taking Risks

Research shows that there are, basically, two different kinds of people when it comes to taking risks. Some people have a high need for achievement and are able to set and meet progressively more difficult goals. They see risk taking as a challenge and a learning experience. Others, afraid of failing, either take very small risks that teach them nothing or set their goals so high that no one could expect them to succeed. Their anxiety prevents them from growing and learning. Fortunately, since calculated risk taking is an important skill for successful living, it is possible to improve your ability to perform this task.

As a skill, risk taking combines the techniques for overcoming anxieties and making decisions. By definition, a risk involves uncertainty or danger. There is the possibility of losing something or suffering some kind of harm. It is reasonable, therefore, to be apprehensive. However, taking a risk is also like making a decision. You choose to do it only when you have determined your goal, examined the alternatives, evaluated the pros and cons, and considered the probability of success. If, after going through that process, you decide the possible outcome is worth the risk, you need to trust in your ability to handle your fears and the discomfort they create—and go for it.

The inability to take calculated risks can be just as paralyzing as the inability to overcome fears. When you use the decision-making model, however, you will often find that the risk is a relatively small one. What is the worst thing that could happen if you ask someone for a date, for example? (Hint: It should not be the end of life on this planet. Nor should it brand you forever as a hopeless geek with a talent for self-deception. Try to evaluate which part of your anxiety is real, and which part is not.) The worst that could happen is that the other person will decline your offer, and then you will get on with your life.

Are you willing to take that chance? Perhaps not. It might be more important for you to hang on to the dream that he or she is harboring a secret passion for you than to actually have a date with this person. This is another point to keep in mind. Know what you are willing to risk or lose. Analyze the probability of the worst happening. Then, if there seems to be a good possibility of losing something you hold dear, don't take the chance.

Keywords: taking calculated risks

Here are some other points to consider about taking risks.

1. Don't try to solve emotional problems with physical risks. You can't solve the problems you have with your parents, for example, by driving carelessly, drinking or taking drugs, or risking pregnancy.

2. Make sure you take your *own* risks, not someone else's, and don't let anyone else take your risks for you. You will not be totally committed to a goal that is not your own, and you can't expect someone else to feel as strongly about your goals as you do. In either case, the risk is likely to fail. (Example: A business is failing. Two people could possibly save it. Assuming they have comparable abilities, who do you think would be more successful, the person who owns the business, or the one who has no financial or emotional investment in it?)

3. Taking risks does not mean taking unnecessary chances. Young people, especially, are prone to taking hazardous risks in order to prove themselves. In truth, however, they prove little except their own lack of understanding. The only kind of risk worth taking is one that takes you a step closer to your stated goal.

4. Taking a risk is taking action. You cannot get to the place you want to be by simply wishing.

5. Do not take a risk unless you are willing to make your best effort. Commit yourself to your goal. As David Viscott says in his book, *Risking,* "If you don't intend to succeed, you intend to fail."

You gain strength, courage, and confidence by every experience in which you really stop to look fear in the face.

—Eleanor Roosevelt

225

Getting Back on Track
If You've Derailed

The advice on the preceding pages may be helpful if you are only thinking of giving up your dream, or if you've been temporarily sidetracked. However, sometimes people get derailed, and they need more help than we can provide in these pages.

That doesn't mean their lives are hopeless, not by any means. Reconsider the stories on pages 204–206, for example. Maybe Miko went back to night school to earn her high school diploma. Perhaps Judy did the same, and then she and Joe shared childcare duties and worked part-time while going on to college or vocational school. Janice might have become an apprentice and learned a skilled craft that paid well enough for her to support her family more comfortably. All of them, though, would need guidance and assistance.

If you've quit school, if you're taking drugs, if you're pregnant or raising a child alone, or if you simply feel lost or abandoned, you may think your future is hopeless. **It's not,** but you must seek out the help you need to get back on track.

Can your parents help? They are probably just as worried as you are about your situation. If you don't feel you can go to them, there are other resources. People who know and care about you are often in the best position to give support, so consider talking with a favorite teacher or coach, a school counselor, your spiritual or religious advisor, or another person you trust and respect. If you prefer to remain anonymous, consider calling local agencies such as the United Way, Alcoholics Anonymous, the Y's, Family Services, and Community Counseling Centers. Whatever you do, don't do it alone. Get help! And one way you can help yourself is to remember this: When sitting on the bottom rung of the career ladder, the only available direction is up.

> Amira dreamed of becoming a doctor since she was a little girl. However, along the way she lost track of that dream and dropped out of high school. Deep down she was still fascinated with medicine, so she went to the local hospital to look for work. Although the only job she qualified for was as a cashier in the gift shop, she remembered her vision and made a commitment to put the energy into getting the education she needed to realize her dream.

Most people would think that Amira's future looks pretty bleak, but she doesn't have to buy into their assessment. She can still reach her dream if she is willing to set a goal, develop a plan, and work at getting the education and training necessary to achieve it. Even if she doesn't become a doctor, the following career ladder will help her visualize her alternatives based on her commitment to education and training.

CAREER BACK-UP PLAN

Keeping your own career area of interest in mind, map out career alternatives based on the chart below. We've included Amira's chart to use as a guide along with an example for someone interested in teaching*.

1. First, write your ideal job title in the box that corresponds with the required training or education. Use a different color pen or all capital letters for that one box.

2. In the starred box ★, write the industry or career cluster with which this career is affiliated.

3. Based on the different commitments to education and training (column 1), choose at least one other job within that career interest area and put that job title in the corresponding box, along with the annual median salary. The *Occupational Outlook Handbook,* print or online (see page 148), will be your best resource.

	ALTERNATIVE CAREER LADDER					
Education/Training Level	Job Title	Median Salary	Job Title	Median Salary	Job Title	Median Salary
	HEALTH SERVICES		EDUCATION		★	
Doctoral or Professional Degree	Doctor	$208,000	District Superintendent	$148,360		
Masters Degree	Nurse Practitioner	$ 113,930	School Principal	$ 95,310		
Bachelor + Work Experience or Certification	Medical Sonographer	$ 67,080	Special Ed Teacher	$ 59,780		
Bachelor Degree	Registered Nurse	$ 71,730	School Teacher	$ 58,600		
Associate Degree	Medical Assistant	$ 33,610	Financial Clerk	$ 39,570		
Postsecondary Vocational Certificate	Medical Transcriptionist	$ 34,770	Executive Secretary	$ 57,410		
Long-term on-the-job training	Pharmacy Technician	$ 32,770	Cafeteria Cook	$ 25,860		
Moderate-term on-the-job training	Pharmacy Aide	$ 26,450	Child Care Worker	$ 23,240		
Short-term on-the-job training	Home Care Aide	$ 24,060	School Bus Driver	$ 34,540		
No High School Diploma	Gift Shop Cashier	$ 21,030	School Janitor	$ 26,110		

Source: Bureau of Labor Statistics, U.S. Department of Labor, *Occupational Outlook Handbook,* 2019.

— Do you see alternative careers that you might consider? Which ones and why?

— What if you were going to school, ran out of money, and needed to go to work for a period of time? Would one of the job titles listed below your ideal career make sense for the short-term? Why or why not?

— What other observations can you surmise from this data? Study your chart and discuss your conclusions with friends and mentors.

* NOTE: The education and training required, as well as the median annual salary, vary from state to state. These are national averages.

CHAPTER 9 CHECKPOINTS
Avoiding Detours and Roadblocks
The road to success is dotted with many tempting parking places

We all know that problems and challenges are a fact of life. You have learned strategies that will help you face them head-on to actively overcome them. Since you are responsible for your own life, you recognize that it is up to you to overcome any perceived limitations. These are powerful lessons, so confirm that you've completed the following objectives before moving on.

☐ I examined common excuses people use for not doing what they can or want to do. I evaluated those reasons and determined what might be done to avoid using them myself.

☐ I started to evaluate my own excuses and look at them in a new way. By accepting responsibility for my problems, I am also opening new avenues for solving them.

☐ After reviewing some unsettling statistics regarding poverty, earnings, and retirement, I better understand how I can address these in my own life.

☐ I examined some common problems and, by projecting into the future, I considered possible long-term consequences of present actions.

☐ I personalized the effect of dropping out of school on my eventual job satisfaction.

☐ I comprehend the financial costs of bad habits, both current and long-term.

☐ I understand how flexibility and salary impact the ability to mix career and family, and recognize that women would do well to consider careers not traditionally pursued by females.

☐ I learned evaluation techniques that I can use before impulsively abandoning a dream or plan.

☐ I am learning to overcome fears I may have by simply imagining myself as successful at that which makes me anxious.

☐ I learned a hierarchical approach to conquering anxieties that might limit my goals for the future.

☐ I started the process of a **10-year Plan** by making long-range plans for someone who could reasonably be expected to fail due to lack of resources.

☐ I observed that taking calculated risks is an important skill.

Success or failure is caused more by mental attitude than by mental capacity.
—Sir Walter Scott

Think you can or think you can't, either way you will be right.
— Henry Ford

CHAPTER TEN

Attitude Is Everything

Learning to accentuate the positive

Section Three:
HOW DO I GET IT?

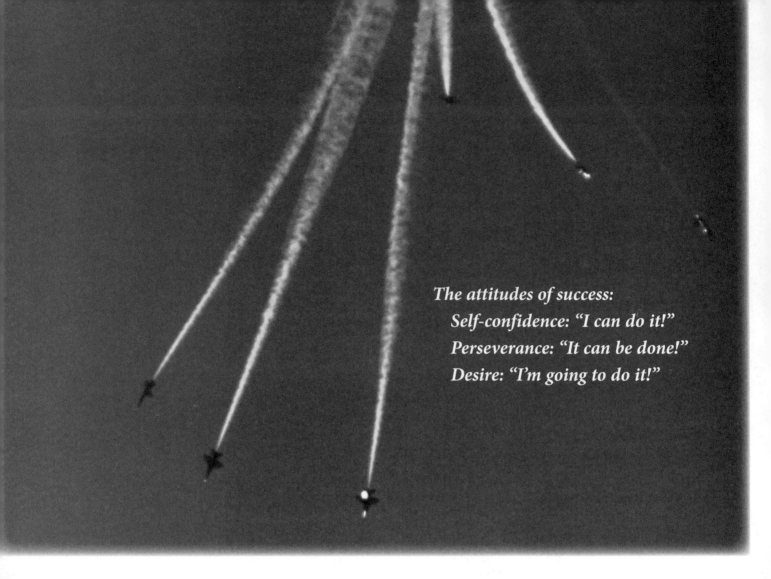

The attitudes of success:
   Self-confidence: "I can do it!"
   Perseverance: "It can be done!"
   Desire: "I'm going to do it!"

According to the old nutritionists' saying, "you are what you eat." Most people feel more like a hero or a failure or a nice guy than they do like a peanut butter sandwich, so more accurate saying might be, "you are what you think you are."

Attitude is everything. Muhammad Ali was telling the world "I am the greatest" long before he became heavyweight boxing champion. In the movie *Funny Girl*, the Fanny Brice character played by Barbra Streisand sings "I'm the Greatest Star" before she becomes just that. During the worst days of the Great Depression, one of the most popular songs was "Happy Days Are Here Again," and soon they were.

It may seem unlikely, but it works: Telling yourself that you are the kind of person you want to become — acting as though you are that person now — helps you achieve your goals. Pretending is a way of practicing. And, without practice, how would we learn to do all the wonderful things we do?

The late actor Cary Grant once said, "I pretended to be somebody I wanted to be, and I finally became that person." In other words, pretending something is true can make it so. Perhaps this is not so surprising. If you want to become more confident, for example, pretending that you already are will probably lead to some kind of reward: getting the job or the date or the good grade on your speech. That experience will help make you more confident, which will help you keep up your act. As you continue to pile up rewards, you will do increasingly less acting. Soon, you may just find that you have become a confident person.

Affirmations Promote Action

Your life is an expression of all your thoughts.

— Marcus Aurelius

Another way to change your attitude is by using affirmations. Think back to the Positive Messages to Yourself exercise on page 53. Affirmations are like the messages you get from other important people in your life, but they come from you—the most important person of all. You can tell yourself anything you like. Since the other messages reached you first, however, it will take time and constant repetition to replace them with new ones.

In order to be most effective, affirmations should also:

1. Be said aloud and repeated throughout the day, or written down. It's even more effective to record them and listen to them while you're in a semi-hypnotic state such as running or lying down.

2. Include your name. "I, _____, am a good student."

3. Be in the present tense. Say that the condition you hope to bring about is true **now**!

4. Be short, positive, and clear. "I, Waldo, am a graceful dancer" is better than "I, Waldo, am going to stop stepping on people's feet, tripping on my shoelaces, and running into the concession stand."

5. Be meaningful and believable to you!

What affirmations can you write about your future? In making your decision, consider reversing any negative messages from the exercise on page 52. For example, if your message from your father is "You can't do anything right," you might include an affirmation that states "I, Violeta, can do anything I set my mind to." If you've received the message "You'll never be good at math," you could benefit from an affirmation stating "I, LeeAnn, am a good math student."

We've included a few statements as examples. Use them if they could be helpful for you. Then write your own affirmations in the space below. Repeat them to yourself often. Act as if they are true now.

I, _____ , am confident when meeting new people.

I, _____ , am capable of getting a good job.

I, _____ , am good at making and keeping friends.

I, _____ , am _____

I, _____ , am _____

I, _____ , am _____

The Six Es of Excellence

If a man has good corn, or wood, or boards, or pigs to sell, or can make better chairs or knives, crucibles, or church organs, than anybody else, you will find a broad, hard-beaten road to his house, though it be in the woods.

> — Ralph Waldo Emerson

Nothing great will ever be achieved without great people, and people are great only if they are determined to be so.

> — Charles de Gaulle

Good is not good where better is expected.

> — Thomas Fuller

To excel means to do something of superior quality, to be the best that you can be — to know you've given your all to the task. By setting high standards and putting in an unusual amount of effort, an individual can go a long way toward assuring a quality existence.

Remember the formula for success from chapter 1:

$$VISION + ENERGY = SUCCESS$$

The formula for excellence takes this one step further:

HIGH STANDARDS + UNUSUAL EFFORTS = EXCELLENCE

This principle holds true in any line of work. By being the best cook or plumber or accountant in town, you can expect to live well. Better still, you can expect to be respected and to have a sense of personal satisfaction.

We want quality in the products and services we buy — even if we have to pay more for them. Doesn't it follow, then, that we should be just as concerned about excellence in the work we do and the way we live our lives? Satisfaction comes, ultimately, not simply from doing something, but from doing something well.

However, excellence requires a conscious and ongoing commitment, a willingness to set high standards and exert unusual efforts. Not everyone is willing to sustain this kind of commitment. How do you acquire excellence? For starters, you can apply the following principles to your life, whether it's the work you do or the plans you make — alone and as part of a team.

As you evaluate your own efforts or that of any team, use the qualities on the following pages as your guide. Incorporate these standards into your work and there is a greater chance you'll meet your goals in an admirable fashion.

> Note: It's important to keep in mind that a team's success depends on all members sharing a common understanding of the importance of these characteristics.

Expectations

The dictionary says that the word expectation "suggests anticipation of success or fulfillment." Actually, it's another word for vision. Expectations are often self-fulfilling prophecies — if you expect to be happy and successful, you have a good chance of achieving your goals. If you expect a poor outcome, that's about what you're likely to get.

Therefore, it is important to have high expectations — for yourself and from yourself. Many people shortchange themselves by expecting only what they think is possible in a negative sense, or what others think they should want. Quite often, good students to whom learning comes easily believe that everything should be easy. When they come up against a task that requires effort on their part, such as learning to play a sport, they give up. They aren't used to making an effort to succeed, so they limit their expectations to those things that they can do most easily.

What should you expect? Review your answers to the exercises in chapter 3. Expect to get what you said you want.

Enthusiasm

Once your expectations are in place, it's easier to generate the enthusiasm you need to accomplish your goals. Enthusiasm is the eagerness, interest, or excitement with which you approach a job or activity. It grows out of knowing what you want and doing what you love. If you have always dreamed of being a teacher, for example, your enthusiasm is likely to show up in your lectures and lesson plans, and you will probably be good at and happy in your job. If you really wanted to be a fire fighter, however, but went into teaching because that's what your parents wanted you to do, you aren't likely to have the same enthusiasm. You won't enjoy your job as much, and you won't do it as well as some others will.

This is the basic thesis of Marsha Sinetar's book *Do What You Love, The Money Will Follow*. When you "discover your right livelihood," as she puts it, your enthusiasm will help assure that you give the job the time and attention it requires if you are to excel at it.

Of course, people don't always land their ideal job — at least, not right away. If that's the case, work up some enthusiasm for the work you do and you'll have a much better chance of moving beyond it to something more challenging and rewarding.

Author Brenda Ueland once said, "Never do anything you don't want to do." Few of us can follow that advice in all aspects of our lives, but it is something to keep in mind. Enthusiasm is the breath of life that can make even the most mundane tasks rewarding. When you plan your career, aim to do something you love, something you value. If you do that, your chances of excelling will increase because of your enthusiasm (love) for your project.

> *Nothing great was ever achieved without enthusiasm.*
>
> — Ralph Waldo Emerson

Energy

You can spend the rest of your life daydreaming about your future — or you can make your dreams happen. But it takes energy to put your plans into action. Fortunately, if you are enthused about what you are doing, the energy will usually come.

Everyone, though, has days when it's hard to get going. It's a good idea to take a day off now and again, but how do you overcome inertia when you know you need to get something done?

First, try repeating your version of the statements on page 121: "I want _____ , therefore, I should _____." If that doesn't work, try easing yourself into the chore. Promise yourself that if you do one small part of the project, or work on it for a short period of time (half an hour?), you can quit. Often, once you get going, the energy will start flowing and you will be able to accomplish much more than you hoped. Finally, if all else fails, "just do it," as they say.

Of course, everyone has only so much energy. It's important to set your priorities and do the most important projects first. Otherwise, they may not get done at all. There are many ways to waste time enjoyably. You should make time to do just that. But, generally, your life will be more productive and your free time more enjoyable if you do the things you must do first. That way, you can spend the remaining time any way you like, without worry.

Keep in mind, too, that energy springs from good health. Without adequate rest, nutrition, and exercise, it is difficult to maintain your energy level.

Enterprise

By "enterprise" we mean the willingness to take calculated risks, the ability to recognize both problems and opportunities, and the creativity to make the best of either situation. The old saying, "When life gives you a lemon, make lemonade," was undoubtedly coined by an enterprising person.

This quality is probably the one most evident in "self-made" people, those who started with little and overcame adversity to become successful.

The secret of success is to do the common things uncommonly well.

— John D. Rockefeller, Jr.

Efficiency

An efficient person is organized. An efficient person gets things accomplished — on time. Efficiency is another aspect of taking control of your life. Without organization and planning, your life is manipulated by other people, or even by inanimate objects. You can prepare a super report, but if you can't find it when it's due, no one is going to give you the benefit of the doubt. Imagine how difficult it would be for an auto mechanic to repair a car if she couldn't find her tools, or consider the absolute need for organization in an operating room.

Just as you are learning to plan your career and family life, you can learn to organize your closet, your desk, your files, your kitchen, your garage, and practically anything else. Books have been written on the subject. Seminars and classes are available. You can even hire someone to come in and teach you how to get organized and how to keep things under control.

Ethics

Ethics is another word for your conscience, your sense of right and wrong. Some things are obviously wrong (embezzling funds from your employer, for example), but in other areas, principles are less clear. If you learn that your co-worker is falsifying their time records, should you report this fact to your boss? Talk to your friend about your feelings? Do nothing? What about violating copyright by downloading music or movies from peer-to-peer networks? Just because it's popular, does that make it right?

Standing up for your beliefs or doing what you believe to be right isn't easy or efficient, but it may be necessary. Without integrity or moral courage, the success you attain may be hollow and have less meaning.

This is one area of life over which you should have complete control. No one can force you to betray your conscience.

RECOGNIZING EXCELLENCE

We all know of individuals who exemplify these standards. Maybe it's a teacher you've had or a food server in the local café? Perhaps it's a public figure. Choose two people who you feel embody excellence and write them a thank you note, commenting on how they personify each of these six traits.

Going For It . . .
Work Is an Aggressive Act

In polite society, aggression is not acceptable behavior. At most parties, headlocks and half-nelsons are not appropriate forms of greeting. Those who attack the refreshment table in a flying wedge are unlikely to be invited back anytime soon. This will not come as news to most readers.

What may surprise you, though, is that aggression is exactly what it takes to succeed at work. Not aggression toward people (unless you happen to be a professional wrestler, a defensive lineman in the NFL, or the like), but aggression toward your work. Aggression takes many forms. It fuels competition as well as many other ways of behaving. Without some form of aggressive energy, we would probably never grow up.

How aggressive are you when you take on a job? Many people find it difficult to identify with the term. It doesn't seem "nice" somehow. Wouldn't the world be a better place if everyone stifled their aggressive urges at work the same way they do at a party? Consider the following situations before you make up your mind.

SCENARIO 1

You are trapped in a burning house. The firefighters arrive, but the doors are locked. Would you prefer to have them

a. wait patiently for a locksmith (the "nice" thing) or

b. kick in the doors and windows and get you out of there (extremely aggressive behavior)?

SCENARIO 2

You are unjustly accused of a crime. During your trial, your lawyer uncovers evidence that proves your accuser is lying. Should your lawyer

a. refuse to confront the witness because it wouldn't be polite or

b. nail him to the wall?

SCENARIO 3

Your car won't start. You need to be at an important conference in an hour. When you call the repair shop, would you rather have the mechanic

a. sympathize with your plight or

b. be at your house within 10 minutes and have you on your way in 15?

SCENARIO 4

You are a doctor. You witness a traffic accident in which a child is seriously injured. Should you

a. try to find out the name of the child's doctor and call him or her or

b. do what is necessary to save the child's life?

SCENARIO 5

You are one of five junior executives in a small corporation. Each of you is asked to write a proposal for increasing sales. Should you

a. be careful not to outdo your co-workers or

b. do your best, for your own sake and the company's?

SCENARIO 6

You are a newspaper reporter who hears a rumor that, if true, could drastically affect the lives of many of your readers. Should you

a. hope someone will call and tell you what's going on or

b. investigate vigorously to either verify the story or prove it's not true?

In his book, *Work and Love: The Crucial Balance,* Dr. Jay B. Rohrlich points out that "the basic aggressive urge . . . underlies all work." Perhaps that helps explain the language people use when they talk about what they do. They *tackle* problems, *wrestle* with alternatives, *make a killing* in the stock market, and so on.

According to Dr. Rohrlich, "'Perfection,' 'greatness,' 'mastery,' and 'excellence' revolve around the instinct of aggression." And, as the exercise you just completed demonstrates, "people who fear and suppress their aggressive drives are usually unsuccessful at work."

The drive is there. Don't be afraid to use it. Try to recognize it and channel it consciously. Whether you are a poet or a firefighter, remember that aggression, properly used, will allow you to do your best work. To quote Dr. Rohrlich once more, aggression "is a constructive, creative, and adaptive drive, the fundamental aim of which is to foster the survival, preservation, and enrichment of ourselves and our communities."

So go for it! It's your life!

You're The Boss

Picture yourself as an employer. Your restaurant, "Chris's Creative Cuisine," has been the center of your world since you started it 16 years ago. For the first three years, you worked 12 or more hours a day, taking charge of everything from setting tables to testing recipes. You saw little of your children, unless your spouse brought them by the restaurant. The personal costs were high — perhaps too high. The business finally became profitable five years after you opened. Now "Chris's" is one of the most popular dining spots in town. Things are looking good, and you are determined to stay successful. It's time for the annual performance review of your employees. What advice would you give to the following people if they worked for you?

SHARON

Sharon is a good waitress. She is late for work several times a week, but she always has a good excuse. She apologizes and says it won't happen again. But it does. Last week, Tim, another waiter, had to serve clients at Sharon's tables in addition to his own for two and a half hours because Sharon's car had broken down. (She says it's in good shape now.) Tim said he didn't mind the extra work, but it bothered you.

What is Sharon's problem? _____

_____

What advice would you give her during her evaluation?

_____

_____

Write and diagram an objective that Sharon might use to change her behavior.

_____

_____

JACKIE

Jackie, your pastry chef, has won several awards for her dessert, Death by Chocolate. She has a tendency, though, to call in sick more often than seems likely. Even more unusual, her illnesses tend to occur on Saturday, your busiest day. Twice you've called her apartment to see how she's doing, but she wasn't home. When the mayor ate at "Chris's" last month, you were left with no desserts until Tim suggested an excellent bakery across town that delivers.

What is Jackie's problem? _____

What advice would you give her during her evaluation?

_____

_____

Write and diagram an objective that Jackie might use to change her behavior.

_____

_____

DOROTHY

Dorothy, your hostess, does a good job, but complains about other people's work a lot. She doesn't get along well with her fellow employees, and sometimes her moodiness affects the way she treats customers. You recently overheard her make a rude remark to a long-time regular client and thought he'd never come back. Fortunately, though, Tim was able to make amends while he served dinner, and the client left smiling.

What is Dorothy's problem? _____

What advice would you give her during her evaluation?

_____

_____

Write and diagram an objective that Dorothy might use to change her behavior.

_____

_____

STUART

Stuart is a reliable waiter. He's never been late or missed a day of work. You've noticed, however, that since he started working for you, you've had to reorder things like candles and matchbooks more often than you did before. After a wedding reception at "Chris's" recently, you saw him walk off with the centerpiece from the bridal table. It's true that the flowers had been left, but Stuart didn't even ask. Tim had offered to deliver the flowers to patients at a nearby nursing home.

What is Stuart's problem?

_____

_____

_____

What advice would you give him during his evaluation?

_____

_____

_____

Write and diagram an objective that Stuart might use to change his behavior.

_____

_____

_____

_____

MAT

Mat is a busboy who would like to become a waiter. He does his job adequately — but no more than that. He usually has to be asked to refill water glasses or empty coffee cups. When a customer asked him for another basket of bread earlier tonight, Mat told him that wasn't his job. You can't help but remember the way Tim did the job when he started working for you.

What is Mat's problem?

_____

_____

_____

What advice would you give him during his evaluation?

_____

_____

_____

Write and diagram an objective that Mat might use to change his behavior.

_____

_____

_____

Unfortunately, we all encounter poor customer service on occasion. Write about three such experiences. How did it make you feel? What did you do about it? Did you tell your friends about it?

Traits of Those Who Get Ahead

Now that you've considered some less-than-perfect workers, can you describe a model employee? It might help to review the profiles on the preceding pages. If the characteristics described are undesirable, what opposite traits would make an employee valued by his or her employer?

Employee	Problem	Desired Behavior
Sharon	Tardiness	_____
Jackie	Untruthfulness	_____
Dorothy	Difficult Personality	_____
Stuart	Dishonesty	_____
Mat	Laziness	_____

What characteristic did Tim display in each of the situations?

_____

_____

Describe the characteristics of people you would like to hire for your business. Who do you want on your "team?"

_____

_____

Chances are your description is a fairly accurate definition of the term "work ethic." Being a good employee means being honest, on time, and so on. However, the best employees — the ones who get ahead — display the traits that Tim does: they are creative, cooperative, and willing to do more than is expected of them. To many employers, a "good work habit" is more important in a prospective employee than knowing something about the job. They feel the job skills can always be learned. It's more difficult to instill the attitude they are seeking.

The work ethic is an attitude. The easiest way to acquire it is by liking what you do. Once again, it becomes apparent that, if you enjoy your work, you will do a good job. And, if you do a good job, you will succeed.

Interview three local employers to find out what they expect of their employees. Ask them to rank the characteristics they look for in order of importance. Would someone with each of those characteristics, but limited work experience, still be a good job candidate? Why? How important are character traits like honesty, dependability, punctuality, respect, and getting along with co-workers?

The Employee of the Twenty-first Century

It was a typical morning at the Millers. "Here's your juice, dear," Mrs. Miller said to her daughter, Angela. "Don't forget to take your cholesterol pill."

"I don't have time," Angela answered. "I'm late already, and I can't find my homework, my list of New Year's resolutions."

"I can't believe it's going to be 2040 in a few days," her mother said. "By the way, dear, you left the time machine on again last night. When your father came home, it was 1956 in here. You know how that always upsets him."

"Gee, I'm sorry, Mom. I was doing some research for my class in early television literature. I guess I just forgot to turn it off."

"I suppose you think you're the only one in the family who needs to travel in time," said her brother, Donald, as he came into the kitchen. "I was going to meet Herb and Joe in 1969 last night."

"Well, I certainly think my education is more important than your pleasure trips with your weird friends. Talk about a waste of time!"

"You see how selfish she is, Mom? I don't know why I can't have my own TM. Lots of other guys do, and I'm almost 16."

Like most stories about the future, the one above is almost certainly inaccurate. Chances are you won't have a personal time machine. You may never be beamed aboard the Starship Enterprise or travel back to the future in a souped-up Delorean.

However, you will live there (in the future, that is — not in the Delorean). You will spend all of your working life in the twenty-first century. And, if you bring along certain attitudes, you might just "live long and prosper."

Although detailed predictions about life in the years ahead are unreliable, it is quite possible to make an educated guess about the general direction of events. Certain trends are already apparent and are becoming stronger.

Most of these trends are related to technology and the ways in which it has made our world smaller. Advancing technology, of course, is nothing new, but its speed is. Thousands of years elapsed between the invention of the wheel and the invention of the automobile, but the first successful airplane left the ground only two-thirds of a century before people landed on the moon. Back in the 1950s, the first commercial computers were called "electronic brains" and were so big they filled an entire room. Because of their expense, only a few of the very largest corporations could afford to use them. Today, computers are as common as TV sets, and the Internet has revolutionized how we work, play, and live.

Keywords: characteristics employee 21st century

Because of advances like these, business has taken on a global perspective. Businesses from around the world work together — or compete against each other — to produce quality products and services at affordable prices. In order to do this, they have changed, and the people who work for them have had to change, too.

How well will you function in this new environment? The following self-evaluation quiz should give you some idea. Select the answer that best describes or comes closest to your feelings.

1. I view computers as:
   - ☐ a. an important tool.
   - ☐ b. useful at times.
   - ☐ c. . . . I don't want anything to do with them.

2. If I need to learn a new procedure while working on a computer, I:
   - ☐ a. figure it out after looking it up in the manual or online tutorial.
   - ☐ b. get help from someone who knows what to do.
   - ☐ c. give up — it takes too much time, and I didn't want to do it anyway.

3. I think of technology as:
   - ☐ a. something we all need to know and understand.
   - ☐ b. . . . I don't think about it much.
   - ☐ c. not very relevant to my life.

4. When I got my diploma I thought:
   - ☐ a. this is really just the beginning of my education.
   - ☐ b. about what I'm going to do now.
   - ☐ c. thank goodness, no more school.

5. When I have a question about something, I:
   - ☐ a. look up the answer on the Internet or call someone who should know.
   - ☐ b. make a mental note to keep my eyes open for the answer.
   - ☐ c. forget about it — it probably wasn't important anyway.

6. I approach change:
   - ☐ a. as an opportunity.
   - ☐ b. with caution.
   - ☐ c. with resistance.

7. If, halfway through a project, it becomes apparent that my plan for completing it won't work, I would:
   - ☐ a. rethink my plan and come up with a better one.
   - ☐ b. worry about the project and hope to come up with a better plan someday.
   - ☐ c. lose interest and scrap the project.

8. When I'm around people from other cultures:
   - ☐ a. I appreciate their diversity.
   - ☐ b. I'm curious — but cautious.
   - ☐ c. . . . I am uncomfortable with people who are not like me.

9. The idea of traveling to other countries:
   - ☐ a. sounds exciting to me.
   - ☐ b. is of some interest to me.
   - ☐ c. does not interest me at all.

10. Learning at least one other language:
   - ☐ a. is important for everyone.
   - ☐ b. is probably a good idea.
   - ☐ c. is unnecessary — I can get by speaking only English.

To score your self-evaluation, go back and give yourself 3 points for every "a" answer you checked, 2 points for every "b," and 1 point for every "c." If your total score is 26 – 30, you have the attitudes that make you a valued employee in the twenty-first century. They include the following:

| X | **EMBRACING TECHNOLOGY**

Today, people at all job levels—from the loading dock to the executive suite—use a variety of technological accessories. From desktop computer to laptop, cell phone to iPhone to Android device, Kindle to iPad, the list seems to change constantly. These devices allow employees to be more productive and efficient. Individuals who capitalize on the power of technology are among the most valuable workers. They have the attitude that they can master new applications and look forward to the challenge.

| X | **LIFELONG LOVE OF LEARNING**

In a rapidly changing society, skills need to be updated frequently. There's always something new to learn. A love of learning will not only keep you employable, it will also enrich your life and make you feel a part of the advances taking place around you.

| X | **FLEXIBLITY**

It's been said, "Nothing is certain but change." How you deal with this fact can greatly affect your future. It's one thing to cope with change; prospering in the face of change is quite another. People who embrace change and can learn to live with some uncertainty are more likely to thrive in today's workplace. Jobs and whole industries change—or even become extinct—and the ability to change with them is critical. Whether you need to upgrade skills or find a new career, how you manage the change process impacts your success and, therefore, your future happiness.

| X | **AN INTERNATIONAL PERSPECTIVE**

With Disneyland® in Tokyo, McDonald's in Moscow, and Starbucks® in Sao Paulo, it's easy to see that the world is becoming a much smaller place. Businesses around the world are entering a global marketplace. Nations are joining together for mutual economic advantage. At the same time, people are celebrating their cultural diversity. They are also traveling more and, quite commonly, they are living and working away from their homeland. For those who can appreciate other cultures and understand the different economic systems around the globe, the future holds endless opportunity.

Do you need an attitude adjustment? If your self-evaluation shows that you could use improvement in any of these areas, make plans now to do something proactive to change. Write some objectives that will help you in the spaces below. (Turn to pages 186–189 if you need to review the process.)

Elliot's objectives are as follows:

Technology:
1. Learn how to build my own website by next fall.
2. Find and follow two blogs about podcasting so I can create three podcasts for the community garden supporters.

Love of learning:
1. Read two books on the publishing industry this summer.
2. Improve my tennis game by googling "tennis instruction online" and asking Andre to coach me during the summer.

Flexibility:
1. Write three different endings for my short story and then choose the best one before handing it in.
2. Try to find a new job in a career area that I'm interested in learning more about instead of going back to work at the supermarket.

International perspective:
1. Join the Russian club at the community center next month.
2. Make three new friends from different backgrounds or cultures by the end of the year.

Your objectives:

Technology:

1. _____

2. _____

Love of learning:

1. _____

2. _____

Flexibility:

1. _____

2. _____

International perspective:

1. _____

2. _____

A Final Note on Attitude

A reporter was interviewing a woman who worked for a famous actress. "What do you think about your employer's enormous success?" he asked as she transferred a load of the celebrity's clothes from washer to dryer. "I'm really pleased that she found something to fall back on," came the reply. "Because she doesn't know beans about doing laundry."

In his book, *Up from Slavery*, Booker T. Washington said, "there is as much dignity in tilling a field as in writing a poem." And that, finally, is what attitude is all about. It makes little difference what you do. If you can find pleasure in a job, if you do it well and with pride, any task becomes noble.

I long to accomplish a great and noble task, but it is my chief duty to accomplish small tasks as if they were great and noble.

—Helen Keller

Whether we find pleasure in our work or whether we find it a bore depends entirely upon our mental attitude towards it, not upon the task itself.

—B.C. Forbes

If you are called to be a street sweeper, you should sweep streets even as Michelangeo painted, or Beethoven composed music, or Shakespeare wrote poetry . . .

—Martin L. King, Jr.

Forget about the fast lane. If you really want to fly, just harness your power to your passion. Honor your calling. Everyone has one. Trust your heart and success will come to you.

—Oprah Winfrey

Keywords: attitude toward work

Nurture your mind with great thoughts, for you will never go any higher than you think.

—Benjamin Disraeli

Optimism is the one quality more associated with success and happiness than any other.

—Brian Tracy

Others can stop you temporarily—you are the only one who can do it permanently.

—Zig Ziglar

Whether you think you can or think you can't, you're right.

—Henry Ford

Your time is limited. Don't waste it living someone else's life. Don't be trapped by dogma, which is living with the results of other people's thinking. Don't let the noise of other's opinions drown out your own inner voice. And, most important, have the courage to follow your heart and intuition. They somehow know what you truly want to become. Everything else is secondary.

—Steve Jobs
Stanford University Commencement address, 2005

CHAPTER 10 CHECKPOINTS
Attitude is Everything
Learning to accentuate the positive

You have begun to develop the attitudes that will lead you to your own definition of success. It may take practice to fully integrate these new attitudes, but you will find that the payoff is well worth it. Check below to make sure you'll have all the tools needed.

☐ I understand the power of affirmation in changing self-limiting attitudes.

☐ I wrote my own affirmations to keep me on track to meet my goals.

☐ I recognize the characteristics and attitudes of excellence.

☐ I realize that aggressive action may be necessary to achieve some goals.

☐ I clarified the concept of the work ethic and can recognize it in others as well as in myself.

☐ I strategized ways to improve work habits to ensure job security and promotion.

☐ I recognize the attitudes most in demand for workers—now and in the future.

☐ I developed an action plan to change any self-limiting attitudes.

☐ I identified the attitudes and skills needed to compete in this ever-changing world of the 21st century.

☐ I recognize the dignity in all work.

Learning without thought is labor lost.
—Confucius

You must either modify your dreams or magnify your skills.

— Jim Rohn

CHAPTER ELEVEN
Your Skills Inventory
The precursor to your Education Plan

Section Three:
HOW DO I GET IT?

Rafael's story

Rafael was an ambitious young man. Born in Mexico, he and his family swam across the Rio Grande River to come to America to make a better life for themselves. He knew from an early age he wanted to be a corporate attorney.

To be able to follow his dream, all he required were resources, commonly known as time, money, and energy. Energy he had a lot of, but time and money were in short supply. He knew he needed to complete his formal education in the shortest time possible so he could help support his aging parents. As for money, his family could not help and the schools he needed to attend were very expensive.

So he worked hard. Graduating from high school at the top of his class, he earned a scholarship to a prestigious university. Upon completion of his undergraduate degree, he applied for and was accepted to a top law school. And while he did get some financial help, he discovered that financial aid for graduate school was a scarce commodity, so he was forced to start taking loans — very big loans.

You can imagine Rafael's dismay when a review of his Skills Inventory at the end of his first year of law school highlighted the fact that his current course of study wouldn't provide all of the skills needed to do the work he wanted to do. He got to work researching possible solutions and discovered an option for combining his law courses with those in the MBA track. If he could make that work, he could be confident he'd have what was required to get the job of his dreams.

Another year of school? How could he afford the time and the money? After carefully reviewing the skills he needed, the question became, "How could he afford not to?" Hunkering down and upgrading his educational plans, Rafael simultaneously registered in the university's MBA program along with his law school. The extra year and money was necessary, and ultimately worth it.

... the individual worker is going to become more and more responsible for managing his or her own career, risks, and economic security.

—Thomas Friedman, Pulitzer Prize-winning author,
The World is Flat: A Brief History of the Twenty-first Century

Today, not only do you need the right attitude, but to stay competitive in the job market you also need the right skills. The best way to do this is to be prepared and to then continue to learn throughout your life. By keeping your professional skills current and adding new ones whenever you have the opportunity, you'll develop a resume that will provide economic resiliency in these constantly changing times.

The more education and experience you get, the more your list of skills will grow. Think about the classes you've taken, the on-the-job learning opportunities you've had. What about the books you've read and the projects you've tackled? Look for any opportunity to acquire new skills. Then keep your skills inventory current by adding new ones whenever you have the chance.

Your Skills Inventory Chart

One of the most important documents you'll need to stay competitive in the workforce is an up-to-date Skills Inventory chart. This is simply a list of the skills you have and those you need to acquire for your chosen career(s). It is the research document you'll use to develop a Skills-Based Education Plan that is focused, efficient, and effective.

During your years in college or post-secondary training, you'll refer to your Skills Inventory to determine:

- Your major

- What courses to take so you'll be prepared for your chosen career

- Which internships, apprenticeships, and/or entry-level jobs will help you gain the skills you require for your chosen career path

- What experiences outside the classroom will round out the skills you require

Once you enter the workforce full time, using your **Skills Inventory** as a checklist of the skills you need to master will keep you competitive for the job market. Then as companies downsize, career duties change, industries become obsolete due to technology, and jobs move off shore, you can re-assess your plans and quickly change direction or careers.

You'll want to keep your **Skills Inventory** updated at all times. This is a dynamic document that should continue to grow over your lifetime. Remember that your resume is what prospective employers look at first when determining if you are a candidate worth interviewing, so be diligent about adding any new skills you've mastered.

How to Create
Your Skills Inventory Chart

A systematic analysis of your skills should precede any education planning or job search. The simplest way to be prepared is by creating a dynamic skills inventory that you keep current on the hard drive of your computer.*

> **Step One** — Throughout this process of developing your **10-year Plan**, you've identified skills you currently have along with additional skills you want to learn. Using a spreadsheet program, start by adding your list of skills from pages 44–48, 132, and 150–155 in the left-hand column. Divide them into two groups with the list of *skills you have* at the top and the list *of skills you want to learn* at the bottom portion.

Remember, skills can be attained through volunteer work, hobbies, and other life experiences as easily as through paid work and formal education. For instance, what does playing video games have to do with work? Well, you practice hand-eye coordination, you reason, and you make quick decisions. With some games you use strategic thinking and must remember sequences. Those abilities can be related to a variety of careers.

> **Step Two** — Go back to your **Skills Inventory** chart and add the skills you've learned from your hobbies, volunteer and life experiences, as well as your formal training and education.

*If you are using My10yearPlan.com®, the computer program does this for you in **My Skills Inventory.**

Adding the Skills of Your Chosen Career

Step Three — To complete your **Skills Inventory**, it is important to add the skills required for your chosen career. Turn back to page 177 and review the choice you made on the **Decision-making Rubric**. Is this still your career choice? If not, work through this decision-making process again to determine the career that matches your personality, goals, and plans.

Once you have a **Career Interest Survey** (chapter six) completed for your chosen career, review your research to question number 11. These are the skills required for this career and must be added to your **Skills Inventory** chart either as *skills you have,* or *skills you want to learn.*

Upgrade Your Skills Inventory List using O*NET

If you haven't already done so, visit the United States Department of Labor's O*NET website.* This is a comprehensive yet easy way to identify the skills you need for your chosen career. With this information you can feel confident that you are on the right track as you develop your Skills-Based Education Plan.

> **Directions:** Once you locate the O*NET** information on your chosen career, you'll find a detailed list of skills required to be proficient on the job. Add them to your Skills Inventory chart.

Rafael's Skills Inventory *abbreviated*

THE SKILLS I HAVE
Legal research
Writing predictive legal memos
Reviewing accounting statements
Projecting cash flows
Drafting documents
THE SKILLS I WANT TO LEARN
Preparing court motions
Drafting legal opinions
Writing publishable legal articles
Negotiation

* If you do not have access to the Internet, you can find the same career specific information in the Department of Labor's publication, *The Occupational Outlook Handbook,* found at the reference desk of most libraries and career centers.

**At the time of this printing found at http://www.onetonline.org

Keywords: most important job skills, most important skills for [career]

The Skills of Your Chosen Career

Below, list the skills for your chosen career outlined on the O*NET website or in the *Occupational Outlook Handbook.* First list those you have mastered under *The Skills I Have.* Then list those you still need to learn under that heading.

My chosen career _____

My Skills Inventory

THE SKILLS I HAVE

THE SKILLS I WANT TO LEARN

Transferable Skills are common to a number of jobs and can be adapted to a particular employer or job's needs. They are skills that can transfer from one career to another without much training. For instance, a teacher can change careers and use the skill of instructing to become a corporate trainer. After they retire, they can use this transferable skill for training their staff in the small restaurant they open.

Job Content Skills are related to *job-specific* tools and tasks. They are usually acquired with specialized or on-the-job training, and are a subset of the more general transferable skills.

Self-management Skills are skills used to describe a good worker, someone with a strong work ethic. Employers look for individuals who have these skills and traits. For examples, review the skills and traits found throughout chapter 10.

You can continue adding to your chart by reviewing the list of general transferable skills below. Note the explanation of each skill as provided by the Department of Labor on its O*NET* website.

O*NET Skills Definitions

Basic Skills	
Developed capacities that facilitate learning or the more rapid acquisition of knowledge	
Skill	**Skill Description**
Active Learning	Understanding the implications of new information for both current and future problem-solving and decision-making.
Active Listening	Giving full attention to what other people are saying, taking time to understand the points being made, asking questions as appropriate, and not interrupting at inappropriate times.
Critical Thinking	Using logic and reasoning to identify the strengths and weaknesses of alternative solutions, conclusions, or approaches to problems.
Learning Strategies	Selecting and using training/instructional methods and procedures appropriate for the situation when learning or teaching new things.
Mathematics	Using mathematics to solve problems.
Monitoring	Assessing performance of yourself, other individuals, or organizations to make improvements or take corrective action.
Reading Comprehension	Understanding written sentences and paragraphs in work-related documents.
Science	Using scientific rules and methods to solve problems.
Speaking	Talking to others to convey information effectively.
Writing	Communicating effectively in writing as appropriate for the needs of the audience.

Social Skills	
Developed capacities used to work with people to achieve goals	
Skill	**Skill Description**
Coordination	Adjusting actions in relation to others' actions.
Instructing	Teaching others how to do something.
Negotiation	Bringing others together and trying to reconcile differences.
Persuasion	Persuading others to change their minds or behavior.
Service Orientation	Actively looking for ways to help people.
Social Perceptiveness	Being aware of others' reactions and understanding why they react as they do.

Complex Problem Solving Skills	
Developed capacities used to solve novel, ill-defined problems in complex, real-world settings	
Skill	**Skill Description**
Complex Problem Solving	Identifying complex problems and reviewing related information to develop and evaluate options and implement solutions.

Technical Skills

Developed capacities used to design, set up, operate, and correct malfunctions involving application of machines or technological systems

Skill	Skill Description
Equipment Maintenance	Performing routine maintenance on equipment and determining when and what kind of maintenance is needed.
Equipment Selection	Determining the kind of tools and equipment needed to do a job.
Installation	Installing equipment, machines, wiring, or programs to meet specifications.
Operation Monitoring	Watching gauges, dials, or other indicators to make sure a machine is working properly.
Operation and Control	Controlling operations of equipment or systems.
Operations Analysis	Analyzing needs and product requirements to create a design.
Programming	Writing computer programs for various purposes.
Quality Control Analysis	Conducting tests and inspections of products, services, or processes to evaluate quality or performance.
Repairing	Repairing machines or systems using the needed tools.
Technology Design	Generating or adapting equipment and technology to serve user needs.
Troubleshooting	Determining causes of operating errors and deciding what to do about it.

Systems Skills

Developed capacities used to understand, monitor, and improve socio-technical systems

Skill	Skill Description
Judgment and Decision Making	Considering the relative costs and benefits of potential actions to choose the most appropriate one.
Systems Analysis	Determining how a system should work and how changes in conditions, operations, and the environment will affect outcomes.
Systems Evaluation	Identifying measures or indicators of system performance and the actions needed to improve or correct performance, relative to the goals of the system.

Resource Management Skills

Developed capacities used to allocate resources efficiently

Skill	Skill Description
Management of Financial Resources	Determining how money will be spent to get the work done, and accounting for these expenditures.
Management of Material Resources	Obtaining and seeing to the appropriate use of equipment, facilities, and materials needed to do certain work.
Management of Personnel Resources	Motivating, developing, and directing people as they work, identifying the best people for the job.
Time Management	Managing one's own time and the time of others.

Desktop Computer Skills

Using a computer for file management and input, manipulation, and effective communication of information

Skill	Skill Description
Navigation	Using scroll bars, a mouse, keyboard shortcuts, and dialog boxes to work within the computer's operating system. Being able to access and switch between applications and files of interest.
Internet	Navigating the Internet to find information, including the ability to use and configure standard browsers; use browser tabs, searches, extensions/addons, and transfer protocols; and send and categorize electronic mail (e-mail).
Word Processing	Using a computer application to type text; insert pictures, graphs, and tables; format, edit, print, save, and retrieve word processing documents.
Spreadsheets	Using a computer application to enter, manipulate, and format text and numerical data; insert, delete, and manipulate cells, rows, and columns; use formulas for computations; and create and save worksheets, charts, and graphs.
Presentations	Using a computer application to create, manipulate, edit, and show virtual slide presentations.
Databases	Using a computer application to manage large amounts of information, including creating and editing simple databases, inputting data, retrieving specific records, and creating reports to communicate the information.
Graphics	Working with pictures in graphics programs or other applications, including creating simple graphics, manipulating the appearance, and inserting graphics into other programs.

*At the time of printing, this information was available at http://www.onetonline.org/skills.

International Perspective

When I was growing up, my parents used to say to me, "Tom, finish your dinner. People in China and India are starving." Today I tell my girls, "Finish your homework. People in China and India are starving for your jobs."

—Thomas Friedman, Pulitzer Prize-winning author
The World is Flat: A Brief History of the Twenty-first Century

Until the last decade, competition for jobs was among individuals who lived within commuting distance of the places they worked. Most people showed up to work each morning in a specific location. Now competitors for the same jobs hail from cities around the world.

Why? Because of technological advances, more and more jobs can be done anywhere. A radiologist in Australia can read a CT scan from Kansas. A graphic artist in Argentina can work for a publisher in Utah. A web hosting service in New Zealand can manage a website for a California-based firm.

A person no longer needs to move to another country to provide products and services for that nation. Your customers, clients, or boss could be anywhere, in any country. Working via phone and the Internet is a viable option for many across the globe.

You'll want to maintain an international perspective by being cognizant of what is happening in the rest of the world, especially as it relates to the economy and job security. Read industry journals and follow news programming on the radio, television, and online. Understanding how international trade and job markets relates to our free enterprise system is crucial.

What skills do you need to be able to compete for jobs in different countries? Fluency in a foreign language is an obvious one. Can you think of other skills you need? Write them here and decide if you want to add them to your **Skills Inventory**.

Skills Needed to Compete in the Global Economy

THE SKILLS I HAVE

THE SKILLS I WANT TO LEARN

KEYWORDS: skills to compete globally

Embracing Technology

On your **Skills Inventory** chart, keep a running inventory of the technology you've mastered and what you want to learn.   You'll want to stay current on new formats and programs, even if you have to learn them on your own time.   If you still struggle with the notion of technology as a whole, turn to page 231 and develop affirmations that will help you change your attitude about this critical area of job performance.

Technology Skills Survey

	Mastered	Some experience	I want to learn	No experience
Typing Speed (at least 50 wpm)	○	○	○	○
Web Navigation	○	○	○	○
Web Browsing Shortcuts	○	○	○	○
E-Mail Management	○	○	○	○
Word Processing	○	○	○	○
Spreadsheets	○	○	○	○
Database Management	○	○	○	○
Slideshow Presentation	○	○	○	○
Graphics Design	○	○	○	○
Digital Cameras	○	○	○	○
File Management	○	○	○	○
Operating Systems Structure	○	○	○	○
Commands & Shortcuts	○	○	○	○
Downloading & Installing Software	○	○	○	○
Videoconferencing	○	○	○	○
External & Flash Drives	○	○	○	○
Scanning, Faxing, Copying	○	○	○	○
Mobile Operating Systems	○	○	○	○
Telephone Conferencing	○	○	○	○
Other:_____	○	○	○	○
_____	○	○	○	○
_____	○	○	○	○

Flexiblity

The ability to adapt is one of the most important traits for success in the twenty-first century. Besides having a flexible attitude, you need some flexibility in your plans so you can be proactive about identifying the need for and adapting to change. Successfully entering the workforce or changing jobs during challenging economic times may require you to recognize opportunities across the spectrum of career options.

Even though you have your heart set on one specific career, you'll want to be vigilant in reviewing and thinking critically about that job's future. The rate of change the global marketplace has experienced over the last decade dictates that you stay on top of this important career-planning step.

Start by conducting an annual audit of the health of your chosen industry and specific job title. For example, is this a job that is growing in the number of positions available, or is technology or global competition making it obsolete? You'll find the most current information available online through United States Department of Labor websites. Check out the *Occupational Outlook Handbook* online. There is a special section that provides an overview of the expected growth for all the major industries.

As they say, "Timing is everything." If you see changes coming because of societal, economic, or technological shifts, such as airlines encouraging customers to book online rather than use a travel agent, or colleges shifting to distance learning rather than classroom instruction, start planning a career move before you get your pink slip.

The world will just keep changing around us. You may sometimes feel helpless in the face of those changes, but you don't have to. What can you do?

Keywords: flexibility job search, future trends [career]

Have a Back-up Plan

Speaking of timing…when Rafael finally completed his formal education, he graduated right into the middle of a major recession. Corporate law firms large and small were laying off staff, rather than hiring.

Undeterred, he put his back-up plan into action. Accepting a clerkship with a federal judge, he continued to add skills to his already impressive list. After all, his long-range plan, following an illustrious career as a litigator, was to sit on the bench as a judge. Recessions end eventually, he reasoned, and by that time he'd have an even more impressive resume.

Identifying and planning for back-up careers is an important part of any career development plan. Economic variables aside, you may still be unable to find work in your chosen field for a variety of reasons, some of which are:

The most successful people are those who are good at Plan B.

—James Yorke

- You discover the competition for this career is so great you have a low probability of getting a job.

- You misjudged the opportunity, and, therefore, getting a job in your chosen field is difficult.

- You find out that you are not qualified to compete for a position in this career.

- Technology has made this career redundant.

- The location of employment opportunities has changed and you don't want to relocate.

- With your skill set or level of education, the path for promotion is not open to you.

- Once working in this field, you find this is not the career you anticipated.

You'll want to identify at least two or three careers as a back-up to your first choice. Start by reviewing all of your **Career Interest Surveys** completed to date, along with the Career Backup Plan in the form of a career ladder on page 227. Then, if you see changes coming within the industry or with that specific career, you can prepare yourself with the necessary skills to shift your career plans.

Transferable Skills

Simply put, transferable skills are those versatile skills that you can apply and use in a variety of careers. You'll want to determine the skills that are transferable between careers in the event you need to explore jobs with a more positive outlook.

While specialized, career-specific skills help you build your career, it is the transferable skills that help guarantee your resiliency in the job market over the long haul. They are the skills that employers across industries look for, so it is essential that you are able to identify them, develop them, add to them and explain them when interviewed.

Transferable skills ensure your marketability in a time of high-employment turnover. This competitive edge helps ease your transition into a new career. Even if you think your current skills are too specialized to qualify you for a career with more promise, it is likely you have a set of valuable skills that are transferable to other careers.

For instance, keyboarding/typing is required in almost every job. Therefore, you'll want to be able to type at least 50 words per minute. Because most jobs require teamwork at one level or another, team building and collaboration skills are important to learn.

By expanding your **Skills Inventory** chart to include your back-up plan, you can easily identify those skills that are transferable between the jobs and industries that most appeal to you.

Identifying Transferable Skills using Your Skills Inventory Chart

- Use your **Skills Inventory** spreadsheet started on page 253. Add three or four columns to the right of your skills list.* Across the top row, list your chosen career along with your back-up careers, adding one in each column.

- Reviewing your **Career Interest Surveys** from chapter six, add all the skills required for your back-up careers. If you don't already have the skill, add it as a skill you'd like to learn.

- Now go back. Under each career title, check the skills required in that specific career.

You'll discover which skills transfer between these different careers by the number of checkmarks in each row. As you develop your education and training plan, you'll want to give the acquisition of these transferable skills priority.

*If you are using My10yearPlan.com®, the computer program does this for you in **My Skills Inventory.**

Keywords: top transferable skills, identify transferable skills

Rafael's Skills Inventory and Back-up Plan

Skills Inventory	Career Back-up Plan and Transferable Skills		
	Chosen Career	Back-up Career #1	Back-up Career #2
	Corporate Attorney with Law Firm	Clerk for Federal Judge	In-house Counsel for Large Corporation
Skills I Have			
Document drafting	X	X	X
Legal research	X	X	X
Cash flow projection	X		
Predictive legal memos	X	X	X
Argumentative legal memos	X	X	
Accounting statement review	X		X
Specialized practice	X	X	
Decision editing and review		X	
Generalized practice of law		X	X
Skills I Want to Learn			
Negotiation	X		X
Drafting legal opinions		X	
Management of large groups			X
IPO preparation	X		
Litigation advocacy		X	
Company-wide decision making	X		X
Private equity due diligence	X		
Preparing articles for publication	X	X	
Accounting statement certification	X		X

Skill Development and Your Education Plan

Employers look for candidates with the skills to match the jobs they are filling. Therefore, the more skills you have for the industry of interest, the more employable you are. As you develop your **Skills-Based Education Plan**, your key goal should be the acquisition of the skills that match your career focus. Once you've identified the skills you need for both your chosen career and your back-up careers, you'll want to get the training and education needed so you can add those to the list of the skills you have.

Start by prioritizing the skills you need to learn. Higher priority should be given to those that are transferable to give yourself the most flexibility in the job market. Use your **Skills Inventory** chart as your dynamic checklist.

Keep your list of skills you need in your wallet, on your mobile phone, or on your electronic tablet. That constant reminder will help keep you alert to every opportunity that will increase your skill mastery.

In addition, you'll want to be sure to:

- Share your **Skills Inventory** with your college advisors and counselors when choosing your major and planning your classes. Choose classes that will help you acquire the skills you've identified.

- Search for online learning opportunities. If your college doesn't have a course that provides some of the skills you need, you can supplement your learning through various online venues. Visit the websites of online universities, technical colleges, industry associations, and online tutorials to identify opportunities.

- Visit video sharing websites such as YouTube. Learn to use their search functions and you'll be amazed at the variety of how-to videos experts from around the world share.

- Read. Books and their electronic counterparts are still one of the best ways to efficiently study a subject or skill. Why? Because books are ordered in a natural learning sequence, and authors are chosen because they are some of the top experts in their fields. Why not learn directly from the masters?

- Seek out internships that offer you the opportunity to increase the skills you need.

- When supplementing your income while in school, choose entry-level jobs within the industry of your chosen careers. If your employer is interested in mentoring and developing personnel, share your **Skills Inventory** chart with them. You never know when you may find a mentor or a stepping-stone to a full-time career.

ARMED WITH THE LIST OF SKILLS YOU WANT TO ACQUIRE, THE GUESSWORK WILL BE TAKEN OUT OF THE DEVELOPMENT OF YOUR SKILLS-BASED EDUCATION PLAN, BOTH NOW AND IN THE FUTURE. CONSIDER IT YOUR ROAD MAP TO A PRODUCTIVE, SELF-SUFFICIENT LIFE.

Begin Drafting Your Education Plan

It's time to add another column to your **Skills Inventory** chart* to the right of the first column. Use the "insert column" command if you are working with an electronic spreadsheet.*

In the far left column enter the list of the skills you want to learn. Title the new column "My Plan for Learning." In the column next to each skill, note how you plan to learn that skill. In other words, where or how are you going to get the training or information you need? (Review the suggestions on page 264.) This is the foundation of your **Skills-Based Education Plan**.

My Chosen Career

Skills I Want to Learn	My Plan for Learning	

chart continued →

*If you are using My10yearPlan.com®, the program provides this dynamic rubric which you can link to from **My Skills Inventory**.

CHAPTER 11 CHECKPOINTS
Your Skills Inventory
The precursor for your Education Plan

By now, you've recognized that it's your skills and your ability to articulate them that will open doors for you. You've recorded the skills you currently have and those you need for your chosen career in a **Skills Inventory**. Make sure you haven't missed anything using the checklist below.

☐ I realize that I must continually build skills throughout my life to remain competitive in my field.

☐ I've created a **Skills Inventory** that I will update regularly and share with my college advisors, potential employers, career counselors, and peers.

☐ I've identified the skills I've gained from work and formal education in addition to those I've gained from my volunteer work, hobbies, and other experiences.

☐ I've figured out which skills I'll need for my chosen career, including those I already have and those I need to learn.

☐ I know that, due to the interconnected nature of the 21st-century world, I'll likely need to cultivate additional skills to be competitive in the global economy and I'll need to stay current on international events.

☐ I've taken stock of my technology-related skills and added these to my **Skills Inventory**.

☐ I'm prepared to be flexible in the face of constant change.

☐ I've decided on two or three back-up careers just in case I have trouble getting a job in my first-choice career or I decide that career is not for me.

☐ I understand that developing transferable skills will be even more important than developing career-related skills since it is likely that I will eventually change jobs or industries.

☐ I've also discovered how many skills are transferable between jobs.

☐ I've started to draft a **Skills-Based Education Plan** for learning the skills I've determined I'll need to acquire.

*Learning is not a product of schooling
but the lifelong attempt to acquire it.*

—Albert Einstein

*Live as if you were to die tomorrow.
Learn as if you were to live forever.*

—Mahatma Gandhi

Study Skills for the Life-long Learner

Developing Your Learning Plans

*Learning is not attained by chance,
it must be sought for with ardor
and diligence.*

—Abigail Adams

Section Three:

HOW DO I GET IT?

We've already discussed the fact that change is one of the only constants in our global, 21st century landscape, a fact that makes the ability to adapt to change critical to your success—not only in the workforce but also in life. However, adapting to change requires more than just a willingness to change. It also requires that you assess what information or knowledge is needed to implement the change and then go about acquiring it.

For instance, many bemoan the speed at which technology changes. Just about the time you learn all of the ins and outs of the latest gadget, along come new products. Making a switch requires more than just the money to purchase a new piece of equipment. It also requires that you build your capacity to effectively use the equipment by teaching yourself about its operation. This takes time, flexibility, and the attitude that you can do it, but it also takes someone directing your learning. And that someone needs to be YOU!

Becoming a self-directed learner is what will empower you to effectively assess and manage your need to acquire new information.

Learning Plans

You'll want to develop your own formal or informal **Learning Plan** for **each** new topic you want to gain knowledge of or skill you want to acquire. By becoming adept at developing your own learning plans, you will master a process for dealing with the life and career changes that are sure to come your way. This will help you develop or refine the kinds of attitudes, dispositions, and skills necessary for becoming a lifelong learner.

Why is this important?

Because there are daily learning challenges at every level of every industry. Being able to anticipate change—or at least look at a change critically and analyze it objectively—can help you position yourself in a way that allows you to navigate the change successfully. Then, when a new policy comes down from the front office, you'll be equipped not just to read it, but synthesize the information, analyze how it will impact your position, and plot a course for adapting to that change—or understand the consequences of not adapting. Most often, this will mean learning something new, possibly on your own and with little input from others.

Self-directed learning strategies in formal educational settings are becoming more important every day as well. As more and more colleges are using online learning to augment or even supplant traditional classroom-based courses, the responsibility for learning falls more squarely on the shoulders of the student. Left more and more on their own, students must embrace the processes outlined as a matter of course in any **Learning Plan**.

In today's knowledge-based economy, what you earn depends on what you learn.

—Bill Clinton

Your Learning Goal

Rather than learning in the abstract, it is always better to learn by applying what you are studying to a project or real world situation.

Why not jump right in and choose a topic or skill that is among your list of *skills to learn* on your Skills Inventory chart started in chapter 11? Throughout this chapter you will develop a **Learning Plan** for that specific skill.

Begin with the end in mind. What do you want or need to learn? Choose something that is going to be a challenge. For instance:

- The course you've put off taking or are struggling with now.
- A technology skill you've resisted learning.
- The language of the country you'd like to visit — or even live in.
- The job-specific task that will earn you a promotion.
- The skill that will propel you to your next career.

Write your learning goal here: _____

_____

What is the Difference Between a **Skills-Based Education Plan** and a **Learning Plan?**

You might be asking yourself, what is the difference between a **Learning Plan** and a **Skills-Based Education Plan**? A **Learning Plan** outlines your strategy for the acquisition of a specific skill or knowledge about a certain topic. **Learning Plans** are usually short term.

A **Skills-Based Education Plan** is the plan for the development of the composite skills you need to meet your ultimate career and life goals. Therefore, a **Skills-Based Education Plan** (the overview) might have a number of different **Learning Plans** (the detail) aligned with it. Think of your various **Learning Plans** as a subset of your **Skills-Based Education Plan**.

A **Skills-Based Education Plan** is long term and may take a number of years to complete. For the lifelong learner, a **Skills-Based Education Plan** is never-ending. As new opportunities or challenges present themselves, your plan for acquiring the necessary skills continues. You'll focus on the development of your **Skills-Based Education Plan** as you build your **10-year Plan** in chapter 15.

Joanie's Story

Joanie wasn't interested in technology. She barely knew how to turn on a computer. That is, until the day the shoe repair shop called with sad news about her beloved slippers — they were D.O.A and not able to be patched again. She had purchased them many years before and, try as she might, she lamented to a friend, could no longer find this brand made by an overseas company.

"Let's boot up my laptop," her friend said. "If those slippers still exist, I can find them, no matter where they are made." Hope is a great motivator. Within 15 minutes of her friend starting the online search, Joanie was giving advice — "Try this, try that," she urged. Within 30 minutes, she had taken over the mouse to control the search herself.

Without knowing it, she had not only learned how to surf the Internet, but she had also picked up some advanced search techniques modeled by her friend. Finally, her efforts resulted in success. After an hour of browsing, Joanie located a merchant in a small village in England who had exactly what she wanted. Not only was it the right style, but color and size as well. A new online shopper was born.

What Is Your Motivation?

Another aspect of self-regulated learning is the *motivation to learn*. Your motivation may be intrinsic (internal) because it is "driven by an interest, purpose, or enjoyment in the task itself." Or, your motivation might be extrinsic (external) because it comes from pressures outside of yourself. For instance, competition might be part of what currently motivates you. Or, perhaps you're motivated to learn because of external rewards you hope to gain, like good grades, money, or professional recognition.

Your motivation can change. You might start learning something for extrinsic reasons, but you may also discover an interest in the subject that makes the motivation more intrinsic.

That's a key goal of the material you are about to encounter: self-discovery. Being aware of your motivation, and thinking critically and objectively in the different learning situations you encounter, will allow you to take ownership of the learning process.

It is helpful to be able to identify and articulate the benefit of learning something new.

Keeping in mind the learning goal you identified on page 269, what is the benefit of expending the energy to learn this new skill?

_____

_____

_____

Keywords: find motivational goal

Vision + Energy = Success

When the first edition of this book was written over twenty years ago, it was an article in a large national publication that prompted the articulation of one of its guiding principles — Vision + Energy = Success. The article addressed the question: "Why are young people in Asian countries better students than those in the United States?"

The researcher found that Chinese children were not necessarily smarter. Rather, the Chinese culture espoused long-range thinking and valued preparing for the future (vision). Therefore, they understood the value of education. These children were also taught that success did not relate to any natural intelligence, talent, or gift but only to **how hard they worked** (energy).

Today, researchers in the United States tell us that one of the main stumbling blocks for American students is the fact that too many believe that they did not inherit the "academic gene." In other words, they don't believe they have what it takes to excel in an academic setting. While there are a variety of intelligences we can all draw on, everyone can learn. With the right study skills and the determination to work as hard as is needed, everyone can graduate or get the training needed to follow their dream.

If you are one of those who feel college, technical school, or learning in general is simply not in the cards for you, it's time to reframe your thinking and retool your mindset. In chapter 10, you learned the process for writing affirmations. Below write affirmations as they relate to your ability to learn new material regarding a particularly challenging topic or course you have on the horizon.

Affirmations for the Self-directed Learner

I, _____, will be successful at learning _____ because I will use proven study skills and strategies.

I, _____, will be successful at learning   because I will work as long and as hard as it takes.

I, _____, will be successful at learning _____ because I can adapt my learning strategies to match my personality and propensities.

I, _____, will be successful at learning _____ because I know my life will be better for it.

I, _____, will be successful at learning _____ because

_____ .

Remember a degree or special certification can be the ticket to a self-sufficient, secure life.

Study Skills
for the Self-directed Learner

Study skills? Didn't you learn those in grade school or high school? Yes, perhaps, but the skills needed to navigate the levels and speed of learning mandated in today's workforce and college settings require a more focused effort. In addition, if you are going to be responsible for managing your own career, it is essential you become a self-directed learner.

The development of good study skills increases your ability to stay on top of new information and develop expertise.

There are multitudes of books and websites devoted to providing ideas and information on how to develop the best study skills. So that readers can experiment and discover the techniques that work best for them, they offer every conceivable strategy and idea related to learning something new. Unfortunately for most people, this can be overwhelming. For too many students the task of trying to understand everything there is to know about study skills defeats them long before they can get started learning.

To make this process manageable for you, begin memorizing these four easy-to-remember steps, known as the four R's.

1. Research
2. Read
3. Reflect
4. Recall

The order is important as you'll discover.

Customizing Your Study Skills

As you develop your **Learning Plans**, you'll want to start with this four-step formula. Once you understand this basic study skill structure, you'll be ready to customize each step with tips that work best for you and feel more comfortable with your learning style. At that point, if you need further assistance you can go online, review the variety of strategies, and then adapt them as your own.

Keywords: study skills, study skills tips, learning styles

Tips for Getting Started

In order to increase your concentration and begin learning, remember these suggestions:

- Take time to organize a **Learning Plan,** which includes breaking larger tasks into smaller ones.

- Avoid cramming. Give yourself plenty of time to follow the four steps of effective learning, taking breaks so you stay fresh and rested.

- Find a comfortable, well-lit setting where you can work uninterrupted and where you have access to all of your equipment (pens, highlighters, Internet connection, calculators, notes, files).

- Bring a positive attitude… "I can learn this if I work hard enough."

Research

Choosing the best vehicle of your learning — the tool or setting that matches your needs — is an important first step. This will take research, but effective answers can be as close as your computer.

The best book on the topic

Books (print or digital) provide opportunities to learn from the top experts on just about any topic. Look up reviews of books online to determine which ones are the best for what you need to know. Just reading a book might not be all you need, particularly if the skill requires hands-on experience. However, starting with the organized overview most books provide, you'll likely have enough knowledge to map your next steps.

The best course: traditional classroom setting or online learning

Course offerings of local colleges, trade schools, and commercial professional development providers can all be found online, along with reviews from satisfied or discouraged consumers. Taking a course, whether it is in a classroom or online, provides the opportunity to interact with an instructor, a valuable part of the learning process.

The best video or video series

Videos can provide a profound learning experience. Let's say you are studying to get into medical school. You can either read about the heart and its functions or you can watch PBS's *The Mysterious Human Heart*. Which do you think would be the more effective learning tool?

Online open-source lectures

A variety of websites have made open-source lectures available on wide-ranging topics. (See page 277 for details.)

Mentor or tutor

A tutor provides one-on-one instruction. For many, this is one of the most efficient and effective ways to learn. Because the teaching is customized to your needs, it is probably one of the most satisfying learning experiences.

Internship or on-the-job training

These opportunities can be wonderful ways to learn. As you accomplish your job duties you are also practicing the skills you require.

Can you think of other ways to learn? _____

_____

...Find the Best Learning Tool or Setting

Every time you identify something that you want or need to learn, remember the first task to tackling that subject and building your **Learning Plan** is to research the best tool or setting that will deliver the knowledge or hands-on skill required. Get in the habit of surveying each one of the following possibilities. To master a skill, your **Learning Plan** will probably include a variety of these opportunities.

Looking at your learning goal on page 269, research the:

Best book: _____
title and author

Best course: _____
title along with location or course provider

Best video: _____
title and production company

Best online open-source lecture: _____
title and URL

Best source for mentoring/tutoring: _____

Best internship or on-the-job training opportunity: _____

Other: _____

Other: _____

Read

Reading: There is recreational reading (usually fiction), and then there is reading to learn something new (usually nonfiction). One of the most important skills you can develop when reading to learn is to assess your own comprehension, retention, and ability to apply the information. Because so much information is presented in print—be it an actual printed text or in digital print—the development of good study habits that focus on reading to comprehend, retain, and apply is important.

Before you begin reading:

✓ Find a quiet place where you can concentrate and won't be disturbed.

✓ Study the table of contents, introduction, or overview to get a sense of the scope of the topic.

✓ Review what you are about to read by previewing the headlines, subheads, notes, and words in bold or italic print.

✓ Write down some questions you hope to answer as you read.

Reflect as you read:

✓ Take notes as you read, either in the margins or on separate pages.

✓ Read one paragraph at a time, stopping to ask yourself what you just learned. If you can't easily recall, go back and read the paragraph again before moving on.

✓ If you encounter a new word or term, stop and look it up so you can grasp the full meaning of the topic.

✓ Read the material more than once, each time pushing yourself to understand and remember more of what you've read.

Recall after you complete your reading:

✓ If you are preparing for an exam or interview, go back and formulate questions that might be asked on the material you've just learned.

✓ Rewrite your notes in a more formal outline, as a study prompt.

✓ Articulate the concepts in your own words, either verbally or in writing.

A capacity and taste for reading gives access to whatever has already been discovered by others.

—Abraham Lincoln

Keywords: read to comprehend

Adaptations for Learning

For some, the physical act of reading is difficult, whether due to poor eyesight, dyslexia, poor reading skills, or a variety of other reasons. If reading is a challenge for you, there are technological adaptations available. It doesn't matter if you are a poor reader or can't read. That is not an excuse for not learning.

Audiobooks: If you can't read, you can listen to someone else read to you. Many people use the time spent in their cars as an opportunity to listen and learn using audiobooks.

Online videos of lectures and demonstrations: If there's a topic or process you want to know more about, there is probably a video that provides an explanation or demonstration. Most of these are readily available online thanks to a growing number of websites such as YouTube, Khan Academy, TED, Discovery Channel, or iTunes, to name a few.

OpenCourseWare is a free and open digital publication of high quality university-level educational materials—often including videos, syllabi, lecture notes, assignments, and exams—organized as courses. For example, MIT (Massachusetts Institute of Technology), one of the United States' most prestigious universities, provides all their courses (over 2,400 of them) on the internet using the OpenCourseWare projects they developed.

In other words, except for access to professors and credit, degrees, or certification, a self-directed learner can access some of the best resources for learning in the world. You can launch your own **Learning Plan** by watching the video of a lecture, studying the lecture notes, completing the assignments, and using the exams to assess your progress. Then remember to add the acquired skills to your Skills Inventory chart.

E-books: Short for electronic book, an e-book can be viewed online or downloaded to a personal computer, special eReader, or handheld device. Most e-books offer hyperlink navigation and keyword searching within the text. As content is digitized, the ability to change text to speech is possible.

Speech recognition and text to speech (TTS) services: Incorporating speech recognition and text to speech (TTS) services can be beneficial to certain types of applications and certain groups of users, such as the visually impaired or individuals who struggle with reading. Speech recognition is the ability of a machine or program to identify spoken words and phrases and convert them to text or a machine-readable format. The speech recognition software "listens" to the user's voice, records and processes the sounds, and converts what is said to text. These applications enable you to talk into your computer or smart phone and have the words you speak dropped into a text message, an email, or an internet search engine. Text to speech services involve having a device "read" written text aloud to the user using a digitized voice.

Even if you are a voracious reader, the above technological learning resources can supplement your Learning Plans and Skills-Based Education Plan. Consider adding these to your learning arsenal and you may astonish yourself with the knowledge you gain.

Here's a learning goal that will save you time in the long run.

Goal: To learn to use speech recognition and TTS software

Time is money. The more time you can save while preparing yourself for the lifestyle and career of your dreams, the sooner you can get on with your life.

Reflect

Padma was always in a hurry. She prided herself on being able to finish a novel in a day, skimming the text for the highlights. She always had another book on her nightstand she wanted to get to, and there was no time to waste.

When Padma went back to college with the goal of becoming a professor of literature, she quickly discovered that her reading strategy didn't serve her well in a learning environment. Nearly failing her first exam, she went online to review study skill strategies for increasing her reading comprehension.

She discovered that reading line by line using 3" x 5" cards forced her to read each word, and that was a start. She also learned to stop at the end of each paragraph and ask herself, what did I just learn? It wasn't long before she no longer needed the cards and automatically paused to reflect on what each paragraph or section taught. Her grades soared, along with her comprehension and knowledge. It's no wonder that 10 years later she was voted the best instructor at her community college.

Taking notes: Along with reading for comprehension, the act of taking notes is important. This process helps embed information in your mind so you retain it and understand it. There are a variety of systems for note taking, such as Cornell notes, graphic organizers, and outlines. Review explanations of each of these online and then choose the one that works best for you.

Take notes when reading, attending lectures, talking to peers and mentors, and watching television or videos. Jot down notes when an idea or question comes to you. Whether you write your notes longhand, tap them into a computer or tablet, or dictate them to be transcribed later for review, taking notes as you learn something new is a lifelong habit you'll want to cultivate.

Re-read: Just as good writing is rewriting, reading to learn is re-reading. Until you can articulate what you've read in your own words, you really haven't learned the material. So if what you are reading or viewing is of critical importance to your future success, count on revisiting it until you can talk about it, lecture on it, and use the information to create new knowledge or products.

Using the keyword search recommendations at the bottom of this page, go online and review the various note-taking options. Which one(s) do you think will work best for you? Describe that strategy here:

_____

_____

Can you think of other tactics you use to help you retain what you study?

_____

_____

Keywords: taking notes, note-taking strategies, Cornell notes

Recall

Recalling what you've learned

Many argue that the availability of information and knowledge online makes memorization obsolete. Unfortunely, there may be times when simply memorizing facts is necessary. As a self-directed learner you don't want to abdicate your brainpower to the computer. You need be able to recall foundational knowledge if you are going to be able to reason and think at the highest levels.

Yet your goal should be the acquisition of knowledge for the long term rather than throw-away information that is quickly forgotten once the test or interview is over. If you clearly understand the material rather than simply memorize it, the information will stay with you so that when you need it, it is easier to recall.

What's the best way to retain knowledge?

Learn by doing

Remember from chapter 6 the saying, "Tell me and I forget, show me and I remember, but involve me and I understand?" Figure out ways to "get involved" and actually use or apply the material you are studying.

- Start discussions about the topic.
- Create a project that requires you to use the information.
- Write or journal about the topic, putting the information in context in your own words.
- Use mnemonics.
- If you are a visual learner, use mind maps, charts, diagrams, drawings, color coding, or whatever works for you.

What are some ways to use and practice the skill you identified as your goal on page 269? Can you think of projects that provide opportunities to apply what you learned?

_____

_____

_____

Learning is an active process.
We learn by doing. Only knowledge
that is used sticks in your mind.

—Dale Carnegie

Demonstrating Your Expertise

Preparing for an exam, interview, or presentation

Once you feel you've learned the new information or skill, you'll have to be able to demonstrate your expertise in a variety of settings. It might be for a test in school, an interview for a job, or a practical, on-the-job application such as a presentation to launch a new project.

The best way to do well on a test, an interview, or presentation is to be prepared. Do your studying or research prior to your exam, interview, or speech. You'll be more relaxed and confident because you'll know your content or skill, and that will reflect in not only your demeanor but also in your results.

You'll find a variety of websites dedicated to tips on taking tests. They go into detail, so whether it's a multiple choice, true/false, essay, oral, or short answer test, you'll find ideas that will help you be successful. Take time to review their ideas and put their suggestions into practice.

As you prepare:

- ✓ Review any notes, reading material, or study guides on the topic and practice articulating the key points in your own words.
- ✓ Ask your instructor or boss to detail what they think is important to know along with tips on what they think will help you perform well.
- ✓ Make a list of questions you might be asked on an exam, by the interviewer, or by your audience. Then be sure you know the answers.
- ✓ Go to review sessions or ask knowledgeable associates to quiz you.
- ✓ Take practice tests if they are available.
- ✓ Ahead of time, assemble the necessary equipment and tools you'll require for your exam, interview, or presentation.
- ✓ Come rested and nourished so you have the necessary energy to perform at your peak.
- ✓ Give yourself time to prepare, thereby avoiding cramming at the last minute.

Overcoming Performance Anxiety

Being put on the spot and asked to demonstrate your expertise on a topic can be stressful. After you do everything you can to prepare, if you still find you are overly anxious about exams, interviews, or presentations, start by revisiting pages 216 to 221 in chapter 9 and use the guided visualization technique to create a plan to overcome this fear. You may also want to seek the assistance of a counselor to help you through this process. Don't let performance anxiety get in your way of following your dreams.

Keywords: test taking strategies, test anxiety, public speaking anxiety

Making Time to Learn

As you just learned, taking the time to prepare for an exam or interview is key to your success. Time is really a component in learning any new skill or concept. Perhaps one of the biggest challenges for all of us is taking—or making—the time to learn something new.

With a well thought-out **Learning Plan**, written using the format of measurable objectives learned in chapter 8, you'll be able to easily break down what might appear to be a formidable task into smaller, more manageable projects.

Time Management Tips

- Make a "to do" list and prioritize your tasks. (See page 301.)
- Start projects early enough so you have plenty of time to complete them.
- Write short-term and long-term learning goals along with quantitative objectives that will form your learning action plan. (See pages 186 and 189.)
- Keep your calendar up to date with your projects and deadlines.
- If in school, plan on at least two hours of studying and preparation for every hour of class.

Failure to prepare is preparing to fail.

—John Wooden

After 25 years as a devoted PC user, Mindy realized it was more benefical to learn the Mac. She wanted to produce online training videos for use in her small business and the Apple computer allowed her to control the process in-house, saving money.

Due to an already full work schedule, Mindy was unable to devote herself to the classroom time of a traditional adult education course, which left her feeling apprehensive about how successful she would be. However, a mentor helped her map out a learning plan, and she set to work, learning one application at time.

After researching her learning options, she chose to take advantage of various training opportunities. She sat through hours of workshops at her local Apple Store, and watched scores of online tutorials, sometimes over and over until she understood the lesson. She also read books on topics of interest and met with tutors who provided personalized support.

Through this process, Mindy discovered something very important about her learning style. She found that if she learned in the abstract, she did not retain the lessons as well as when she used the new skill or information in a project. "Use it or lose it" became her most important study skill tip. Upon realizing this, Mindy rescheduled her short one-to-one tutorial sessions for longer project-based learning sessions where she brought an assignment she was working on.

Before long, she was developing and producing online training videos. Her customers found them valuable and her business grew. Mindy had a goal: Learn to use the Mac so she could stop toting around two heavy laptop computers. The day she retired her PC was the day she celebrated meeting her goal.

Throughout this chapter, you've started building a **Learning Plan** for the goal you identified on page 269. On the following page, either formalize your plan for that goal using the format provided, or identify a new topic you'd like to learn or skill you'd like to acquire, and create an appropriate **Learning Plan**. In the future, when faced with the need to learn something new, use this format and you'll be able to map the most direct path to acquiring your desired skill.

Learning is a treasure that will follow its owner everywhere.
—Chinese Proverb

Your Learning Plan Rubric

Your Learning Goal: _____

What is the benefit of learning this?_____

    Affirmations

        I, _____, will be successful at learning _____ because I will use proven study skills and strategies.

        I, _____, will be successful at learning _____ because I will work as long and as hard as it takes.

        I, _____, will be successful at learning _____ because I can adapt my learning strategies to match my personality and propensities.

        I,_____, will be successful at learning _____ because I know my life will be better for it.

        I, _____, will be successful at learning _____ because

        _____ .

Timeline and Priorities: _____

    Write at least 2 quantitative objectives for each of the 4 Study Skill Steps :

Research the best learning tools:

_____

_____

Read for comprehension:

_____

_____

Reflect to understand:

_____

_____

Recall to demonstrate expertise:

_____

_____

Project-based learning opportunities:_____

_____

CHAPTER 12 CHECKPOINTS
Study Skills for the Life-long Learner
Developing your Learning Plans

You have now discovered the necessity of being a self-directed, life-long learner, and you've experienced a wide variety of resources and techniques for learning new things. Most importantly, you understand that anyone has the ability to learn if they are motivated by a future goal and willing to put in the effort. Before you start working toward achieving the learning goal you set, look over the following checklist to review all the tools presented in this chapter.

☐ I understand that I will need to constantly learn new things to keep up with unceasing changes in technology, the workplace, and lifestyles.

☐ I've begun to explore the wealth of learning opportunities aside from formal education.

☐ I see the benefit in "learning by doing," putting my new knowledge into practice as soon as possible to improve my comprehension.

☐ I've developed my **Learning Plan** for a skill I'll need in my future career.

☐ I've identified my motivation for learning that skill, which will allow me to take ownership of the learning process.

☐ I realize that anyone can learn and that my success in life will be a function of the effort I put in rather than any natural ability.

☐ I've written affirmations to build my confidence in my potential to learn.

☐ So that I can continue to learn new skills throughout my life, I've learned the study skill steps to becoming a self-directed learner: "Research, Read, Reflect, Recall."

☐ I've researched learning tools and settings that make the most sense for my learning goal.

☐ I've improved my reading strategies and determined alternative methods of learning if I struggle with reading.

☐ I've begun reflecting on what I've read and I'm taking notes with the intention of better retention of new information.

☐ I recognize the importance of learning for the long term, since new information will only be useful if I know it well enough to use it.

☐ I'll demonstrate my expertise by recalling what I've learned whether on an exam, in an interview, or in a presentation.

☐ I understand that doing well requires preparation and I've created a plan that will help me eliminate apprehension or anxiety.

☐ I've learned new time management strategies to help me achieve my learning goal.

☐ I understand the importance of creating a **Learning Plan** for each of the skills I need to learn, and realize **Learning Plans** are a subset of my **Skills-Based Education Plan**.

Better do it than wish it done.
—Scottish proverb

*It is better to look ahead and prepare
than to look back and regret.*
—Jackie Joyner-Kersee

CHAPTER THIRTEEN
Making Changes
The inevitable process

*Action may not always bring happiness, but
there is no happiness without action.*
—Benjamin Disraeli

Section Three:
HOW DO I GET IT?

As the date for her college graduation approached, Mandy began to panic. For four years, she'd been confident that her decision to major in business was a good one — she'd always dreamed of working for a big corporation. Now, however, the idea of finding a job seemed overwhelming. Maybe she should go to graduate school or get married instead, she thought.

When Ike accepted his job with the state historical society, the future looked promising. He would be involved with setting up a new museum in a building that was to be beautifully restored. Then, because of budget cuts, the project was cancelled. Ike was transferred to the society's library, where he spent most of his time cataloging bits of information. He was disappointed and bored.

Mary Catherine hadn't considered becoming a police dispatcher until she saw the job listing on a bulletin board, but she thought it might be okay. When she was offered the job, she took it. Before long, though, she knew it wasn't for her.

Roberto and Ellie's dream had always been to have their own bookstore. It took years to save enough money, but they were finally able to open their shop. Things were going quite well until online booksellers entered the marketplace. Then the recession hit, and Roberto and Ellie were forced to close their doors permanently.

When Paul left his job at age 58, everyone thought he was retiring. Paul, however, had watched his own father lose his appetite for life upon his retirement, and he had no intention of following that path. Instead, Paul took part of his savings and set up an employment agency for other older people. Work is something we all need, he thought.

It's been said that, over a lifetime, people change jobs an average of seven times. A good attitude, a little knowledge, and a workable plan can make the process easier but, for many people, change is still unsettling and even frightening. In this chapter, we'll try to make the process more understandable and, we hope, a bit less intimidating. Let's start by seeing what we can learn from the preceding stories.

Like many students about to enter the work world, Mandy is anxious. The change from school to work is a major life transition. Anxiety about change can lead to self-doubt and, perhaps, the down scaling of goals for the future. To feel fear is perfectly normal, but giving in to it is not the best way to plan a life. If you find yourself suddenly making decisions that go against everything you thought you wanted, stop and ask yourself what's going on. It's a good idea to talk with a friend, mentor, or counselor to get a more objective viewpoint. Keep in mind that you're not the only person who's going through these kinds of career dilemmas.

Ike had no interest in changing until his circumstances did. He must now decide to stay with his present employer or look for a new job. Ike's circumstance may seem unusual to you, but changes in a job or work environment affect almost everyone. Even if your job doesn't change, you may find it difficult to adjust if your company changes ownership, or if you get a new boss, or if your best friend or mentor quits. In cases like these, the best course may be to wait and see what happens. You might find that you can deal with the changes, or that you actually like them. Ike, too, may want to give himself some time. Even if he knows he'll never like his present position, he should consider the likelihood that his project will be refunded and his other job restored. It might be a good idea for him to set a date six months or a year off and make his decision then.

Just making a change won't do Mary Catherine much good. Leaping blindly into another job is likely to result in the same dissatisfaction. Unless she takes some time to determine what she wants and then works out a plan to get it, she is unlikely to choose a job that she finds truly rewarding.

Roberto and Ellie had change forced upon them. They knew going in, however, that their bookstore venture was a risky one. Opening the bookstore was something they both wanted to try, and they were confident that, if things didn't work out, their education, skills, and experience would leave them with other options for the future. The odds of achieving success in certain fields are not great. Small businesses often fail. At least half of all politicians are losers in any given election. Only a fraction of those wishing to be professional athletes, actors, or musicians are successful. This is not to say that you shouldn't pursue your dream, but it's a good idea to have a back-up plan, as well.

Paul embraced change as an opportunity for him to achieve a new and, perhaps, exciting career. He planned well, moved with confidence, and never looked back. Of course, this probably wasn't the first time he made a major change in his life, and we rather suspect that it won't be the last.

If you don't like something change it. If you can't change it, change your attitude.

—Maya Angelou

As the preceding stories illustrate, sometimes you choose to change, and sometimes you have no choice—change is forced upon you. Either way, the success of your venture is likely to depend on your ability to analyze the situation, make a considered plan to change it, and then follow through with persistence.

Before you take any of those steps, however, it's important to gauge your attitude toward change. How do you feel about it? Has your previous experience with change been positive, negative, or neutral? Does your history indicate that you are too quick to change? Too reluctant to go after something you want? Do you approach new challenges and situations with enthusiasm or apprehension? The better you know yourself, the more likely you are to make change successfully.

How Do You Feel About Change?

Each of us reacts to change in our lives in different ways. Review the following situations and check the response that best describes your feelings or reactions.

1. When you were in second or third grade, as you got ready for the first day of a new school year, you felt:
   - ☐ a. enthusiastic.
   - ☐ b. curious.
   - ☐ c. apprehensive.
   - ☐ d. anxious.

2. Think about the most recent time you changed your residence. During the week following your move you:
   - ☐ a. were eager to explore your new neighborhood and enjoyed the process.
   - ☐ b. felt challenged and systematically set about discovering your new locale.
   - ☐ c. were apprehensive but knew with time you would adjust.
   - ☐ d. didn't explore at all and resented the move.

3. As graduation approaches (approached) and you plan (planned) for your career search you feel (felt):
   - ☐ a. excited.
   - ☐ b. optimistic.
   - ☐ c. apprehensive.
   - ☐ d. anxious.

4. Imagine your supervisor has just offered you a position that will require you to take on more responsibility and learn new skills. This comes as a surprise to you. That evening you:
   - ☐ a. celebrate.
   - ☐ b. strategize how to get the skills you need.
   - ☐ c. make a list of questions you need answered before accepting.
   - ☐ d. figure out how to turn the offer down.

5. Imagine you have just received an offer for a job that is exactly the kind of work you want. The job is in another part of the country that has some appeal to you. As you receive this information, your very first thoughts are:
   - ☐ a. This is exciting and could be an adventure.
   - ☐ b. Sounds interesting…
   - ☐ c. I'll have to think whether I want to move.
   - ☐ d. Stop! I don't want to hear anymore. I don't want to move!

Attitude and ...

Your attitude toward and experience with change are important because they help determine how you will make the decisions that affect your life and your happiness.

What can you learn from your responses to the questions on page 289? If your attitude corresponds most often to the responses following the letter "**a**," you are very comfortable with change and welcome new situations. Be aware, though, that you may tend to rush into change before examining the situation carefully and analyzing your chances for success.

If the "**b**" responses most often mirror your feelings, you are comfortable with change, but unlikely to act impulsively.

Did you choose mostly "**c**" responses? You are likely to be more methodical in your approach to change. You need to allow more time for thinking and planning before you will be entirely at ease with your decision.

If a majority of your feelings matched those listed beside the letter "**d**," you are not comfortable with change. Perhaps you've had some bad experiences in the past, or maybe you haven't made enough conscious changes to feel confident that you can survive them.

Remember, though, that change is inevitable. Attempts to avoid it or deny it often lead to disastrous consequences. Before proceeding further, try to analyze your resistance, and then vow to develop an attitude that will make change less traumatic for you. The following information will help you start that process. (You may also want to review the section on anxiety tolerance, pages 216-221.)

The greatest discovery of all time is that a person can change their future by merely changing their attitude.

—Oprah Winfrey

Keywords: accept change

... Experience

What has been your experience with change? On the lines below, in the first column, list as many of the changes you have made as you can. Consider changes in address, different schools you've attended, all the jobs you've held, relationships entered and/or left behind, changes in attitude or personal philosophy, financial gains or setbacks, losses of loved ones you've endured, physical or emotional crises you've overcome, and so on.

Changes I've made	My feelings about change	Success of change

There exists limitless opportunities in every industry. Where there is an open mind, there will always be a frontier.
— Charles F. Kettering

Now consider your attitude toward these changes at the time you made them. Were you enthusiastic or anxious? Curious? Optimistic? Doubtful? Confused? Confident? Enter your feelings in the second column on the chart on the preceding page.

Do you see any relation between your attitude and the degree of success you had in making the change? Analyze each situation and record your recollections in the third column, using a "+" to indicate a positive experience, a "-" to mark those that were negative, and a "*" to indicate mixed experiences.

> Mandy's relative inexperience with change makes the situation uncomfortable for her. However, if she can achieve a good attitude and create an appropriate plan, she may be a real pro by the time she reaches Paul's age. And, each time she makes a decision to change, she'll bring a little more wisdom and a little more confidence to the task.

What about your present attitude to all the changes you've succeeded in making? (You did succeed. The degree of success may vary, but you survived, didn't you?) Review your responses from page 289 and, below, write a statement or two about your present attitude toward change.

_____

_____

_____

_____

To get a better understanding of your comfort level with the process, review these responses when you need to make a decision about change.

Recognizing the Need to Change

In his book *Megatrends,* John Naisbitt stated, "We experience change when there is a confluence of changing values and economic necessity." In other words, if you're bored with school and you can't afford to pay tuition for next semester anyway, you are a candidate for change. Your values have changed (you're no longer interested in pursuing higher education) and so has your economic situation (you're broke). The idea of finding a job may seem like the perfect solution to both your problems.

You may need to make a change even if there's been a shift only in your values or only in your finances. If you've lost your job and you need to support yourself and your family, you obviously don't have a choice: you must change.

Sometimes change may only be partial or temporary. For example, if you're that student who's run out of funds but you don't want to give up your education, you may need to find a part-time job or to leave school until you can make other financial arrangements. Don't make a permanent change based on economic necessity alone, however. Don't give up your dream.

293

Don't assume that values are less important than finances in deciding to make a change, either. Being in the wrong job can be just as painful and cause just as much anxiety as being short of funds. How do you know you're in the wrong job? Here are some possible symptoms:

1. **You're bored.** You find yourself checking the clock too many times during the day. The only thing you look forward to is the weekend.

2. **You're overworked and/or burned out**. Constantly exhausted, you may find you catch more colds than you used to, or you feel older than your years. You can't remember the last time you were in a good mood.

3. **Job pressures are beginning to have physical consequences** like nightmares, headaches, stomach problems, and so on.

4. **You feel you've settled for too little**. Perhaps you took this job when your level of skills or self-confidence was low. Now you're feeling more ambitious and you don't see much room for advancement in your present position.

5. **You feel you've taken on too much.** Your job doesn't give you enough time for your family or your outside interests, and you think you'll be happier in another career, even if it pays less.

6. **The job responsibilities conflict with your personal principles** (for example, you're a strict environmentalist working for a company that makes pesticides).

7. **You feel you're the victim of discrimination or harassment.** (These actions are illegal, of course, and you may want to file charges.) You may simply choose to move on, instead. Staying on in a situation like this is damaging to your self-esteem and not recommended.

Can you add any other symptoms to this list? Deciding what it is you want to change can help you figure out where to go from here.

_____

_____

_____

_____

People change when the pain and anxiety of change
is less than the pain and anxiety of the status quo.

_____

Getting Ready for Change

If you have a choice, it's easier to make a change when you are physically, emotionally, and financially prepared for it.

Change Takes Energy

We don't often realize that change takes a great deal of energy, both physical and emotional. It's important to consider this factor before you make your move (if you have a choice). If you're not in good physical or emotional health, if you've just passed through some personal crisis, or if you're simply exhausted from a history of constant change, you may need a period of recovery before you're ready to move on to new vistas.

Listen to your heart. Consider your physical reactions (a knot in your stomach is a sign to proceed with caution). Evaluate your physical and emotional stamina. Talk with people who know you. In short, get in shape for change.

Likewise, if change is inevitable, pay particular attention to your health. Pamper yourself as much as you can. Eat right, get plenty of rest, and exercise appropriately. Surround yourself with positive people. Guard both your physical and emotional health.

The checklist below will help you evaluate how physically and emotionally fit you are to take on a change right now.

When I think about changing my job or career I feel:
- ☐ a. enthusiastic.
- ☐ b. interested.
- ☐ c. anxious.

My current emotional stability can best be described as:
- ☐ a. strong – I feel confident I can handle the uncertainties of change.
- ☐ b. normal – With support I will eventually adjust to the rigors of change.
- ☐ c. delicate – When I run into a "roadblock" I might collapse or run away.

Currently my physical condition can be described as:
- ☐ a. excellent.
- ☐ b. good.
- ☐ c. poor.

My present feelings of esteem and self-confidence are:
- ☐ a. high — I feel I am in control of my life's plan and my destiny.
- ☐ b. average — I feel confident in most situations and relatively comfortable with my decisions.
- ☐ c. low — I feel somewhat insecure right now, as though I need to "get permission" from others before considering a change.

Sometimes Change Takes Money

Will you need money to make the change you want? If so, is it financially feasible? Evaluate your present financial condition, and determine as closely as you can how much money your desired change will require. Can you do it immediately? If not, think about and list below the steps you will take to earn or save the needed funds.

Desired Change:

_____

_____

What are the financial considerations? How will your financial situation change? Will you have less or more money to support yourself/family? Will this condition be temporary or permanent? If temporary, how long do you think it will last?

_____

_____

_____

_____

Do you need to save money before making the change? Describe your plan below — step by step — using quantitative objectives like the ones found on pages 186 to 190.

_____

_____

_____

_____

_____

_____

_____

_____

Support Makes Change Easier

Making a major life change can be difficult and too important to do alone. There may be demanding times ahead, and you will need encouragement and support to keep on going. Where will you turn for help when you need it?

Can you count on your family or your best friends? If they are supportive of your plans, you're fortunate. You will always have a cheerleader nearby. Unfortunately, the people closest to you may not always be enthusiastic about your determination to make a change — especially if it means they will have to change, too.

List your closest family members and friends below. Include people with whom you have daily contact, or whose opinion is very important to you. After each person's name, write a word that describes his or her attitude toward your considered change. For instance, are they supportive or nonsupportive? Interested or uninterested? Enthusiastic or anxious?

Name	Attitude about your change
_____	_____
_____	_____
_____	_____
_____	_____
_____	_____

If it seems unlikely that these people can give you the support you need, there are other options. Do you know of someone who is going through a similar process? He or she might be more helpful and sympathetic than a close friend who doesn't know what you're experiencing. Support groups have been formed to help members get through all kinds of changes. You can probably find a group to keep up your spirits as you adjust to whatever change you have in mind. Most colleges and technical schools offer career counseling services, or you might consider a community workshop or adult education class.

Professional counselors and therapists are also available, and often well worth the fee they charge. In addition to support, you can count on them for insights, advice, undivided attention, and unprejudiced suggestions.

A lot of people have gone further than they thought they could because someone else thought they could.

— Anonymous

Mentors

And then there are mentors. Most successful people have had them, and most have found their help to be invaluable. You can't go out and hire a mentor, but they are around. The trick is to recognize one when you see him or her. A mentor may be a teacher, a boss, or just a more experienced person who can offer informal advice and support. The best way to attract one is to do a good job and show some promise in the field of the mentor's expertise. If a mentor offers assistance or advice, listen carefully and show your appreciation. You don't necessarily have to take the advice, especially if you don't know the person well. It's up to you to decide if it is wise or right for you.

Finally, be a friend to yourself. Be firm in your resolve that you know what you want, you deserve it, and you are willing to work for it. Don't let anyone diminish your enthusiasm or your self-esteem.

List your support team below.

Family

_____

Friends

_____

Peers in the same situation

_____

Professionals/Counselors/Therapists

_____

Mentors

_____

Keywords: find career mentor

Is Your Job the Real Problem?

Wendell had always wanted to be a lawyer, but when he lost his first case he was devastated. Obviously, he thought, he wasn't fit to hold such a responsible position.

Linelle loved the sales part of her job, but doing the necessary paper work was less than exciting. She wondered if she might be in the wrong line of work.

Every few years, Barrett would change not only her job, but her apartment, her hobbies, her hairdo, and her wardrobe. However, all these changes never seemed to make her happy.

An external change won't solve an internal problem. Until Wendell stops expecting perfection from himself, he's unlikely to find satisfaction in any career. Barrett needs to discover the real source of her unhappiness, perhaps with the help of a counselor.

Just as there are no perfect workers, there are no perfect jobs. If Linelle finds most of her job enjoyable, she should consider keeping it.

Here are a few more workers who may think they need a new job when they really need something else. Recognize anyone?

1. The overly responsible person who takes on extra work, and then feels put upon.

2. The harried worker who can't or won't delegate responsibility to others.

3. The sociable person who resents it when work gets in the way of having a good time.

4. The "caretaker" who's too busy solving other people's problems to complete a job on time.

5. The person who is going through a temporary personal crisis (divorce, illness of a family member, adjusting to a new baby, and so on).

6. The person with major personal problems to address (life-threatening illness, severe emotional problems, chemical dependency, or the like).

7. The individual whose many outside commitments make it impossible to give a job the attention it requires.

Can you think of any others?

_____

_____

If any of these descriptions fit, you may certainly need to make some changes, but changing jobs right now may be unnecessary and perhaps even unwise.

Changing Your Life Often Means Changing Your Priorities

As a full-time homemaker, Merylee took pride in keeping a spotless house and cooking a three-course dinner for her family every night. When she went back to school, however, and got a part-time job to help pay her tuition, trying to maintain her previous standards left her feeling exhausted and resentful of her husband and children, who had never been expected to help before. One night when, for the third time that week, she ordered pizza instead of cooking dinner herself, she felt so guilty she almost decided to abandon her education plans.

Most often, setting new goals means making other changes, as well. As we said back on page 191 (now's a good time to re-read it), new goals often reflect new values, and vice versa. Change is an ongoing process that leads to continual growth.

To keep your daily life in step with your hopes for change, however, it is often necessary to set new priorities as well. If Merylee intends to give her education the attention required for her to succeed at it, for example, she needs to make that her priority. She will probably have to lower her standards for housework and get the rest of the family to pitch in, too.

Setting priorities is not a complicated process. It simply involves deciding which tasks are most important for you to accomplish in light of your current goal. For most people, problems arise not because they don't know what they need to do, but because they don't take the time to accomplish these tasks. They may not be willing to set aside their old priorities, or perhaps they're too busy doing what other people want them to do.

Setting Priorities

It's a good idea to formally set your priorities even if you haven't set a new goal. Identifying what's most important to you right now will help you use your time wisely and keep you on track. If you consciously plan your priorities and then write them down, you are more likely to follow through with your plan.

An easy way to do this is, with your goal (old or new) in mind, list all of the tasks you hope to accomplish in the course of your day. After you've made your list, go back and determine which things you absolutely need to do within a specific time frame.

Mark with an **A** those tasks that are both vital for success and urgent in nature. Do them first.

Put a **B** beside the things that are important to get done, and do those after you've worked through your **A** list.

Put a **C** by the things you'd like to do — but don't really need to — and get to them only if you have the time.

Keep this list current by using a digital spreadsheet program. Then you can easily sort your tasks based on the letter assigned and periodically print it out for your to-do list.

Will the changes you are considering require you to set new priorities? What tasks will you need to put at the head of your list? What activities will you need to give up or devote less time to? Are you willing to commit yourself to these changes?

GOAL: Go back to college to become an Registered Nurse	Priority Ranking
Save enough money to put towards my tuition	A
Apply to nursing school and get accepted	A
Get a job at the local hospital	B
Reduce my lifestyle so it is easier to go back to school.	B
Interview three RNs for a real-world perspective of nursing school	C
Do what I can to make sure my family and friends support my decision	C

List below your goal and the tasks required to make the change you are contemplating.

GOAL:	Priority Ranking

So, What Do You Want?

If you know you want to change jobs or careers, but you're not exactly sure what kind of change you want, the following brainstorming activity might be helpful. Review the following situations and make a list of two or three possible jobs or careers that might interest you in each category. Once you've tried it by yourself, you might like to brainstorm this with a friend or mentor. Come back to this exercise several times over the next few days. Give yourself some time to think.

Situation 1: Staying with your current employer, but changing positions within the company.

_____

_____

Situation 2: Seeking a similar job with a different company.

_____

_____

Situation 3: Seeking a job with a company in a different but similar industry.

_____

_____

Situation 4: Working for yourself in your present field.

_____

_____

Situation 5: Going to work in a completely new field that holds tremendous appeal for you.

_____

_____

Now turn back to pages 156 and 157 to review the techniques of visualization. Imagine yourself holding each of the jobs you listed. What might a typical day in each of those jobs be like? Does any particular situation make you feel energized? What seems to be the best fit for you? Circle the jobs or careers that give you that special feeling.

In general it's likely that:

Situation 1 might appeal to you if you are in a dead-end position and want to move ahead. You might even consider a job that pays less but offers advancement opportunities.

Situation 2 might be a good idea if you want a different corporate culture or office environment, more opportunity for advancement, more interesting assignments or tasks, or more security (if your present job is not secure).

Situation 3 might appeal to you if you want to use current skills and knowledge in a new industry.

Situation 4 might be a good choice if you want the freedom that comes with working for yourself and the challenge of starting a new business.

Situation 5 could be your ideal solution if you feel you're ready to realize the dream you've been harboring for some time now.

Note that each descending situation requires more commitment and is more risky than the situations listed above it. Changing jobs within your present company is less threatening than going to work for a competitor. The greater the change you want to make, the more time, energy, and/or money you are likely to require. A bigger change is also more likely to call for retraining or relocation.

Career Interest Survey

If you are considering a career change, be sure to complete a Career Interest Survey if you haven't already. Don't skip this important step. Making a career choice on a whim goes against all you've learned.

JOB TITLE _____

1. What specific tasks would I perform on this job? (For example, a sales clerk would answer questions, tidy displays, unpack merchandise, ring up sales, make change, and so on.)

   _____

   _____

2. What is the job environment likely to be? Is this compatible with the setting I said I wanted on *page 126?*

   _____

   _____

3. What would be the rewards of working at this job? Are they the same as the ones I listed on *page 129?*

   _____

   _____

4. I would find this job particularly satisfying because: (Review your passions, values, interests, and life goals for guidance.) *See page 27.*

   _____

   _____

5. Is this job compatible with my work behavioral style? If so, in what ways? *Review pages 38–43.*

   _____

   _____

6. How much training or education would I need? Review your options (college, technical school, apprenticeship, work experience, etc.). *See pages 340–341.* What commitment am I willing to make? *Review pages 114–120.*

   _____

   _____

7. Does this job require specific physical attributes or abilities (strength or health requirements, 20/20 vision, and so on)? If so, what are they? Do I meet them?

   _____

   _____

8. What could I expect to earn as a beginner in this field? _____

   What is the average mid-career salary? _____

9. Does this meet my salary requirements? *See pages 93 and 131.*   Yes   No

_____

10. Will there be many job openings when I am ready to go to work? How might societal, economic, and technological changes impact this career? *Online resources will be helpful.*

_____

_____

11. What aptitudes, strengths, and skills does this job call for? Are they transferable to another career if I change my mind or this job title becomes obsolete? *See page 132.*

_____

_____

12. What can I do today to begin preparing for this job?

_____

_____

13. What classes must I take in high school to qualify for this job?

_____

_____

14. Where in this town or state could I find a job in this field?

_____

_____

15. How does this career mesh with my family plans? Is it consistent with my desired lifestyle? *See page 130.* Does it offer opportunities for flexible hours or part-time work? Is the income high enough so I could maintain my family on it alone if necessary? Could I afford the kind of day care I'd like for my children?

_____

_____

_____

16. Are there opportunities for self-employment in this field (business owner, freelance work, consulting, and the like)?

_____

_____

Create a timeline outlining how this career has changed over the last 10 years and predicting how it might change in the next 10 years. *Start with online resources.*

Your Plan for Making a Change

Have you made up your mind? Are you ready to make a change?

Write your goal for the change below:

_____

_____

_____

_____

Now write your plan, taking into consideration any remediation you need to do before beginning the change. Keep in mind that the transition from student to the full-time workforce is a change, and a major one at that. You'll want to conscientiously plan for that eventuality using these prompts.

Ask yourself:

Do you have a positive feeling toward change, or do you need to work on that? If so, how?

Are you physically and emotionally ready for change?

What can you do to get into shape?

What financial planning do you need to do?

Where will you get the support you need?

If you found that you need to make personal changes rather than professional changes, how do you plan to begin?

If it is a career or job change you need, what are your beginning strategies?

Begin to chart your plan below. Try to write each step as an affirmative statement (see pages 230–231) with measurable objectives (see pages 186–190).

_____

_____

_____

_____

_____

_____

_____

_____

_____

_____

_____

_____

_____

_____

_____

_____

_____

_____

_____

_____

_____

_____

_____

_____

CHAPTER 13 CHECKPOINTS
Making Changes
The inevitable process

You have come to understand that change is inevitable in life and have learned strategies for making smart choices when the need for change arises. Check that you've accomplished all of the goals listed below.

☐ I assessed my attitude toward change and, if necessary, have made progress toward improving it.

☐ I learned to analyze change as it relates to my work, personal values, and the economic realities in my life.

☐ I understand the difference between the need for a job change and the need for personal changes.

☐ I learned about planning for changes, financially and emotionally.

☐ I know how to choose an optimal time to make a self-imposed change.

☐ I learned to identify individuals who can support my change process.

☐ I learned that a variety of issues impact job satisfaction and that identifying the true problem is an important first step in the change process.

☐ I observed that change may require that life goals and daily responsibilities be reprioritized.

☐ I considered options for career changes.

☐ I developed a plan for change, if a change is indeed in order.

Belly dancing is the only profession where the beginner starts in the middle.

—Anonymous

We learn by doing.

—Aristotle

CHAPTER FOURTEEN
Beginning the Job Search

Just do it!

Section Three:
HOW DO I GET IT?

Following in the footsteps of his uncle, Jon decided to pursue a career in commercial real estate. A young man who always had a plan, in college he chose internships and jobs that gave him sales experience. No one was surprised when he graduated and immediately landed a job with the largest broker in the state.

What he didn't plan for was an economic downturn that left him struggling to make ends meet as a commissioned salesman. Lamenting to a family friend, he was stunned when she asked, "Jon what are you passionate about? What could you do all day long and the time would pass in the blink of an eye?" "Mountain biking" was Jon's immediate response. "Well then," the friend offered, "get a job in the biking industry. They need good sales people."

After doing his research, Jon started cold-calling all the bike manufacturers in his area. A persuasive guy, he finally convinced one company to give him an entry-level job in inside sales. Because he loved everything about bikes, his enthusiasm translated to the customer, which in turn converted to sales. He quickly moved up the company career ladder. It wasn't long before he was the sales manager.

Making Your Move

Thanks to the Internet, the process of finding a job has changed dramatically over the last decade. However, whether you're looking for your first job or seeking a career change, there are certain "tried and true" tools and processes with which you must become familiar.

On the following pages we will go over these traditional topics and offer a few hints you may find useful. But there is much more to be said about these subjects so don't stop here. You can find entire books and websites on looking for work, writing a resume, or interviewing for a job, and we urge you to read them. You'll also find a wealth of information online. We suggest starting online with *America's Career InfoNet** and O*NET.** Helpful articles appear regularly in professional and general interest magazines, and in the financial or employment sections of newspapers. Why not start saving these whenever you come across them and filing them for future reference?

* At the time of this printing, the web address was http://www.careeronestop.org/toolkit

** At the time of printing, the web address was http://www.onetonline.org

Keywords: best job search sites

Your Skills Inventory and the Job Search Process

Revisit your **Skills Inventory** chart prior to beginning your job search. Knowing the skills you have mastered will help you narrow down the kinds of jobs to apply for. You'll want to match the skills you have with what the employer is looking for. By studying your **Skills Inventory** in advance, you'll write better resumes and cover letters. In addition, you'll be better prepared for your interviews.

Update Your Skills Inventory Chart

In preparation for a job search and interview, revisit your **Skills Inventory** chart. In a column to the right of your list of skills that you have, make note of situations where you have demonstrated your mastery of that skill. Then:

✓ In your cover letter, mention a couple of the skills the employer is seeking along with examples of your expertise.

✓ On your resume, be sure to list the most desirable skills for the vacant position along with these qualifiers.

Jon's Skills Inventory Chart *abbreviated*

Skills I Have	How I Use Them
Face-to-face sales strategies	Top sales person three months in a row last year in my division
Service oriented; helping customers find the best solution for their needs	I developed a customer needs survey to pinpoint their requirements
Customer contact management software	Managing my client list of 1,200 leads
Writing to communicate clearly	Writing sales proposals, editor of our company newsletter
Persuasive communication skills	In sales plus on the debate team in college
Socially perceptive	I "read" people's motivation in order to close a sale

Jon's Story *Continued*

Jon's sales experience in the real estate industry easily transferred to the bike industry, particularly given his love and expertise for anything on two wheels. Fifteen years later, Jon is a COO for one of the most prestigious down-hill bike manufacturers in the country.

Your Resume

A resume is a summary of your abilities, education, and work experience. It introduces you to possible employers, who will use it to help decide whether you are qualified for a job. Writing it will help you define your talents and abilities, clarify your career aspirations, and outline your related experience.

A resume gives you an opportunity to present yourself in the best possible light. Everything you say must be true, of course, but you can include information that may not come out on an application form. If your resume makes you seem more creative, responsible, and energetic than other job applicants, it may lead to an interview with the employer. That is its most important purpose: a resume won't get you a job, but it can give you the opportunity to meet the employer in person. Final decisions about whom to hire are usually made from interviews.

A resume's appearance can also add to or detract from its effectiveness. Computers make it relatively easy to make a good visual impression with your resume. Be sure, though, that the impression you are making is an appropriate one for the field in which you are seeking employment. A banker, for example, should have a more conservative-looking resume than someone looking for work as a creative director for an advertising agency.

Format is important and we suggest you check the various websites, books, and articles written on the subject for examples. And it should go without saying that you must check your resume carefully to make sure there are no misspellings or typographical errors.

You can send the same resume to each prospective employer, but include a personalized cover letter, as well. It gives you an opportunity to explain why you would like to work for that company, and what skills and talents you can bring to their job. It is even better to tailor your resume to the job you are applying for, in addition to customizing each cover letter.

Keywords: resume tips, sample resume, sample resume [occupation]

Which Type of Resume Is Best for You?

There are three basic resume styles: chronological, functional, and combination.

The chronological resume is used most often, and is generally the appropriate form for individuals without a lot of job experience in the field in which they are seeking employment. Under this format, schools attended and jobs held are presented in reverse chronological order, with the most recent experiences listed first. You'll find an example of a chronological resume on the facing page.

A functional resume sometimes works better for people with a history of relevant job experience — that is, in jobs calling for some of the same skills as those required for the desired position. It is also often a good choice for individuals who have been out of the workforce for periods of time.

Instead of listing all of your job titles and duties, in a functional resume you list only those skills related to the job for which you are applying. For example, if you've been a real estate agent and a boutique owner, and now you want a job as a luxury car salesperson, you might head one of your major topics *Sales Skills* and, underneath, say something like: "Nine years sales experience with products ranging in price from $2 to $750,000. Regional sales award winner, 2017." Other headings would relate to any other requirements listed in the job description (people skills, administrative abilities, or whatever). Following these, under separate headings, list your employers and education (no dates), your personal qualities, and your references.

The combination resume usually begins like the functional style but may, for example, include dates of employment (in reverse chronological order) to show the extent and continuity of your experience.

1. **Your name, address, phone number, and email.** These should be clear, complete, and at the top of the page. Don't use abbreviations, titles (Mr., Ms.), or nicknames. If you have your own website that you are using in support of your job search, include it here as well.

2. **Your job objective or goal.** This is probably the first thing an employer looks at to determine if they are going to read on. Employers want to know if your career goals match their job offering. Therefore, this is a part of your resume that you'll edit with each resume you send.

This statement will also help you decide what other information to include in your resume. As much as possible, the information in the resume should relate to your qualifications for the job for which you are applying. An executive summary that defines your career goal in addition to summarizing your most important accomplishment is particularly effective.

3. **Your education.** If you have graduated from college or had other training beyond high school, list the schools, their location, the year you graduated, and any degrees, certificates, or licenses you earned. Include any honors earned.

If you are still in school, list the school you are attending, along with the city and state, and note what level you have completed. If you have attended other schools, list them in reverse chronological order (start with the most recent school, and work your way back to the first one you attended). There is no need to list elementary or junior high schools.

4. **Your skills.** Use this category to list the skills that are relevant to the job you seek. Your hobby of rebuilding small engines is definitely of interest if you are applying for a job as a mechanic's apprentice. However, if you want a sales job at a local department store, it may not be worth mentioning.

Turn back to your **Skills Inventory**. From the list of *Skills I Have,* choose those that match the skills of the job for which you are applying require. Usually these are listed in the employment advertisement. If not and you need help determining what those might be, review the list of required skills found online on O*NET* under that job's classification.

*At the time of printing, the address was http: www.onetonline.org

5. Your work experience. Include all paid work in this category, using reverse chronological order. Start with your current job, or the last one you held, and work your way back to your first career-level job. Include the company name, the city and state in which it was located, along with the date range you were employed at that position. Follow with your job title and the specific duties you performed on the job.

Describe your duties with action words, such as "prepared," "delivered," and "collected." Include any duties related to the job you seek and any awards you received. You might also want to include any character traits that relate to doing well on the job, such as "like a challenge," "always on time," or "never missed a deadline." Review your responses on page 39 to trigger your thinking.

If applying for your first job, be sure to include volunteer work. If you have served in the military, list the branch and dates of service. If you were honorably discharged, say so.

If you have a break in the time you are in the workforce, be prepared to explain why. Were you out of the workforce caring for children or another family member? Employers will pay close attention to gaps in your work timeline.

6. Your references. References are professional associates, usually supervisors, who can vouch for your work ethic, your skills, and your drive. They are not relatives or friends. Think of several people who would give you a good reference and ask if you may include their names as a reference. Provide their names, addresses, home phone numbers, and email addresses. Do not give a business phone number unless you have permission.

Many people simply say "references available upon request" on their resume. This is perfectly acceptable, but you must still be prepared to provide the names, titles, and contact information if you are asked. Get permission ahead of time and prepare your list even if you don't include it on your resume. If you are a finalist for a position you'll be asked for it, so be sure to have a copy with you at your interview(s).

Sample Resume

Elvira Lopez

1245 Steephill Avenue, San Francisco, CA 94000

(415) 555-1200   Fax (415) 555-1234

elvira.lopez@website.com

EXECUTIVE SUMMARY

Fashion-savvy women's apparel buyer for national clothing chain seeks to leverage ten years of progressive experience in the industry toward a career in fashion marketing. Applies extraordinary insight into the target market to select most profitable merchandise and to advise marketing design team. Capitalizes on social skills by successfully negotiating favorable vendor contracts and effectively managing a team to derive greatest human resource value.

SKILLS

Intuitive trend selection, motivational team leadership, negotiation, effective oral & written communication, relationship building, financial math literacy, long-range planning, design (fashion & graphic), ERP software expertise, InDesign knowledge, Microsoft Word & Excel proficiency.

EXPERIENCE

Modern Outfitters   San Francisco, California
Buyer, Women's Apparel   September 2014 – present

- Negotiate favorable contracts with new and existing vendors, saving the company an average of 5% on merchandise expenses
- Approve merchandise selections to achieve optimal balances of products and labels
- Analyze item sales performance and cancel or refill orders accordingly, contributing to increased profit
- Advise marketing team on advertising and website design strategy to best complement current fashion trends, contributing to 18% increase in online sales
- Develop long-range plans that take trends, seasons, and business goals into account, resulting in more streamlined operations and a more relevant, competitive chain
- Manage team of 14 employees with attention to encouraging efficiency and loyalty

Assistant Buyer, Women's Apparel   June 2012 – September 2014

- Researched and selected new vendors in addition to selecting merchandise for stores, contributing to observable improvement in the quality and value of merchandise offered in stores
- Maintained relationships with current vendors, revitalizing vendor relationships
- Assisted production team with supply chain management and improved efficiency enough to eliminate the need for an additional employee despite company expansion
- Managed six employees and oversaw their professional development

Stevensons Day   San Francisco, California
Retail Buyer Intern   January 2012 – May 2012

- Monitored regional merchandise reports to make appropriate merchandise purchase recommendations
- Assisted with product selection, choosing a record number of wildly popular items
- Managed inventory levels and received praise for keeping a proper selection of styles, sizes, and colors in stock far more satisfactorily than the previous intern
- Developed a system to track and process samples more efficiently

Bette's Boutique   San Francisco, California
Assistant Manager   April 2010 – January 2012

- Consulted with manager on improved merchandise selection, reducing the quantity of merchandise that did not sell and was returned to the warehouse by 10%
- Communicated with vendors regarding store orders and improved vendor relations
- Coordinated annual fashion show, which attracted four times the audience of previous years
- Maintained financial records and improved credit score by 78 points

Sales Associate   June 2008 – April 2010

- Created appealing displays to attract shoppers, contributing to increased store traffic and 20% growth in sales
- Helped customers choose merchandise to fit their needs and formed relationships to create repeat customers
- Resolved customer service issues to increase customer satisfaction with the store

EDUCATION

San Francisco State University   San Francisco, California
Bachelor of Science in Business Administration   May 2012

Academy of Art University   San Francisco, California
Associate of Arts in Fashion   May 2008

PERSONAL

Hobbies include: shopping frequently and intensively at department stores, boutiques, consignment shops, and antique stores; designing and sewing some of my own clothes; reading fashion blogs and magazines; and collecting vintage shoes. I am a clothes fanatic with a reverence for quality and an eye for detail.

REFERENCES

Available upon request

Cover Letters

Your cover letter is your opportunity to expand on the information in your resume and to relate it to your suitability for the position. The goal is to distinguish yourself from other job applicants as the best person for the position.

The first paragraph should contain the name of the position for which you are applying and how you found the listing, but you have some flexibility in choosing how to structure the rest of the letter. Be sure to visit the company's website and study the job description to determine how best to appeal to the company's needs for the position. Think of some specific examples from your past experience that you can use to demonstrate how you meet the requirements and desired qualities listed in the job description. Even if you don't have any work experience, you can still write a compelling letter by drawing examples from your classes, volunteer work, or roles in clubs or other organizations. Don't make any apologies, be positive, and focus on the value you can bring to the company.

The cover letter also serves as a writing sample, so you must ensure that your writing is strong and completely free of errors. Use the active voice whenever possible, keep your paragraphs short, and keep your entire letter on one side of a piece of paper. You can browse the Internet for examples of well-written cover letters to get started. If you feel your writing skills could use a bit of polishing in general, consult a guide like *The Elements of Style* by William Strunk & E. B. White.

Regardless of your confidence in your writing, it is always a good idea to have your cover letter and resume proofread. Career counselors at your school, whether you're still enrolled or have already graduated, will likely review your job application for free, as well as your local One-Stop Career Center.* At the very least, ask a trusted acquaintance to proofread your letter.

*At the time of printing, the address was http://www.servicelocator.org

Keywords: writing cover letters, sample cover letter

Elvira Lopez

1245 Steephill Avenue, San Francisco, CA 94000

(415) 555-1200   Fax (415) 555-1234

elvira.lopez@website.com

Genevieve Nguyen
2356 Grand Avenue
San Francisco, CA 94000

Dear Ms. Nguyen:

I am writing to express interest in the Marketing Manager position at Heritage Cloth posted on LinkedIn. Skilled at understanding trends, consumers, and the numbers behind them, I have an interest in and an aptitude for fashion merchandising and I feel that I can be an asset in marketing the up-and-coming Heritage Cloth brand.

Currently working as Buyer of Women's Apparel for the national chain Modern Outfitters, I have utilized an intimate understanding of our target consumer to choose the ideal selection of products and contribute to the company's tremendous expansion during my tenure. I am confident that I will quickly develop a keen insight into the similarly mod-retro yet more feminine customer of Heritage Cloth, as well, and market the company's merchandise to accelerate demand and profits. In addition to possessing exceptional fashion sense, I am skilled at motivating teams of employees and managing a variety of personalities.

My experience on the creative side of marketing involves guiding the Modern Outfitters marketing team to generate advertising and website content with current trends in mind. I have also refined my technique in persuasive copywriting through negotiating with vendors, "selling" our chain as an ideal market for their products.

My resume further details my experience and education. I am dedicated to a career in fashion marketing and I look forward to having the opportunity to discuss what I can offer Heritage Cloth. Thank you for your time and consideration.

Sincerely,

Elvira Lopez

Elvira Lopez

Finding a Job

You may want to begin your job search by browsing the internet. You'll find the most up-to-date career advice and job seeking tips to get you started. You'll also find the most extensive job listings and be able to apply for jobs online. Many job sites will allow you to post your resume so that employers can find you when they're looking to fill jobs.

Most experts agree that, ultimately, the best way to get a job is to decide where you want to work and then contact that company to apply for a job there. How to decide?

Once you've determined the industry you want to work in, start by considering companies you already know about and respect. Go online and research companies that employ people in your chosen field. Read trade magazines and professional journals (almost every occupational area has them) and stay on top of current events. Which companies are making news? Not only will you have the best idea of which companies you'd most enjoy working for, but your knowledge of industry happenings will make a good impression on prospective employers.

Networking has the potential to tremendously accelerate your job search. Share your career aspirations with everyone you know, because tips and leads can come from unlikely sources. Attend job fairs in your area, which provide an opportunity to meet and learn about a lot of employers at once. You should also learn more about social media as a tool to market yourself and connect with the companies you are interested in. Browse the Internet for ideas on using such sites as LinkedIn and Twitter to maximize your exposure to recruiters.

Keywords: job seeking tips, job search advice, using the internet for job search, how to choose a company to work for, best companies to work for

Networking

Your relationships with others can have a large role in how soon you find your dream job. Don't hesitate to mention to your friends, family members, professors, or other acquaintances what kind of job you are looking for and to ask if they happen to know of any related opportunities. You never know who they might know that is looking for someone just like you.

You should also consider attending job fairs, especially ones focused on your industry. Job fairs allow you to meet a lot of employers in a short amount of time and can give them a glimpse of your personality before they make the decision to interview you. Search online to find upcoming job fairs in your area.

Consider joining a professional association in your desired field. If you're in school, find out if your campus has a club for your interest. Such organizations offer information about current happenings in the industry and job opportunities. They also give you the opportunity to meet people at all stages of their careers in occupations similar to the one you are seeking.

Keep in mind that networking is most successful when it benefits both parties. If you hear of an opportunity that one of your contacts might be interested in, go the extra mile to tell him or her about it and provide a reference, if applicable. It may sound cliché, but it really is true that the more you help others, the more they will be willing to help you.

Keywords: networking tips, job search, job fair [city], attending a job fair, social networking job search

Social Media

One of the latest phenomena to expand the definition of networking and change the face of the job hunting scene is social media. You may already have one of these accounts for keeping in touch with your friends, but do you know that you can also use such sites to enhance your exposure to employers?

Having social networking profiles that portray an intelligent, professional image while distinguishing you as an individual can help employers get to know you, your personality, and the strengths you will bring to the workplace. Since companies often prefer to hire people they know and trust, providing more information about yourself and demonstrating your worthiness of a job in your field can increase the probability that you will be invited in for an interview.

Check out the following strategies for enhancing your networking efforts. You can read more about any of them online, consult a book about social media, or ask an acquaintance that is familiar with social networks to learn more about how to use them in your job search.

LinkedIn (linkedin.com) is specifically designed for professional networking and is probably the most important social media site for job seekers. It displays your work experience and a summary of your qualifications, which provides recruiters easy access to your resume when they have a position to fill. Like other social networking sites, it also allows you to add contacts, but it has an additional benefit in that it allows you to view and search your contacts' professional connections. You can search for the companies you are interested in and find any of your contacts that work there or know someone that does. Such connections could possibly give you an informational interview or even recommend you for a position.

Twitter (twitter.com) gives you the opportunity to connect with just about anyone, whether you've met or not. You can search for and contact people at companies or with job titles that you are interested in and you can also participate in conversations on topics that interest you with people you weren't previously connected to. It's a good way to meet people, and each person that reads your bio just might keep you in mind if they hear of a job opportunity for which you would be a good fit. You should also use Twitter to share information about your field in the form of "tweets," which further enhance your image as a desirable candidate.

A **blog** can also be a good way to showcase your personality and your knowledge when you choose topics relevant to the job you're seeking and post regularly. There are several good websites for starting a blog: wordpress.com, tumblr.com, medium.com, and squarespace.com to name a few.

Keywords: social media job search tips, linkedin profile tips, twitter job search, blogging for job seekers

Job Hunting Website

It is probably not too far in the future when you'll link prospective employers to your job hunting website or your profile on a social networking site. There employers, hiring managers or recruiters will find all they want to know before deciding whether or not to proceed with the interview process.

Consider developing your own website now. This will help you stand out as an innovator and forward-thinking individual. As with any written information you provide a prospective employer, it must be professional in appearance and well — designed and written.

Your website would include your written resume.

It could also include:

- A picture of you
- A portfolio of examples of the work you've done
- Interviews of former employers as a video reference
- A video resume

Video Resume: If you have a dynamic personality, you might benefit from recording a brief introduction to your background and your career objective for an online video resume. If a recruiter likes what he or she sees of your personality in your video, you may get invited in for an interview even if the experience on your resume might not have distinguished you from other candidates. If you feel your personality won't do you any favors on film, don't worry. Video resumes are far from being expected of job candidates and your job search will likely be just fine without one.

What Is Your Online Persona?

A word of caution: Just as providing positive information about yourself online can attract employers, conveying negative content can repel them. A majority of employers now search for your name on the Internet before inviting you to an interview or hiring you and will eliminate your name as a candidate if they don't like what they see. Take care to avoid posting embarrassing pictures, writing about inappropriate or illegal activities, using profanity, or providing access to any content that an employer might find unprofessional. You may decide that it would be wise to increase your privacy settings on personal profiles so that only friends can see them, but be aware that information could still potentially leak.

Keywords: video resume tips, clean social media profile, personal website job search

The Informational Interview

Another thing most experts agree on is the value of the informational interview. This is nothing more than talking with someone who works in a job like the one you hope to find. What better way to learn more about your chosen career? Here's how it works:

A personal recommendation is the best way to find an interview subject, but if you can't find anyone who knows someone in this field, try another route. Search online or call the Chamber of Commerce. Professional organizations or unions may be able to help. Use your imagination.

Then call and ask for an appointment. It's okay. People do this all the time. Simply say something like "Hello, my name is Bob Johnson. My friend, Ted Garner, said you might be willing to talk with me about your job as a radio announcer. Could I take half an hour of your time to ask some questions?"

There are a few rules to follow: Be on time. Dress neatly. Be polite. Don't stay longer than you said you would. Send a thank you note afterward. It's not appropriate to ask for a job, but you can explain your situation and ask for any leads that might help you get the experience you want.

Here are some questions you might use during your interview. Add some of your own.

- How long have you had this job?
- What kind of education or training did you need?
- If you were still in school, would you do anything differently?
- What advice would you give me about preparing for this career?
- What advice would you give about working in this field?
- What parts of the job do you find most enjoyable?
- What do you like least about your job?
- Do you have any plans for a career switch? If so, what would you like to do?

Dean's Story

Dean didn't know anyone in his new city. Looking through connections on his college roommate's LinkedIn network, he located a mutual friend who lived a few miles away and had a job in the industry he wanted. He made a telephone call, set up an informational interview, and, before he knew it, he was offered the job of his dreams.

Keywords: informational interview tips, informational interview questions

Your Skills Inventory Chart and the Interview

Review your Skills Inventory chart prior to an interview

In job interviews, you'll want to be able to define your skills and achievement concisely as well as give examples as to how you've used them in the past. Research indicates that the most common interviewing mistake is the inability to articulate one's job skills, so you'll want to practice this important process prior to any interview.

Reinforce your examples by giving measurable data along with results. For instance, Josie, interviewing for a sales associate position, can list face-to-face sales as an important skill she possesses. During an interview, she follows that declaration by explaining she's worked in sales for five years and that, in her last job, she increased the sales in her department by 50% in one year. She might even want to tell a short story of a particularly successful sales effort.

As you prepare for an interview, practice describing those situations and briefly telling your stories. Video and critique your efforts. With practice you'll be confident each time you outline a skill that is required by the prospective employer.

In the end, employers don't usually hire based solely on the formal education you've completed or your number of years of experience. They make most hiring decisions based upon the skills the applicant has acquired and the results of their workplace efforts. You'll want to be sure to look for opportunities to highlight these points in your interview.

The Job Interview

The personal interview is usually the final step in the job hunting process. The decision to hire you — or not to hire you — will probably be based on the impression you make here. Give yourself every opportunity to succeed by following these four rules:

1. **Be on time.** An interviewer who's been kept waiting for even 5 minutes will already have serious doubts about your work habits.

2. **Look good—but not flashy.** The interviewer's first impression of you will be based on your appearance. Hair should be clean, combed, and off your face. Clean and trim your nails, too. Your clothing choice should be conservative rather than trendy. Ties and jackets for men, a blouse and slacks or knee-length dress for women. Take it easy on the jewelry and cologne, and silence your cell phone and put it away.

3. **Look confident.** Sit up straight. Speak clearly. Make eye contact with the interviewer. Keep in mind that few people actually feel confident while being judged by a total stranger. The interviewer knows this and will make some allowances, this is one of those situations where it helps to pretend you feel confident. With practice, you'll begin to feel more at ease.

4. **Be prepared.** You can expect to be asked a number of questions. Take time to plan your answers before the interview. If possible, practice with a friend, taking turns being the applicant and the interviewer. Better yet, capture your practice interviews using the camera on your phone. That way you can see for yourself how to improve your presentation.

It's also a good idea to convince yourself that you want this job more than anything else in the world. The interviewer will pick up on your confidence and enthusiasm, and that can only help you. Be prepared, too, to tell the employer what you can do for the company, how you will be of value.

Keywords: interview tips, interview attire

Preparing for the Job Interview

There are many good ways to prepare for a job interview. You can read some of the numerous books and articles on the subject. You can ask other people about their interview experiences. If you know someone who actually interviews people for jobs, you might be able to get some extremely helpful and personalized advice! Videos presenting interview techniques are available online, and web sites offer practice using common interview questions.

Many communities offer free or reasonably priced seminars and classes. Call your community education office for information. It may cost more, but you might consider workshops or private sessions offered by a professional career development agency. Many such agencies record simulated interviews, review your performance with you, and offer advice on improving your technique.

Try to think of interview situations as learning experiences. Everyone is nervous at first, but as you go along you'll know what to expect and feel more at ease.

Interview Dos and Don'ts

- Do listen carefully to what the interviewer is saying or asking, and respond appropriately.

- Do be prepared to make a clear, honest statement about your strengths — and weaknesses (nobody's perfect). Mention what steps you've taken, or plan to take, to overcome any negative points.

- Do think about your past successes and be prepared to list them.

- Do study the company's web site beforehand to learn something about them. Show an interest in their services and products.

- Do prepare thoughtful questions to ask the interviewer about the company or the position.

- Do answer questions concisely. Any reply more than a minute in length is probably too wordy.

- Do display enthusiasm, energy, and optimism.

- Do pay attention to any signals the interviewer is sending. Is she bored? Is he impatient? Interested? Concerned?

- Do practice interviewing, preferably on videotape.

- Do make eye contact and smile.

- Do show confidence.

- Don't be arrogant or insulting.

- Don't make negative comments about the company or its products.

- Don't put down former employers.

- Don't be self-deprecating.

- Don't misrepresent your experience or abilities.

Sample Interview Questions

Here are some questions commonly asked in various forms at an interview. Make notes here on your responses and then practice answering these questions aloud. Practice with a friend who can give you feedback and suggestions.

- What attracted you to this job?

- Why do you think you would be good at this job?

- Why do you want to work here?

- Tell me about the experiences that qualify you for this job.

- Tell me about your educational background.

- What are your strengths?

- What are your weaknesses?

- Why did you leave your last job (or any other job on your resume)?

- May we contact your present (or any past) employer?

- What are your plans for the future?

- When would you be able to start work if offered the job?

- What salary do you need to earn?

- Is there anything you'd like to ask me about this position?

Keywords: behavioral interview questions, questions to ask employer, interviewer, interview thank you

You should also be prepared to answer behavioral interview questions, which are increasingly asked at interviews with more competitive companies to assess your potential based on your past experiences. Look for more sample questions like the ones below and think of several good examples from your past that you could use in an interview.

- Describe a time when you showed initiative to go "above and beyond" what was expected of you.

- Tell me about a time when you made a mistake.

- Give an example of a goal you set and how you achieved it.

- Recall a stressful situation and how you coped with it.

- Tell me about a time when you didn't agree with an authority figure.

- Discuss a situation in which you worked with a group that was not successful.

- Give an example of a time that you effectively resolved a conflict.

Make sure you receive a business card from your interviewer so that you can mail or email a thank you note after the interview. This message should thank him or her for taking the time to interview you, reinforce your interest in the position, and restate a couple key reasons as to why you are the best person for the job.

Job Applications

In most cases, you will be asked to fill out an application form. Every employer has its own form, but most ask for the same kinds of information.

You will usually complete your job application at the employment site. Be prepared to do it right. Neatness counts. Read each question carefully and think about your response before you begin to write. Crossed-out answers give a bad impression. It's also a good idea to bring your own pen — one with a fine point that does not drip or smear.

You will need to have a social security number for any job you get in the United States. Do you have yours? If not, apply for your card now. Call the social security office in your city or visit the Social Security Administration web site for information on how to do this and to locate the office nearest you.

You might also need to have your birth certificate in order to prove your age. If you don't have this document, you can get a certified copy from the Department of Health in the state where you were born. Google "vital records" and the state where you were born.

Some jobs might require a driver's license, as well. If you have one, bring it along.

Bring your resume along. Information on your education and work experience will certainly be needed. You might be asked to include your supervisor's name and phone number and your salary when listing previous employers. Be prepared to list your references, too.

Keywords: job application form

Some questions you should be prepared to answer include the following:

Do you have the legal right to work in the United States?   Yes   No
(If you are a U.S. citizen or have a work visa, answer yes.)

Previous addresses if you've moved in recent years _____

How will you get to and from work? _____

When are you available to work (days and hours)? _____

How many hours a week do you want to work? _____

What salary do you expect? _____

Have you served in the military?   Yes   No

Have you ever been convicted of a misdemeanor or felony?   Yes   No

Most forms ask you to sign and date your application before you turn it in to the employer. Your signature indicates that the information you have provided is true and complete. It also gives the employer the right to contact schools, former employers, or references to verify your answers.

Dealing with Rejection

No one likes to be rejected. However, at one time or another, everyone gets turned away. This is especially true in the working world. There may be dozens, or even hundreds, of applicants for a single job. Since all except one will be rejected, your chances of being in the larger group are extremely good.

Your first response, of course, will be to take it personally. This self-blame can be on either the micro ("if only I'd parted my hair on the other side") or the macro level ("I'll never get a job if I live to be 150"). It's fine to review your performance so you can make improvements in the future. But the fact that you didn't get the job has nothing to do with your worth as a person. Nor does it doom you to a life of failure.

The best way to deal with rejection is to brush off your ego and try again. If you truly want to work at the firm that has rejected you, apply again. Employers respect persistence. Apply for other jobs, as well. When you are hired, you will find your sense of self-worth miraculously restored. If you give up, however, you will have to keep living with the idea that you failed, and you didn't. You just didn't try long enough.

Until you get that job, though, here are some things that might help you feel better:

- Seek out and spend time with people who make you feel good about yourself. Stay away from those who are quick to find fault with you.

- Do something you're good at. Playing the piano or shooting baskets or writing a poem can help you remember that you have many talents and are a capable person.

- Improve your job hunting skills. Practice your interview style.

- Watch your favorite inspirational movie — one where the hero or heroine overcomes unbearable tragedy or unspeakable evil (and you thought you had problems!) to become the champion or the star or save the world. If he or she can do it, so can you. As Rocky Balboa once said, "Go for it!"

Accepting a Job

The day finally arrives — you are offered a job. What do you do now? Assuming that this is a job you want, there are still a few things to get straight. If you have decided you don't want this job, thank the employer for the offer and explain that you have taken another position, or you realize that the position is not a good match for you or whatever. Don't burn any bridges though. Don't say anything negative about the job or the employer. Even though you don't want to work there now, you might someday.

Before you accept a job, make sure you clearly understand what it entails. What are your duties and responsibilities? If there is a written job description be sure to see it if you haven't already. Ask to see a copy of the company's personnel policies. Meet with the person offering you the position to find out such points as when you will start, what days and hours you will work, what the overtime expectations and arrangements are, and the all-important question — what are the salary and benefits?

At professional or higher skill levels, salaries are usually negotiable. If the salary offered is not what you need or want, the best time to negotiate an increase or a future raise is before you accept the position. Now is the time to bring up previous experience or special training that might entitle you to a higher salary. If you can't think of any reason why you should get the higher rate, or if you have a pressing need or desire for the position, it may be best to accept the amount offered.

If you don't have experience negotiating, it might be wise to brush up on these skills. There are a number of good books and articles available at your local library or online.

Hang in there. The day will finally arrive — you will be offered a job you want with the circumstances that fits your needs and requirements. Your personal satisfaction and contentment with life will make all the training, planning, strategizing, and, yes, even the rejection well worthwhile.

Making Connections

When you start working at your job, also start looking for mentors. One thing most successful people have in common is that, throughout their lives, they've had help from others. The word mentor means counselor or teacher. But employers or co-workers, parents, neighbors, coaches, and others can be mentors as well.

What do mentors do? Basically, they give you advice and encouragement. They "show you the ropes." If you've ever started a new job and found someone to tell you about different co-workers and projects or advise you on what to wear, how to speak, and so forth, you've had a mentor.

Why are they important? For one thing, they save you time. Imagine how much longer it would take to learn the customs of a new workplace without advice: What is the one excuse you should never use when you're late? What's the best thing to order from down the street? Where do people go after work on Friday? When you go to work for a new company, a mentor can answer these sorts of questions to help you feel comfortable and look competent.

Mentors are valuable sources of information. If they can't tell you what you need to know, they can often tell you where to look or who to ask. Because of their experience, they can teach you things you won't learn anywhere else. They can introduce you to other people in the company or in your field. They can help you become better known.

Best of all, mentors encourage you and push you to do your best. They applaud you when you do well. They build your confidence.

So where do you find them? Some people seem to know instinctively that they can benefit from these contacts, and have no problem recognizing potential mentors. Others haven't given the subject much thought, but it's not that difficult.

Professors, coaches, and employers are the most obvious sources of help. Not surprisingly, the best way to get their attention is to do a good job. Instructors and coaches, especially, love their subject or sport and find great satisfaction in helping young people excel in their field. Similarly, employers are often more than willing to help promising employees learn their trade.

From time to time, you are likely to meet other people who could enrich your life. It's never a good idea — or proper behavior — to be a pest or to force your attentions on anyone. However, most people are willing to answer a question or offer information. You can follow up with a thank you note. Perhaps a mentor relationship will develop. Perhaps not. Again, don't push it.

The best relationships develop naturally. If there's no friendship or rapport between two people, the association won't last.

We've talked about what a mentor can do for you, but what can you do for a mentor? Well, you can carry on in his or her tradition or trade. Better yet, you can continue the practice. As you establish yourself in your career, extend a hand to those who follow. Become a mentor yourself.

Can you think of people who have served as mentors for you in the past? List them below. What did they do that you found helpful?

_____

_____

_____

How about now? Are there potential or actual mentors in your life? List them here. How have they, or how could they, help you?

_____

_____

_____

Think about the training or work you are currently planning to get or do in the next 10 years. What kinds of mentors do you need? List them by title or classification below.

_____

_____

_____

_____

Have you ever been a mentor? To whom? What did you do? How did you feel about it?

_____

_____

_____

_____

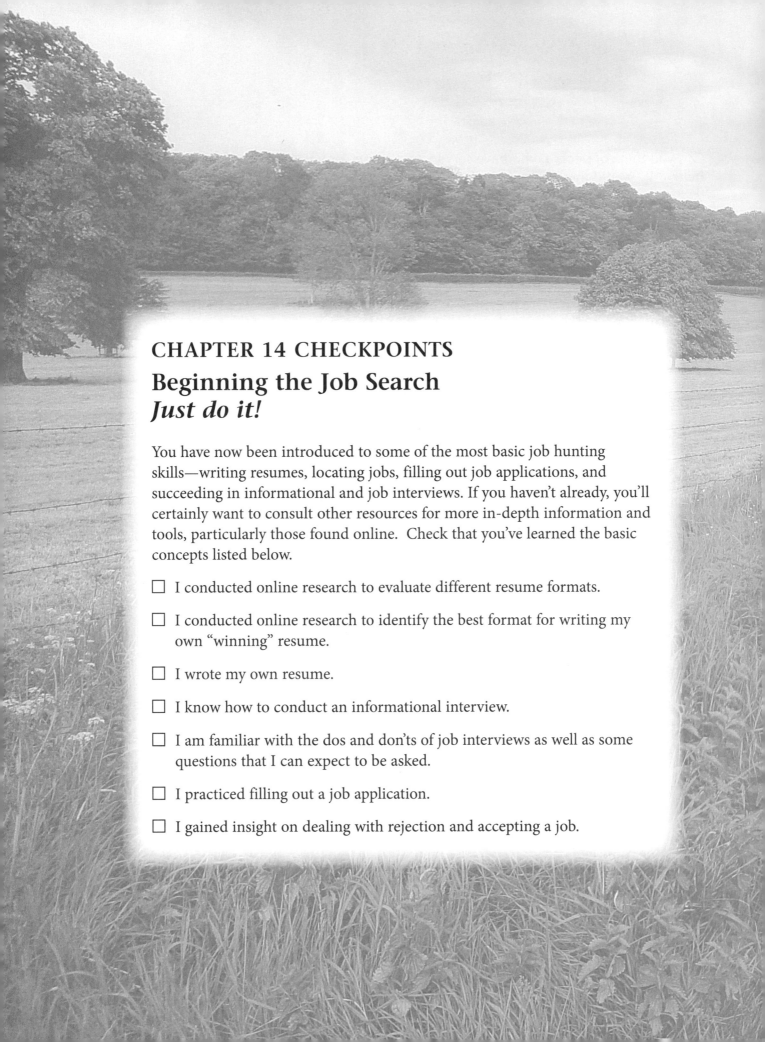

CHAPTER 14 CHECKPOINTS
Beginning the Job Search
Just do it!

You have now been introduced to some of the most basic job hunting skills—writing resumes, locating jobs, filling out job applications, and succeeding in informational and job interviews. If you haven't already, you'll certainly want to consult other resources for more in-depth information and tools, particularly those found online. Check that you've learned the basic concepts listed below.

☐ I conducted online research to evaluate different resume formats.

☐ I conducted online research to identify the best format for writing my own "winning" resume.

☐ I wrote my own resume.

☐ I know how to conduct an informational interview.

☐ I am familiar with the dos and don'ts of job interviews as well as some questions that I can expect to be asked.

☐ I practiced filling out a job application.

☐ I gained insight on dealing with rejection and accepting a job.

Even if you're on the right track, you'll get run over if you just sit there.

—Will Rogers

A journey of a thousand leagues begins with a single step.

—Lao-tzu

CHAPTER FIFTEEN

Where Do You Go from Here?

Writing your 10-year action plan

Section Three:
HOW DO I GET IT?

We know what we are, but know not what we may be.

—William Shakespeare
Hamlet

He that would eat the fruit must climb the tree.

—Scottish Proverb

The one who removes a mountain begins by carrying small stones.

—Chinese Proverb

As we said in chapter 1, success depends largely on two factors: vision and energy. By now, if you have completed the exercises in this book, you should have a better understanding of who you are and what you want; you should have a vision. You have also learned a number of skills and techniques to help realize that vision, a task that required no small amount of energy. But, truthfully, your work is just beginning.

In this final chapter, you will write your own **10-year Plan**. You will think about and list the actions you need to take over the coming years to achieve your goals. It may look like an overwhelming task, but do your best to complete it because "if you don't know where you're going, you're likely to end up someplace else."

Your plan should be a flexible guide, though. Unexpected problems and opportunities are sure to turn up, and you will need to adjust your plans accordingly.

Think of this chapter as a map. You know where you are. You know where you want to go. Your plan should serve as one route to your destination. You may decide to follow it all the way, or you may find an alternate path that suits you better. Perhaps you'll change your plans and head off in an entirely different direction.

That's fine, but make your decisions consciously. Have a reason for changing your mind. Then make a new plan, using this model if you like. Having a guide helps you remember your long-term goals and makes it easier to avoid actions that could keep you from reaching them.

Let's get started.

Sometimes, I think, the things we see
Are shadows of the things to be;
That what we plan we build…

—Phoebe Cary
Dreams and Realities

Getting the Education or Training You Need

Education is a companion which no misfortune can depress, no crime can destroy, no enemy can alienate, no despotism can enslave. At home a friend, abroad an introduction, in solitude a solace, and in society an ornament. It chastens vice, it guides virtue, it gives, at once, grace and government to genius.

—Joseph Addison

The things taught in schools and colleges are not an education, but the means of education.

—Ralph Waldo Emerson

A whale ship was my Yale College and my Harvard.

—Herman Melville,
Moby Dick

There are many ways to get the training and/or education you need, but most of them require one thing—**a high school diploma**. You also need a high school degree to be eligible for most kinds of employment. Without this ticket to opportunity, you are likely to end up with a low-paying, dead-end job—or no job at all.

If you've already dropped out and can't go back to school, consult your local school district or college about adult education or other options. You might be able to earn a GED or high school equivalency certificate.

After you have your diploma or certificate, you have a variety of choices:

339

FOUR-YEAR COLLEGES AND UNIVERSITIES come in all sizes and varieties. Some are small liberal arts schools that usually stress a broad, general education. Other colleges specialize in certain kinds of training. State colleges and universities are usually large institutions that offer both liberal arts and more directed studies. Some four-year schools are very expensive and/ or hard to get into. Others are quite accessible. To learn more about them, check the library and online for guides such as the annual *Peterson's Four-Year Colleges,* or browse web sites like CollegeScorecard.ed.gov that provide comprehensive information on every college and university in the United States.

Keywords: community college [city], community college [state], tips on choosing a college, how to choose a vocational school, apprenticeship [state], how to find an apprenticeship, military options

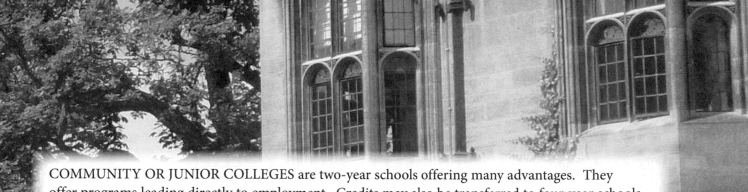

COMMUNITY OR JUNIOR COLLEGES are two-year schools offering many advantages. They offer programs leading directly to employment. Credits may also be transferred to four-year schools. Usually, tuitions are low at community colleges, and, since there are so many of them (1,200), it's often possible to cut expenses even further by living at home. In addition, admission requirements are lower than at most four-year schools. So, if you didn't excel in high school, you have a chance to redeem yourself here. If you are interested in attending a particular school, visit its website and drop it an email requesting more information. You can also visit the American Association of College's at http://www. aacc.nche.edu or http://CollegeScorecard.ed.gov.

PUBLIC AND PRIVATE VOCATIONAL SCHOOLS offer specialized training in a wide variety of careers. Attending one of these schools for a year or two can lead to jobs paying as much or more than many of those requiring college degrees. Like junior colleges, public vo-tech schools usually offer low tuition and convenient locations.

APPRENTICESHIPS allow you to become a skilled worker through an arrangement between you and an employer, a union, and a school of some kind. According to the Department of Labor, more than 450 jobs can be mastered in this way. As an apprentice, you will spend part of your time on the job and part in the classroom. Usually, you will earn 40 to 60 percent of the normal wage while you are learning. Visit the Department of Labor's Bureau of Apprenticeship and Training web site,* or contact them for more information.

ON-THE-JOB TRAINING is available from many companies. It can take several different forms. You might receive instruction from fellow workers during and after work, you might be sent to classes elsewhere during the work week, or you might take classes on your own, with the company paying the tuition.

ONLINE OR DISTANCE LEARNING opportunities are becoming more and more prevalent in the post-secondary arena. For-profit schools along with traditional colleges and universities offer a variety of courses and majors to students who are self-directed learners. You'll find detailed information online. Consult with a career counselor to find the best match for you.

THE MILITARY offers both training for specific jobs and help with tuition once you are discharged. If you can get appointed to one of the military academies, you receive an excellent college education at no charge. (In return, you spend several years in the service after you graduate.) For more information, contact your local recruiters.

Ask your career counselor or librarian to help you find sources on any of these options. Extensive information is available. Before making your decision, you may also want to interview someone who has attended the school you are considering, or who has taken the path that appeals to you most (been an apprentice, served in the military, or whatever).

*At the time of this printing, the web address was http://www.dol.gov/apprenticeship

Your Skills Inventory and Education Plan

Wendy was a natural entrepreneur. At age 9, her lemonade stand had a loyal following. In junior high, her coupon shopping business grossed wages an adult would envy. So when she graduated from a top university with a degree in both business and entrepreneurship she thought she was set. She was headed for a career in the high-tech field and the sky seemed to be the limit.

Until she couldn't get a job to match her aspirations. Reviewing her Skills Inventory, she realized there were gaping holes in her skill sets. So she went back to school — vocational school. Upon completion of both traditional classroom-based and distance learning courses, she attracted the attention of a mentor who provided an apprenticeship opportunity. That position eventually segued into an entry-level job that offered great on-the-job-training.

She had a plan and she worked the plan. As a lifelong learner she continually sought and added new skills to her list of those mastered. Fifteen years later, Wendy is a partner in an educational publishing firm that is quickly moving into the digital world.

As the above true story illustrates, the complex learning necessary to be competitive into today's workforce doesn't end when you walk across the stage at graduation. While traditional schooling is a good foundational start, and most people can get their entry-level job in their chosen career with a carefully planned college or vocational education, it's probably not the last test you'll take or book you'll read.

Also, keep in mind, schooling is expensive, both in time and money. Each semester you dither without a focused direction can cost thousands of dollars and hundreds of hours. So having a plan that allows you to get the education you need in the quickest way possible is even more critical today.

A clearly laid out plan is essential to this goal. With so many choices, where do you begin?

Updating Your Skills Inventory Chart

Start by reviewing your **Skills Inventory** chart, begun in chapter eleven. Focusing on the skills you need to acquire, in the column to the right of that skill, list the opportunities you have for attaining that skill. Can you master it in your college work? If not, do you need to seek out opportunities online or in apprenticeship assignments? Might you be able to get the training you need in the military or from an entry-level job? Perhaps you can develop these skills in a variety of settings. If so, list them all.

After you complete this exercise, step back and review your chart. What you've created is a master educational plan. On the next pages, translate this information to both your 10-year Action Plan and your Lifelong Learning Graph.

And, remember, your **Skills Inventory** chart will continue to grow throughout your lifetime. When you identify a new skill that you need to master (and in this fast-changing world that will be a fact of life), be sure to add it to your **Skills Inventory** and then determine the best way to obtain it.

Wendy's Skills Inventory				
		CHOSEN CAREER	Back-up Career #1	Back-up Career #2
Skills I Need to Learn	My Plan for Learning	Educational Publisher	College Professor Business	Documentary Film Producer
Graphic design on the computer	Certification courses at community college	X		X
Sales and persuasion techniques	Extension courses at local college, on-the-job training	X	X	
InDesign software	Online tutorial	X		X
Video production and editing	Community television workshops	X		X
Building web pages	Online tutorial, adult education class, hire tutor	X		
Copyright law	Read a book, question my mentor	X		X
Negotiating publishing contracts	On-the-job training, read best book on the topic	X	X	
Project and time management	College coursework in business administration	X	X	X

My Education Plan for My Career Path

My chosen career_____

My Skills Inventory				
		CHOSEN CAREER	Back up Career #1	Back up Career #2
Skills I need to learn	My Plan for Learning			

For ideas to help you complete the column titled *My Plan for Learning*, review chapter 12. Why not complete a **Learning Plan** rubric from page 283 for each skill you want to master.

Your Skills Inventory continued

As you master a skill you'll want to be sure to transfer it to your **Skills Inventory** under the headline as a *Skills I have*. Then be sure to identify *How I use them*, and utilize that information as a prompt for your resume, cover letters and interview examples. Being able to articulate examples of your expertise is important in the job-finding process.

You'll want to update this listing of the skills you have throughout your life. Watching this list grow will give you confidence and help you stay occupationally competitive.

My Skills Inventory *continued*		CHOSEN CAREER	Back-up Career #1	Back-up Career #2
Skills I have	**How I use them**			

To stay competitive in today's ever-changing workforce, learning is a lifelong pursuit. On the following pages you'll want to complete a timeline of your efforts using the 10-year education and training plan along with your first draft of a lifelong learning graph. Review your **Skills Inventory** chart to get the data you need to be focused and efficient as you prepare for the career of your dreams.

What Is Your Commitment to Education?

On page 177 you indicated the career for which you want to prepare. Write that job title in the space below.

Chosen Career _____

How much education and/or training will you need to complete before you can get an entry-level job in this field? If you haven't already, update your **Career Interest Survey** on pages 150–153 for this particular career.

EDUCATION or TRAINING	DURATION
_____	_____
_____	_____
_____	_____
_____	
	Total _____

Use the information above to determine how many more years of formal education or training you need. Enter that number here.

_____ years

Your College Major

If you are in or plan to attend college list the major(s) that match both your career goals and the skills you need to acquire as outlined in your **Skills Inventory** and **Skills-Based Education Plan**.

_____

What educational requirements must you meet during each of your college years (classes you need to take, grades you must maintain, and so forth)? List them on the following chart. What specialized training or skills do you need? How are you going to get them?

Keywords: choosing college major

Your Education and Training 10-Year Plan

List College, Vocational, Post-Graduate, On-The-Job and Special Training

This year:

_____

_____

Next year:

_____

_____

The three:

_____

_____

Year four:

_____

_____

Year five:

_____

_____

Year six:

_____

_____

Year seven:

_____

_____

Year eight:

_____

_____

Year nine:

_____

_____

Year ten:

_____

_____

Lifelong Learning Graph

Success generally depends upon knowing how long it takes to succeed.

—C. L. de Montesquieu

It is never too late to be what you might have been.

—George Elliot

If you are planning to have a career that takes a great deal of education, the preceding exercise may have given you pause. Do you really want to spend that much time in school? Before you decide it's all too overwhelming, turn back to pages 114–119. Review the information there regarding the future dividends you can expect to earn for each year of education. Is it worth the effort?

Remember, too, that although the investment of time may seem huge from your current perspective, you will earn the rewards over a lifetime.

Now that you have completed most of this book, rethink the chart from page 118, paying particular attention to the next 10 years. How do your initial thoughts relate to the training and preparation you need to reach your career goal? We have redesigned the chart to give you room to expand on your plans for the next 10–15 years. On each line, write your major activity for that year, whether it's education, training, or work opportunities.

You'll want to review the education and training alternatives you've listed on:

✓ Your **Career Interest Surveys** (pages 150–155)

✓ Your **Career Back-up Plan** (page 227)

✓ Your **Learning Plans** and **Skills-Based Education Plan** (pages 265, 275, 344)

Consider the scenarios you might substitute if circumstances dictate a change in plans. You don't want to give up your career goal if you preparation phase is interrupted. Outline a back-up plan on the right side of the page using pencil.

Now add what you think may be your major activities in the decades to come — your 30s, 40s, 50s, and so on. Include your initial thoughts on growth opportunities.

How will the next 10 years of preparation impact the balance of your life?

Give a person a fish and you feed them for a day.
Teach them to fish and they eat for a lifetime.

—Chinese Proverb

Age		Write your vision of each decade below.
90		80s _____
		_____
80		70s _____
		_____
		60s _____
70		_____
		50s _____
60		_____
		40s _____
50		_____
		30s _____
		_____

Write your Education and Professional Growth Plan
for each of the next 10 years.

Age		Year
40		10th _____
30		9th _____
		8th _____
		7th _____
20		6th _____
		5th _____
10	High School and Grade School	4th _____
		3rd _____
		next year _____
0		this year _____

He that can have patience can have what he will.

—Benjamin Franklin

Self-Mastery Techniques

If getting the right amount of education was all you needed to have a satisfying and rewarding future, your path could be pretty straight-forward. However, your future also hinges on how well you manage yourself with all the other choices you make. You've learned self-control techniques for:

- Delaying gratification
- Facing fears and anxieties
- Overcoming roadblocks and solving problems

You'll want to incorporate these strategies into your planning process, so you won't be tempted to scale back your goals and dreams as you complete your 10-year plan.

Delaying Gratification

Following a plan necessarily means delaying gratification. Turn to page 183 to review this concept. Admittedly, that's not always easy to do. It helps, though, if you are motivated and prepared. Answering the following questions should help you be both.

Can you think of sacrifices you might need to make in order to achieve your goal? Might you need to give up some social activities, for example? To enable you to take a cut in pay, will you have to spend some of the money you now use for clothes or recreation for tuition? List them below.

_____

_____

_____

_____

What commitments are you willing to make? Will you study for a certain amount of time every day? Will you take a job to earn money for school? Will you accept a simpler lifestyle for long-term life satisfaction?

_____

_____

_____

_____

List the rewards you hope to gain from those commitments and sacrifices below.

_____

_____

_____

Do the rewards make the sacrifices and commitments seem worthwhile?

_____

_____

Turn back to page 121 and review the decision-making model on "the path of least resistance." Use it to complete the following statements.

Jodie's example: What do I want? *I want to be a lawyer.*

What are my choices right now? *To register for the advanced math course that will help me get into law school, or to take the art class that would be more fun.*

I want to *be a lawyer,* **therefore, I will** *take the math class.*

What do I want? _____

What are my choices right now? _____

_____

_____

I want to _____ **, therefore, I will** _____

_____

The only place where success comes before work is in the dictionary.

—Vidal Sasson

351

Facing Fears and Anxieties

He has not learned the lesson of life who does not every day surmount a fear.

—Ralph Waldo Emerson

Courage is being scared to death but saddling up anyway.

—John Wayne

One of the best ways to overcome anxiety is to anticipate it, face it squarely, and take personal responsibility for overcoming it. Remember that courage doesn't mean being without fear. It means acting in spite of fear. It's natural to be afraid or apprehensive at times, but don't let your fears get in the way of your goals.

In the space below, anticipate your fears by listing every excuse you can think of for giving up your dream.

_____

_____

_____

_____

Now list every reason or excuse you can think of for not successfully completing the preparation or training you need to have the career you want.

_____

_____

_____

Your Plan for Overcoming Fears

Now that you've faced your fears, take responsibility for them. For each excuse listed above, write an affirmation that counters the fear and gives you power. (See chapter 10.)

_____

_____

_____

_____

_____

They are able because they think they are able.

—Virgil

If your ship doesn't come in, swim out to meet it.

—Jonathan Winters

Your Plan for Overcoming Roadblocks and Solving Problems

Just as you are responsible for overcoming your own fears, you must take responsibility for solving your own problems. Can you think of any roadblocks or detours that might get in the way of your success during the next 10 years? (Review pages 203–215.) List those possibilities below.

1. _____

2. _____

3. _____

4. _____

Imagine your life 15 years from now. What will it be like if one of these events actually occurs?

_____

_____

_____

_____

_____

Remember that you are in control of the situation. Can you think of things you can do now to avoid these problems? Write a goal and two objectives that will help you do that in the space below.

GOAL: _____

Objective: _____

_____

Objective: _____

_____

Your Action Plan
for the Next 10 Years

*Long-range planning does not deal with future decisions,
but with the future of present decisions.*

—Peter Drucker

The secret of success is constancy to purpose.

—Benjamin Disraeli

On the following pages, you will write a detailed action plan for the next 10 years. Before you begin, sit down and visualize your life over this period of time. (See page 217 on visualizations.) How old will you be in 10 years? What do you think you'll look like? How do you want to feel about yourself and about your life?

Your plan takes into account your education and training, living arrangements, employment, and finances for each year. You already have a detailed plan for your education. Turn back to page 347 for that information.

Your living arrangements include both where you live and with whom you live. Will you live with your family? In a dorm or apartment? Will you live alone or with a roommate? Do you think you will be married in 10 years? Will you buy a house? Use your imagination.

Think about your probable employment. Will you be working for pay? Part-time or full-time? At what point will you begin working in your chosen career? Will you need to take jobs just for the money while you continue your education?

Whether you are employed or not, you will need money (finances). Where will you get it? Will your parents or spouse support you? Will someone else? Do you think you might qualify for scholarships or financial aid, or will you need to support yourself? How much money do you think you will need each year? Make an educated guess.

Your 10-Year Goal: _____

_____

_____

_____

Once you have a clear picture of where you'd like to go and how you might get there, write your plans below. Word them as measurable objectives. See pages 186 to 190.

YEAR ONE — (Next Year)   Your age _____

Education and training: _____

Living arrangements: _____

Employment: _____

Finances: _____

YEAR TWO

Education and training: _____

Living arrangements: _____

Employment: _____

Finances: _____

YEAR THREE

Education and training: _____

Living arrangements: _____

Employment: _____

Finances: _____

YEAR FOUR

Education and training: _____

Living arrangements: _____

Employment: _____

Finances: _____

YEAR FIVE

Education and training: _____

Living arrangements: _____

Employment: _____

Finances: _____

YEAR SIX

Education and training: _____

Living arrangements: _____

Employment: _____

Finances: _____

YEAR SEVEN

Education and training: _____

Living arrangements: _____

Employment: _____

Finances: _____

YEAR EIGHT

Education and training: _____

Living arrangements: _____

Employment: _____

Finances: _____

YEAR NINE

Education and training: _____

Living arrangements: _____

Employment: _____

Finances: _____

YEAR TEN

Education and training: _____

Living arrangements: _____

Employment: _____

Finances: _____

A master will tell you what he expects of you. A teacher, though, awakens your own expectations.

—Patricia Neal

You know, when you're young and curious, people love to teach you.

—Dede Allen

Supporters of My Plan

It's one thing to be responsible for your own actions, but quite another to feel you have to do everything on your own. Part of responsibility is knowing when to get help and where to get it. Review page 334 on the importance of mentors. Can you think of people in your life right now who could be of assistance in reaching your goals? If so, list them below. If not, start watching for these important people to turn up in your life. Whether or not you know any now, you are sure to meet others in the next few years. Learn to recognize them, and be open to the things they have to teach you.

_____

_____

_____

_____

My Definition of Success

In the first chapter, you began the process of writing your own definition of success. You've probably updated it along the way as you learned more about yourself. Has it changed? Take a moment to refine that statement and write it here.

_____

_____

_____

My Mission in Life

Back on page 61 you stated your mission in life. Is it still the same? Restate or rewrite it below and refer to it often. Although your mission may change, it will keep you on course. In the end, you are likely to judge your own success or failure according to how well you have lived up to this purpose.

_____

_____

_____

_____

*If your success is not on your own terms, if it looks good
to the world but does not feel good in our heart,
it is not success at all.*

—Anna Quindlen

What happens next is pretty much up to you. If you apply enough energy to your vision, there is no reason why you won't someday be able to say, as Samuel Johnson did more than two hundred years ago, "I knew very well what I was undertaking, and very well how to do it, and have done it very well." Good luck!

Some people see things as they are and say "Why?"
I dream things that never were and say "Why not?"

—George Bernard Shaw

Hats off to the past; coats off to the future.

—American Proverb

In the ordinary business of life, industry can do
anything which genius can do, and very many
things which it cannot.

—H. W. Beecher

Keep your eyes on the prize,
Hold on, hold on.

—Traditional civil rights song

We are a success:
When we have lived well, laughed often and loved much. When we gain the
respect of intelligent people, and the love of children. When we fill a niche and
accomplish a task. When we leave the world better than we found it, whether
by an improved idea, a perfect poem or a rescued soul. We are successful if we
never lack appreciation of earth's beauty or fail to express it. If we look for the
best in others, and give the best we have.

—Robert Louis Stevenson

CHAPTER 15 CHECKPOINTS
Where Do You Go from Here?
Writing your 10-year plan of action

You now should have the resources you need to move forward. You have gathered the information and developed the skills to write a comprehensive and meaningful 10-year plan that is personalized to your own unique goals, personality, and mission in life. You have also learned decision-making techniques that will continue to help you throughout your life as you encounter change. Make sure you've covered all of the following topics, and you'll be on your way!

☐ I conducted a final review of my **Career Interest Surveys** and decision-making rubrics to determine the career that most closely matches me and my plans for the future.

☐ I conducted online research and understand the various education and job training opportunities that are available to me, particularly for my chosen career field.

☐ I not only developed an Education and Training 10-Year Plan, but I also understand that life-long learning is necessary in the 21st century.

☐ I recognize the importance of delaying gratification by identifying the sacrifices and commitments required to achieve the greatest reward.

☐ I wrote affirmations to empower me as I overcome fears that might hold me back from achieving my dream.

☐ I identified things I can do now to avoid roadblocks I'm likely to encounter.

☐ I defined my 10-year goal and wrote my 10-year action plan to get there, taking education, living arrangements, employment, and finances into account.

☐ I acknowledge my responsibility to ask for help when I need it and I know how to recognize potential mentors when I meet them.

☐ I refined my own personal definition of success.

☐ I confirmed or refined my own personal mission statement and understand the role it plays in guiding me through future choices and changes.

Congratulations!

You may have reached the end of this book but, as you are aware, not the end of what is a lifelong journey. Follow the process you've learned and throughout your life, the pay-off of a self-actualizing life will be, as they say, priceless.

Keep your **10-year Plan** current, updating your goals and objectives each year so you continue to envision and plan for a productive future. The process you've learned is ageless. Whether you're 18, 28, 48, and 68 years old, it will guide you through the steps necessary to make the best choices for a life of personal fulfillment and happiness.

This step-by-step process can be used for all major decisions in your life. When you face life-defining choices — where to live, who and when to marry, whether and when to have children, which career you want and what level of education and training to pursue — you'll want to remember to ask yourself these three questions:

Who Am I?
What Do I Want?
How Do I Get It?

You've learned a decision-making process that will pay dividends throughout your life. What you do with the plan you've developed will help determine how happy you are and how successful you feel. Couple this productive vision of your future, with the energy to put your plan into action and you're bound to experience personal success.

You've got to find what you love. That is as truthful for your work as it is for your lovers. Your work is going to fill a large part of your life, and the only way to be truly satisfied is to do what you believe is great work and the only way to do great work is to love what you do. If you haven't found it yet, keep looking and don't settle. As with all matters of the heart you'll know when you find it. And, like any great relationship, it just gets better and better as the years roll on.

—Steve Jobs, Stanford University Commencement address, 2005

Index

Acknowledgments

We want to recognize the following individuals for their contributions to the publication of *Career Choices and Changes* and My10yearPlan.com®, We appreciate their talent and suggestions throughout the development and editorial process.

Editorial Assistants: Kelly Gajewski; Rafael Garcia, J.D., M.B.A.

Programmer and Online Program Developer: Brad Owen

Consultants and Advisors: Diane Hollems, Ph.D.; Lauren Wintermeyer, Ed.D.; Penelope Paine; Rebecca Dedmond, Ph.D., L.P.C.; Kristen Lunceford; Victoria Bortolussi, Ph.D.; Bill Benjamin; Andy Arnold; Jim Comiskey; Wendy Bingham; Carl Lindros, M.B.A.; Russell Rumberger, Ph.D.; Laurel Phillips, Esq.; Rosa Ramos, M.A.; Maria del Rocio Pacheco, M.S.

Designers: Itoko Maeno, Brittany Owen

Research and Development: Matt Jenkins; Charles "Chip" Campbell, M.B.A.

We'd like to thank our peer reviewers for their important contributions to the original edition of this work:

Kenneth B. Hoyt, Ph.D., University Distinguished Professor (retired), Kansas State University; James C. Comiskey, Author and Lecturer, *How to Start, Expand and Sell a Business and Successfully Self-Employed,* Santa Barbara, California; Carl E. Lindros, M.B.A., President, Santa Barbara Securities; Sarah Lykken, M.Ed., former National Sales Manager, Carlson Learning Corporation, Minneapolis, Minnesota; Susan A. Neufeldt, Ph.D., Clinical Psychologist, Santa Barbara, California; Diana Frank, Community Volunteer and Philanthropist, Homemaker and Designer, Goleta, California; Rochelle Friedman, Ed.D., Principal, Murray High School, Career Vocational Education Administrator, Albemarle County Schools, Charlottesville, Virginia; Laura Light, M.Ed., Reading Specialist/Language Arts Teacher, Murray High School, Charlottesville, Virginia.

Notes

1. *Chicago Tribune,* "Nearly half of U.S. workers consider themselves underemployed, report says." June 28, 2016.

2. U.S. Census Bureau, *Current Population Reports, Income and Poverty in the United States: 2017.* September 2018.

3. Ibid.

4. Bureau of Labor Statistics, U.S. Department of Labor, *The Economics Daily,* April 2018.

5. Bureau of Labor Statistics, U.S. Department of Labor, Economic News Release, "Average hourly and weekly earnings for all employees on private nonfarm payrolls by industry sector, seasonally adjusted," April 5, 2019.

6. Bureau of Labor Statistics, U.S. Department of Labor, Economic News Release, "Quartiles and selected deciles of usual weekly earnings of full-time wage and salary workers by selected characteristics, fourth quarter 2018 averages, not seasonally adjusted," January 17, 2019.

7. Ibid.

8. Bureau of Labor Statistics, U.S. Department of Labor, Worker Displacement: 2015–2017, August 28, 2018.

9. *The New York Times,* Times Health Guide, "Alcohol Use Disorder." Retrieved April 8, 2017.

10. Agency for Healthcare Research and Quality, *Healthcare Cost and Utilization Project, Statistical Brief #246,* December 2018.

11. U.S. Government Accountability Office, "Retirement Security: Most Households Approaching Retirement Have Low Savings, an Update," March 26, 2019.

12. U.S. Government Accountability Office, GAO Highlights, Retirement Security, "Most Households Approaching Retirement Have Low Savings," May 2015.

13. *USA Today,* "Is 70 the new retirement age?" September 16, 2016.

MINDY BINGHAM

Best-selling author, entrepreneur, CEO, and educational activist, Mindy's mission is to help individuals realize their fullest potential. The genesis of this book was when Mindy was a part-time instructor at Westmont College in Santa Barbara in the late 1970s. Over the last 20+ years, as author or co-author, Mindy Bingham's titles have sold over two million copies. In addition to this title, her award-winning textbook, *Career Choices*, is used in over 4,800 secondary schools, along with the interdisciplinary companion books, *Lifestyle Math* and *Possibilities*. Her children's picture books include the Ingram number-one bestseller, *Minou; My Way Sally,* the 1989 Ben Franklin Award winner; and *Berta Benz and the Motorwagen,* inspiration for a soon-to-be-released animated movie.

SANDY STRYKER

Sandy Stryker, co-author of the first edition of this book is also co-author of the bestselling *Choices: A Teen Woman's Journal for Self-Awareness and Personal Planning* series. Her first children's book, *Tonia the Tree,* was the 1988 recipient of the merit award from the Friends of American Writers.

TANJA EASSON

Along with her duties as editor of this book, as the Vice President of Curriculum and Technical Support, Tanja has helped educators around the country initiate and expand their educational programs using the Academic Innovations titles and websites. Her creativity and talent is evident in her work with author Mindy Bingham on the Internet enhancement My10yearplan.com®.

CHRIS NOLT

Owner of Cirrus Book Design, in Santa Barbara, CA, Chris is responsible for the design, typesetting and production of *Career Choices and Changes.* Working with Academic Innovations for over twenty years, Chris' skill and artistry brings these publications to life in a user-friendly format.